I0400951

كلام كل يوم

Kalaam Kull Yoom 1

Situational Egyptian Arabic

Alaa Abou El Nour
Matthew Aldrich

lingualism

ISBN: 978-1-949650-04-4

Written by Alaa Abou El Nour and Matthew Aldrich
Edited by Heba Salah Ali and Matthew Aldrich
Illustrated by Heba Khater
Audio by Mohamed Ibrahim and Heba Salah Ali
Cover art: © Shutterstock / LexyK

website: www.lingualism.com
email: contact@lingualism.com

Table of Contents

Introduction .... *ii*

How to Use This Book........ *iv*

Taking a **Taxi** 1

Asking for **Directions**........ 18

Taking the **Subway**........ 33

Taking a **Microbus**........ 49

Taking a **Train**........ 62

At the **Airport**........ 74

At a **Restaurant**........ 87

At the **Coffee House**........ 101

Making **Small Talk**........ 117

Visiting Someone's Home........ 131

Making **Appointments**........ 146

At the **Doctor's**........ 160

At the **Pharmacy**........ 175

At the **Gym**........ 190

At a **Barbershop**........ 207

At a **Beauty Salon**........ 222

Introduction

This is the book I wish I had when I first went to live in Egypt. I had a pretty good grasp on colloquial Arabic grammar. I could conjugate verbs and form basic sentences. I knew "lots of words"... or so I thought. But I would so often find myself in situations unable to express my thoughts and needs and struggling to understand what people were saying to me. I was always worried that my awkward exchanges with locals made me come across as rude because I didn't know the right things to say at the right times. Understandably, I wanted to prepare before I tried to tackle specific communicative challenges–such as getting my hair cut. But how? I found myself flipping through various course books and pocket dictionaries looking for words and phrases to use with the barber. I would bring lists to my teacher. How do you say "not too short"? What's the word for "sideburns"? How do I make small talk with my barber? (I knew that Egyptian barbers were chatty!) It was a lot of research to accomplish a simple task I'd taken for granted back home.

Kalaam Kull Yoom: Situational Egyptian Arabic was written to help intermediate learners succeed at critical moments during everyday communicative tasks. This is the first of two books in a series. I have divided each book into 16 chapters, which are not meant to be studied in order and do not increase in the level of difficulty. Instead, you should find the chapter to navigate your way through a particular transactional or social situation that is relevant to your needs.

Time for a haircut? Gentlemen, check out the chapter At a Barbershop on page 207. Ladies, try At a Beauty Salon on page 222. Each chapter has several dialogues, vocabulary lists, bonus expressions, footnotes, and cultural information. (See How to Use This Book on the next page to learn more about the organization and features of the chapters.)

I am deeply grateful to Alaa Abou El Nour, who carefully wrote the dialogues with an eye to reflect authentic, everyday Egyptian

Arabic as well as to include high-frequency vocabulary and phrases likely to be heard and used in specific situations. I wrote the texts on cultural tips and information based on my own experiences living in Egypt and information from several Egyptian and expat friends alike who were kind and patient enough to share their advice and feedback. I would also like to thank Heba Salah Ali for her help proofreading the dialogues and vocabulary lists (ensuring the tashkeel and phonemic transcriptions are accurate). Special thanks also to Heba Khater for providing illustrations and to Mohamed Ibrahim and Heba Salah Ali for producing the audio of the dialogues.

Matthew Aldrich

Audio

Visit www.lingualism.com/audio, where you can find the free accompanying audio to download or stream (at variable playback rates).

Anki Flashcards

Enhance your learning with our Anki digital flashcards, available for separate purchase on our website. This comprehensive deck features all the vocabulary and expressions from this book, complete with audio, to help you memorize and master the material more effectively.

How to Use This Book

This is not a coursebook with chapters that build on each other and need to be studied in order. Use the **Table of Contents** at the front of the book (also located on the back cover of the paperback edition, for your convenience) to find the topic that interests you for your immediate or future communicative goals. Of course, you're not going to go out into the real world and have conversations with people that follow the dialogues line by line. The purpose of the dialogues is to teach you different words and phrases that you can use and that you may hear. Synonyms, alternative expressions, and supplementary vocabulary are provided to help you form your own sentences to express yourself and to be prepared for the variety of possible things you may hear Egyptians say to you.

Introductory Paragraph

On the first page of each chapter, you will see an illustration above the chapter's title in English and Egyptian Arabic. An introduction to the topic follows and presents some key vocabulary.

Mini-Dialogues

Next, we have several short dialogues. Each dialogue has a title that shows you the goal of the specific "subtask"–for example, paying the bill, offering your seat to someone, reporting a theft.

Symbols

Notice that the lines of dialogue are preceded by symbols.

○ You–the foreigner, the customer. (Things you might need to say.)

◇ An Egyptian person–merchant, barber, waiter, landlord, friend, etc. etc. (Things you might hear other people say.)

The symbols are there to help you decide whether you need to memorize the phrases so you can actively use them yourself, or if you just need to be able to passively understand them when you hear them.

Arabic Script

Each dialogue appears three times on the page. The first is written in Arabic script with tashkeel (diacritics). At first glance, it may seem that many letters are missing diacritics. A final consonant is assumed to take sukuun, as Egyptian Arabic does not have case endings as MSA does.

We write كتاب *kitāb* **book** (and not كِتَابْ). Non-final consonants without diacritics are understood to take the short vowel fatha (ـَ): شمْس *šams* **sun** (and not شَمْسْ). This was done intentionally to keep the texts from being cluttered with redundancies and streamline fluent reading. You can find a detailed online guide with printable PDFs on Egyptian Arabic pronunciation and Lingualism's system of orthography in the Resources section of this book's product page on our website.

Phonemic Transcription

Each dialogue also appears as phonemic transcription. This can be helpful for learners who are not yet comfortable enough with the Arabic alphabet. Some of the phonemic characters may seem unfamiliar and confusing, but by investing just a short time learning the sounds each character represents, you will find the system intuitive and easy to read. The Arabic script does not adequately show all of the sound changes (vowel lengthening, shortening, and elision) and shifts in word stress that occur in Egyptian Arabic. So even learners who prefer Arabic script can benefit by referring to the phonemic transcription. Follow the link above for a guide to Lingualism's phonemic transcription system.

English Translation

Between the dialogues of Arabic script and phonemic transcription, English translations appear to help you understand the dialogues and quickly find words and phrases you want to learn. Some style was sacrificed in the translations to keep them direct and true to the original Egyptian Arabic. This allows you to easily match up phrases and words by comparing the translations to the Arabic.

Footnotes

Underlined words and phrases are followed by superscript numbers that reference footnotes:

- Synonyms are preceded by equal signs (=). These show you words and expressions which can replace those in the dialogue without significantly changing the meaning.
- Alternative expressions show examples of other things you might want to say or might hear instead. These are followed by English translations.

Culture and Information Notes

The real focus of the book is, of course, the language itself. Other information–on culture and services in Egypt–is provided as a bonus. Hopefully, you will find some information useful and interesting, but keep in mind that the comments on culture are generalizations–there are always exceptions. Likewise, the information on services (companies, procedures, transportation options, etc.) is subject to change. You should always double-check such information from other sources, especially Egyptian friends and acquaintances.

The Extended Dialogue

The mini-dialogues in each chapter are followed by a longer dialogue that combines several of the subtasks into a full communicative exchange.

Vocabulary

Vocabulary lists in three columns (English, phonemic transcription, and Arabic script) follow the dialogues. These are not glossaries containing all of the words from the dialogues, but rather lists of keywords related to the topic and those likely to be needed in various circumstances–that is, they are there to save you time searching in dictionaries for the words you need.

Expressions

Expressions are divided into two sections, preceded by the same symbols used in the dialogues. First are expressions you may need to use, and second are statements and questions you may hear others say.

Audio

All of the dialogues have been recorded by professional voice artists from Cairo, Egypt. You can download or stream the audio free of charge from our website.

Taking a Taxi في التّاكْسي

Cairo is one of the easiest cities in the world in which to hail a taxi, with tens of thousands of them flooding its streets. Simply signal an approaching taxi with your arm stretched out, the palm of your hand facing toward the ground, and optionally calling out تاكْسي *táksi* or تاكْس *taks* **taxi!** But hailing a taxi is the easy part. Not only do you need the driver to agree to your destination (he may not want to go to an area that has a lot of traffic congestion or is too remote), but you also need a strategy regarding the fare. سوّاقين *sawwaʔīn* **drivers** are reluctant to use عدّادات *3addadāt* **fare meters** (if they have working meters in their taxis at all!), which results in arguments between passengers, who feel they are being taken advantage of, and drivers, who are aggrieved (sincerely or theatrically) by what they see as underpayment. While Egyptians are not immune to this headache, foreigners tend to be especially subject to this frequent source of unpleasantness. Most taxi drivers are polite and satisfied to receive a fair fare, but many view foreigners as unsuspecting targets for gouging. **Acting confident and knowing the language to show that you are no newbie to Egypt can go a long way to being treated more fairly and avoiding confrontations.**

1

Agreeing on the Destination and a Price in Advance

o ميدان التّحْرير ياسْطَى[1]؟

◇ ماشي اِتْفضّل.

o هدْفع ٢٠ جِنيْهْ تمام؟

◇ ماشي يا باشا، اِرْكب. مِش هنِخْتِلِف.

o Tahrir Square, sir?
◇ Okay, get in.
o I'll pay 20 LE, all right?
◇ Okay, sir. Just get in. We won't argue.

o *midān ittaɧrīr yásṭa*[1]*?*
◇ *māši, itfáḍḍal.*
o *hádfa3 3išrīn ginēh, tamām?*
◇ *māši ya bāša, írkab. miš hanixtílif.*

[1] ياسْطى *yásṭa* is the polite form of address for a taxi driver. It is a contraction of the words يا أُسْطى *ya ʔúsṭa.*

Taxi drivers have a big say in the destinations they prefer to take and which to avoid. You might have to ask several taxis to go to a particular destination before you have any success. Be patient. The norm is to tell the driver your destination through the window before you get in. If he agrees, you might hear an اِتْفضّل *itfáḍḍal* / اِتْفضّلي *itfaḍḍáli* or just get a nod or grunt. Otherwise, he will mutter something (it doesn't matter what) and/or simply drive off.

Ask a local shopkeeper or passerby how much the fare should be before you hail a taxi, especially if your destination is common, like وِسْط البلد *wisṭ ilbálad* **downtown.** لَوْ رِكِبْت مِن (هِنا) لِـ__، أدْفع لِلتّاكْسي كام؟ *law rikíbt*ᵊ *min (hína) li-__, ádfa3 li-ttáksi kām?* **If I take a taxi from (here), how much should I pay?** or ...التّاكْسي ياخُد مِنّي حَوالي كام؟ *...ittáksi yāxud mínni ɧawāli kām?* **... how much will the taxi [driver] charge?**

2

Turning on the Fare Meter

o أسْتأْذِنك[1] تِشغّل العدّاد؟

◇ تمام يا أُسْتاذة و لَوْ إنُّه مِش جايِب همُّه[2].

o Could you turn on the meter, please?

◇ Okay, ma'am, although it won't be worth it for me.

o *asta?zínak*[1], *tišáɣɣal il3addād?*

◇ *tamām, ya ustāza wi law ínnu miš gāyib hámmu*[2].

[1] You can replace أسْتأْذِنك *asta?zínak* (lit. I ask you permission) with مُمْكِن *múmkin* (lit. possible) in making requests.

[2] هتْخسّر معايا. *hatxássar ma3āya.* **It'll be a loss for me.; I'll lose money on it..**

Although you might spot a fare meter on the dashboard of a تاكْسي إسْوِد *táksi íswid* **black taxi**, you will notice that it is as antiquated as the vehicle itself. It has not worked for decades. Asking the driver of a black taxi to turn on the meter would give him a good laugh... but also expose how wet behind the ears you are. The newer تاكْسي أبْيَض *táksi ábyaḍ* **white taxi** should have a working meter. If it does not, you may opt to pass and wait for one that does. But even when a taxi has a fare meter, the driver may tell you that it مِش شغّال *miš šaɣɣāl* **doesn't work / is broken.** Or he may turn it on with some reluctance while giving you a guilt trip, as in this dialogue. In fact, a common complaint among drivers of white taxis is that the metered fare is too low. Keep in mind that, after fuel and other expenses, your taxi driver takes home less than half of what you give him. Be sure to give him a few pounds' بقْشيش *ba?šīš* **tip**.

When the meter is turned on, it is best to specify the route you prefer; otherwise, the driver may take you on a "scenic route." Of course, when you negotiate a flat fare ahead of time, it is in the driver's best interest to take the most efficient route.

3

Paying the fare

o ماشي، هنْزِل هِنا على جمْب[1].

◇ اِتْفضّلي. الحِساب ٣٧.

o ماشي، خُد الـ٤٠ دوْل[2] ياسْطى. مُتْشكِّرة.

◇ خلّي[3] يا أُسْتاذة!

o Okay, I'll get out here on the side [of the road].

◇ There you go. The fare is 37 LE.

o Okay, take this 40 LE, sir. Thank you!

◇ Keep it[3], ma'am!

o *māši, hánzil hína 3ála gamb*[1].

◇ *itfaḍḍáli. ilħisāb sáb3a w talatīn.*

o *māši, xud ilʔarbi3īn dōl*[2] *yásṭa. mutšakkíra.*

◇ *xálli*[3] *ya ustāza!*

[1] = على جمْب لَوْ سمحْت! *3ála gambᵊ law samáħt!* (lit. On the side [of the road], please!)

[2] If you don't expect change, you can also say خلّي الباقي عشانك *xálli -lbāʔi 3ašānak* **Keep the change!** Or, to make it clear that you do want your change back, say something like الباقي لَوْ سمحْت. *ilbāʔi, law samáħt.* **The change, please.** or معاك فكّةْ ٥٠؟ *ma3āk fákkit xamsīn?* **Do you have change for a fifty?**

[3] When you go to pay your taxi driver, and he tells you خلّي *xálli* **keep it!**, he is not offering you a free ride. This is merely a figure of speech embedded in the language and reflects the importance of hospitality in Egyptian culture. Think of it simply as a humble thank-you.

TELLING THE TAXI DRIVER TO TAKE A CERTAIN ROUTE

o مكْتبةْ إسْكِنْدِرية؟

◇ ماشي، اِتْفضّل. نمْشي بحْر وَلّا أبو قير؟

o لا[1] خلّينا بحْر أحْسن عشان مِسْتعْجِل جِدّاً و لازِم أكون هِناك خِلال نُصّ ساعة.

◇ تمام، سيبْها على الله.

o Alexandria Library?

◇ Okay, get in. Shall we go along the sea[side] road or Abou Eer Road?

o Let's stick to the sea[side road], as I'm in a hurry, and I need to be there in 30 minutes.

◇ Okay, don't worry [lit. leave it to God].

o *maktábt iskindiríyya?*

◇ *māši, itfáḍḍal. nímši baħrᵊ wálla ábu ʔīr?*

o *lā̤*[1]*, xallīna baħr áħsan 3ašān mistá3gil gíddan wi lāzim akūn hinā̤k xilāl nuṣṣᵊ sā3a.*

◇ *tamām, síbha 3ála -llāh.*

[1] You may notice لا *lā/laʔ* in responses where the English translation 'no' would not make much sense, as in response to the 'either-or' question in this dialogue. Realizing this usage of the word will help you avoid confusion when speaking with Egyptians.

You can find words and expressions for giving directions in the vocabulary section at the end of this chapter and the next chapter (p. 28).

Notice that the passenger in this dialogue tells the driver his destination but doesn't negotiate the fare ahead of time. This is always a judgment call on the passenger's part, but as a general rule of thumb, if you have taken the same route several times and know the normal, expected fare, you can just hand the driver the amount on arrival. In this case, have the exact change on you, hand... [continued on p. 12]

5

ASKING YOUR RIDESHARE DRIVER TO MAKE A STOP ON THE WAY

o كابْتِن[1] حُسام؟

◇ آه تمام. أُسْتاذ أنْوَر؟

o أَيْوَه، محطّةْ القطْر في سيدي جابِر إن شاء الله.

◇ تحْت أمْرك يافنْدِم.

o أسْتأْذِنك بسّ هنُقف دِقيقة في رُشْدي آخُد شنْطِةْ سفر معايا؟

◇ مفيش مشاكِل يافنْدِم. قولّي قبْلها بسّ.

o Mr. Hossam?

◇ Yes, that's right... Mr. Anwar?

o Yes... [we're going to] the train station in Sidi Gaber, God willing.

◇ Yes, sir.

o Could we just stop by Roshdy for a minute so I can pick up my suitcase?

◇ No problem, sir. Just tell me again ahead of time.

o *kábtin*[1] *ḫusām?*

◇ *āh, tamām. ustāz ánwar?*

o *áywa, maḫáṭṭit ilʔáṭrᵊ f sīdi gābir in šāʔ allāh.*

◇ *taḫtᵊ ámrak yafándim.*

o *astaʔzínak bassᵊ hánuʔaf diʔīʔa f rúšdi, āxud šánṭit sáfar ma3āya?*

◇ *ma-fīš mašākil yafándim. ʔúlli ʔabláha bass.*

[1] While it is polite to address a taxi driver as ياسْطى *yásṭa* (see p. 2), you should address your rideshare driver as يا كابْتِن *ya kábtin.*

Rideshare services, such as Uber and Careem, are growing in popularity in Egypt, as many find them to be safer, have better customer service, and even lower fares.

Pink Taxi (www.pinktaxi.net) is a rideshare option for women only and has only female drivers.

6

Paying your rideshare driver

o ماشي، أنا هنْزِل بعْد التِّرام على طول.

◇ تمام حضْرِتك تِحِبّي أنْهي الرِّحْلة؟

o آه عشان يِلْحق يِجمّع[1].

◇ الحِساب ٣٦ يافنْدِم.

o طيِّب، خُد الأرْبعين دي و حُطّ الباقي رصيد.

◇ تمام يافنْدِم، حمْدِلله على السّلامة[2] و متِنْسيش التّقْييم[3].

o Okay, I'll get out right after the tram tracks.

◇ All right, ma'am. Would you like me to end the trip [on the app]?

o Yes, so that there's time to calculate the fare.

◇ It's 36 [LE], ma'am.

o Okay, take this 40 LE, and add the change into my credit.

◇ Okay, ma'am. Thank God you arrived safely... and don't forget [to leave] a rating.

o *māši, ána hánzil ba3d ittirām 3ála ţūl.*

◇ *tamām, ħadrítik tiħíbbi ánhi -rríħla?*

o *āh, 3ašān yílħa? yigámma3*[1].

◇ *ilħisāb sítta w talatīn yafándim.*

o *ţáyyib, xud il?arbi3īn di wi ħuţţ ilbā?i raşīd.*

◇ *tamām, yafándim, ħamdílla 3ála -ssalāma*[2] *wi ma-tinsīš ittaqyīm*[3].

[1] = (الحِساب) يِحْسِب *yíħsib (ilħisāb)* = يِعْمِل الحِساب *yí3mil ilħisāb* **calculate (the fare)**

[2] حمْدِالله على السّلامة *ħamdílla 3ála -ssalāma* is a formulaic wish to someone who has completed a journey (or recovered from an illness). The response is الله يِسلِّمك *allāh yisallímak.*

[3] متِنْسينيش في التّقْييم *ma-tinsinīš fi- ttaqyīm* **Don't forget to rate me.**

7

Renting a taxi for an extended time

○ بقولّك ياسْطى، كُنْت عايِز أروح الزّمالك و أعْمِل كام مِشْوار كِده. فاضي؟
◇ ماشي حضْرتِك بسّ فينْ المشاوير دي؟
○ هنْروح الأوِّل الزّمالك هاخُد حاجات و بعْديْن هنِطْلع على مدينِةْ نصْر أوَصّلْها.
◇ بسّ إحْنا كِده هنْجيبْها مِن شرْقها لِغرْبها.[1]
○ هراضيك يا عمّ متِقْلقْش. ١٥٠ جِنيْه تمام؟
◇ ماشي يا بيْه، اللي إنْتَ عايْزُه.

○ Hey, sir, I wanted to go to Zamalek along with a few other destinations. Are you free?
◇ All right, sir, but where are these destinations?
○ We'll first go to Zamalek to pick up some stuff and then head to Nasr City to drop it off.
◇ But it'll take us so long.
○ I'll make it worth your while (lit. make you content). Don't worry. Is 150 LE good?
◇ All right, sir. As you wish.

○ *baʔúllak yásṭa, kuntᵊ 3āyiz arūḫ izzamālak w a3mil kām mišwār kída. fāḍi?*
◇ *māši ḫaḍrítak bassᵊ fēn ilmašawīr di?*
○ *hanrūḫ ilʔáwwil izzamālak hāxud ḫagāt, wi ba3dēn haníṭla3 3ála madīnit naṣr awaṣṣálha.*
◇ *bass íḫna kída hangíbha min šarʔáha li-ɣarbáha.*[1]
○ *haraḍīk ya 3amm, ma-tiʔláʔš. míyya w xamsīn ginēh tamām?*
◇ *māši ya bēh, íll- ínta 3áyzu.*

[1] (lit. take it from east to west); بسّ إحْنا كِده هنْلِفّ كْتير أَوي *bass íḫna kída hanlíffᵊ ktīr áwi* **But we'll be driving all over the place.**

Extended Dialogue

(stops a black taxi)

○ الحيّ السّابِع ياسْطى؟

◇ لا حيّ سابِع مين دِلْوَقْتي؟[1]

(stops a white taxi)

○ الحيّ السّابِع لَوْ سمحْت؟

◇ معلِشّ والله يا بِنْتي بسّ مِش طريقي خالِص.

(stops another black taxi)

○ الحيّ السّابِع؟

◇ ماشي بسّ هاخُد ٦٠ جِنيْه.

○ لا ٥٠ بسّ.

◇ لا يِفْتح الله[2]، سلامُ عليْكو!

(stops another white taxi)

○ حيّ السّابِع مِن فضْلك؟

◇ آه تمام اِتْفضّلي[3].

○ هتْشغّل العدّاد؟

◇ العدّاد هَيْخسّر معايا في الجّوّ و الزّحْمة دي.

○ خلاص تمام، مُتْشكِّرة.

(orders an Uber)

○ مِن فضْلك، حضْرِتك فيْن دِلْوَقْتي؟

◇ أنا داخِل على مُجمّع التّحْرير. مكان حضْرِتك عَ الـ GPS مظْبوط؟

○ آه بسّ مضْمنْش يِكون مظْبوط أَوي في الجّوّ ده. بُصّ أنا عنْد محطِّةْ المِترْو اللي هِناك.

◇ تمام أنا شُفْت حضْرِتِك. أنا داخِل عليْكي دِلْوَقْتي.

(gets in the car)

○ سلامُ عليْكُم. إن شاء الله الحيّ السّابِع.

◇ تحْت أمْرِك يافنْدِم.

(approaches destination)

○ أنا هنْزِل النّاصْيَة الجّايّة دي على طول.

◇ حمْدِلْله عَ السّلامة يافنْدِم. كِده الحِساب ٤٧.

○ تمام اِتْفضّل الخمْسين دوْل.

◇ تمام هحُطّ لِحضْرِتِك التّلاتة جِنيْهْ دوْل في الرّصيد.

○ لا خلاص مفيش مُشْكِلة. مُتْشكِّرة جِدّاً لِذوْقك.

◇ العفْو يافنْدِم.

(stops a black taxi)

○ 7th District, sir?

◇ No, how can we go to the 7th District now?

(stops a white taxi)

○ 7th District, please?

◇ I'm sorry, young lady, but it's not on my way at all.

(stops another black taxi)

○ 7th District?

◇ Okay, but I'll take 60 LE.

○ No, just 50 LE.

◇ No can do. Goodbye.

(stops another white taxi)

○ 7th District, please?

◇ Yes, okay. Get in.

○ And will you turn on the fare meter?

◇ The meter will make me lose out in such weather and traffic.

○ Never mind then. Thank you.

(orders an Uber)

○ Excuse me, where are you now?

◇ I'm just coming toward Mogamma Tahrir. Is your location on the GPS accurate?

o Yeah, but I can't guarantee it will be accurate in such weather. Anyway, I'm at the subway station over there.

◇ Okay, I've spotted you. I'm just coming toward you.

(gets in the car)

o Hello! [We're going to] 7th District, God willing.

◇ As you please, ma'am.

(approaches destination)

o I will get out right here at this corner coming up.

◇ Thank God you arrived safely, ma'am. The fare is 47 [LE].

o Okay, take this 50 [LE].

◇ All right. I'll add the remaining 3 LE to your credit.

o No, that's okay. Thank you so much for your thoughtfulness.

◇ You're welcome, ma'am.

(stops a black taxi)

o *ilḫáyy issābi3 yásṭa?*

◇ *lā, ḫayyᵊ sābi3 mīn dilwáʔti?* [1]

(stops a white taxi)

o *ilḫáyy issābi3, law samáḫt?*

◇ *ma3alíšš, wallāhi ya bínti, bassᵊ miš ṭarīʔi xāliṣ.*

(stops another black taxi)

o *ilḫáyy issābi3?*

◇ *māši bassᵊ hāxud sittīn ginēh.*

o *laʔ, xamsīn bass.*

◇ *lā, yíftaḫ allāh*[2]*, salāmu 3alēku!*

(stops another white taxi)

o *ilḫáyy issābi3 min fáḍlak?*

◇ *āh, tamām, itfaḍḍáli*[3]*.*

o *hatšáɣɣal il3addād?*

◇ *il3addād hayxássar ma3āya fi -ggawwᵊ wi -zzáḫma di.*

o *xalāṣ tamām, mutšakkíra.*

(orders an Uber)

- O *min fáḍlak, ħaḍrítak fēn dilwáʔti?*
- ◇ *ána dāxil 3ála mugámma3 ittaħrīr. makān ħaḍrítik 3a -l* [GPS] *maẓbūṭ?*
- O *āh, bass^{ə} ma-ḍmánš^{ə} yikūn maẓbūṭ áwi fi -ggaww^{ə} da. buṣṣ ána 3and^{ə} maħáṭṭit ilmítru -lli hināk.*
- ◇ *tamām, ána šuft^{ə} ħaḍrítik. ána dāxil 3alēki dilwáʔti.*

(gets in the car)

- O *salām 3alēkum. in šāʔ allāh ilħáyy issābi3.*
- ◇ *taħt^{ə} ámrik yafándim.*

(approaches destination)

- O *ána hánzil innáṣya -ggáyya di 3ála ṭūl.*
- ◇ *ħamdílla 3a -ssalāma yafándim. kída -lħisāb sáb3a w arbi3īn.*
- O *tamām, itfáḍḍal ilxamsīn dōl.*
- ◇ *tamām, haħúṭṭ^{ə} l-ħaḍrítik ittalāta gnēh dōl fi -rraṣīd.*
- O *laʔ, xalāṣ, ma-fīš muškíla. mutšakkíra gíddan li-zōʔak.*
- ◇ *il3áfw^{ə} yafándim.*

[1] = حيّ سابِع إزّاي دِلْوَقْتي *ħayy^{ə} sābi3 izzāy dilwáʔti?*

[2] يِفْتَح الله *yíftaħ allāh* is commonly used by merchants when they do not agree on a price offered. It is a shortened version of the Egyptian proverb بينْ البايِع و الشاري يِفْتح الله *bēn ilbāyi3 wi -ššāri yíftaħ allāh.* (lit. May God open [a way] between the seller and buyer.) **If you don't like my price, you don't have to buy it.**

[3] اِرْكبي! *irkábi!* **Get in!**

[continued from p. 5] ... it to the driver quickly and get out... or better yet, get out first and hand the driver the money through the window, which is common practice in Egypt. This way, you can get away before... an argument erupts. Whatever you do, do not ask بِكام الأُجْرة؟ *bi-kām ilʔúgra?* **How much is the fare?** at the end of the trip; this is basically asking to be overcharged. Likewise, asking the fare beforehand for short trips (of just a few blocks) shows that you do not know the system. Keep in mind, however, that traffic congestion on longer trips can merit a higher fare, and your driver might insist on a bit more for a route you've taken before during a less congested time.

As taxi drivers are almost always male, it is important to follow cultural norms depending on your gender. It is fine for male passengers to sit in the front seat next to the driver. However, female passengers should always sit in the back seat lest be sending an unwanted message to the driver. It may be prudent to send a friend the taxi's license plate number (often printed on the side of the vehicle, as well) and an "ok" message upon arriving safely.

When a taxi is not using a meter, don't be surprised if the driver stops to pick up another passenger if their destination is on the way (or if a taxi with a passenger in it already stops for you). Of course, this doesn't mean you're sharing the fare with fellow passengers!

Chatting with your taxi driver is a great opportunity for practicing your Arabic. You may get to listen to interesting stories and be asked all sorts of personal questions. As an added benefit, becoming chummy with your cabbie will reduce the chance of an argument over the fare at the end of the trip. For expressions related to small talk, see the chapter **Making Small Talk** on p. 116.

In the greater Cairo metropolitan area, you will see taxis in two colors: تاكْسي إسْوِد *táksi íswid* **black taxi** (with white fenders) and تاكْسي أبْيَض *táksi ábyaḍ* **white taxi** (with a checkered strip on the side). The iconic black taxis are slowly being replaced by white taxis, which have air-conditioning and fare meters. In Alexandria, taxis are yellow and black. In other parts of Egypt, you will notice taxis in other colors (blue, green, orange, etc.).

Taxis parked outside 5-star hotels charge double or triple the going rate. Walk a block from the hotel to hail a taxi and prices will plummet. The same situation exists at airports, where taxi drivers have their fingers crossed that unsuspecting new arrivals will pay whatever they ask. Use a ridesharing service such as Uber or Careem instead.

Vocabulary

taxi	*táksi*	تاكْسي
(rideshare) app	*aplikēšan* *taṭbīʔ*	أبْليكيْشن تطْبيق

driver	*sawwāʔ*	سوّاق
meter	*3addād*	عدّاد
fare	*úgra*	أُجْرة
change (money back)	*ilbāʔi*	الباقي
change (small change, change for a larger bill)	*fákka*	فكّة
the next corner	*innáṣya -ggáyya*	النّاصْيَة الجّايّة
street	*šāri3 (šawāri3)*	شارِع (شَوارِع)
narrow street, side street, alley	*zuʔāʔ*	زُقاق
tram	*tirām*	تِرام
subway, metro (UK: underground	*mítru*	مِتْرو
police report	*máɦḍar (maɦāḍir)*	محْضر (محاضِر)
police station	*ʔism*	قِسْم
traffic, congestion	*záɦma*	زحْمة
traffic sign	*išāra*	إشارة
police checkpoint	*lágna*	لجْنة
license	*rúxṣa*	رُخْصة
credit	*raṣīd*	رصيد
rating, evaluation	*taqyīm*	تقْييم
square, plaza	*midān*	ميدان
bridge	*kúbri*	كوبْري
tunnel	*náfaʔ (anfāʔ)*	نفق (أنْفاق)

highway	*(ṭarīʔ) sarī3*	(طريق) سريع
roundabout, traffic circle	*dawarān*	دَوَران
corniche, waterfront road	*kurnīš*	كورْنيش
taxi door	*bāb ittáksi*	باب التّاكْسي
window	*šibbāk*	شِبّاك
front seat	*ikkúrsi -lli ʔuddām*	الكُّرْسي اللي قُدّام
back seat	*ikkánaba ílli wára*	الكّنبة اللي وَرا
trunk (UK: boot)	*šánṭa (šúnaṭ)*	شنْطة (شُنط)
hood (UK: bonnet)	*kabbūt*	كبّوت
tire (UK: tyre)	*kawítš*	كاوِتْش
(car) horn	*kaláks*	كلاكْس
seat belt	*ḫizām ilʔamān*	حِزام الأمان
windshield wipers	*massaḫāt*	مسّاحات
mirrors	*ilmirayyāt*	المِرايات
gas tank (UK: petrol tank)	*tank (ilbanzīn)*	تانْك (البنْزين)

Expressions

○

I want to go to...	*ána 3āyiz arūḫ...*	أنا عايِز أروح...
Do you know...?	*ínta 3ārif...?*	إنْتَ عارِف...؟
If you don't mind, I would like to open the window.	*3āyiz áftaḫ iššibbāk ma3alíšš.*	عايِز أفْتح الشِّبّاك معلِشّ.

Excuse me, I will stop here for a minute to get something.	*háʔaf hína diʔīʔa, min fáḍlak, āxud/agīb ɧāga*	هقف هِنا دِقيقة مِن فضْلك، آخد/أجيب حاجة.
If there is a shortcut, I'd be grateful.	*law fī ṭarīʔ muxtíṣir yarēt.*	لَوْ فيه طريق مُخْتِصِر ياريْت.
You're taking [us] for a long ride when the trip is actually short!	*ínta bitlíffᵊ ktīr raɣm inn issíkka ʔuṣayyára!*	إنْتَ بِتْلِفّ كِتير رغْم إنّ السِّكّة قُصيرّة!
Can we take the 6th of October bridge?	*múmkin nāxud kúbri uktūbar?*	مُمْكِن ناخُد كوبْري أُكْتوبر؟
Please, drive faster as I'm in a hurry.	*ya rēt tísri3 3ašān mistá3gil.*	يا ريْت تِسْرِع عشان مِسْتعْجِل.
Could you please slow down a bit?	*min fáḍlak, múmkin tiháddi šwáyya?*	مِن فضْلك مُمْكِن تِهدّي شْوَيّة؟
Go straight.	*3ála ṭūl.* *ṭawwāli*	على طول. طَوّالي
Turn right.	*xuššᵊ ymīn.*	خُشّ يمِينك.
Turn left.	*xuššᵊ šmāl.*	خُشّ شِمالك.
Here is fine. (Stop here.)	*hína kwáyyis.*	هِنا كُوَيِّس
The next street on the right/left.	*iššāri3 iggáyyᵊ ymīn/šmāl.*	الشّارِع الجّاي يمِين/شِمال.
The corner after the next one.	*innáṣya -lli ba3d iggáyya.*	النّاصْيَة اللي بعْد الجّايّة.

How much is the fare, please?	*ilɧisāb kām min fáḏlak?*	الحِساب كام مِن فضْلك؟
Do you have change?	*ma3āk fákka?*	معاك فكّة؟

◇

Do you want me to open the trunk for you?	*aftáɧlak iššánṯa?*	أفْتحْلك الشّنْطة؟
May I fill the tank? It will only take five minutes.	*asta?zínak amáwwin bass xámas da?āyi??*	أسْتأْذِنك أموِّن بسّ خمس دقايِق؟
Where will you get out?	*nāzil fēn ɧaḏrítak?*	نازِل فينْ حضْرِتك؟
Wait, I'll pull over in a comfortable spot.	*istánna, a?áflak fi -lwás3a.*	اِسْتنّى أقفْلك في الوَسْعة.
Look, I'll drop you off at the end of the bridge, and you will just need to cross the road.	*buṣṣ, hanazzílak āxir ikkúbri w ínta 3áddi -nnáɧya -ttánya.*	بُصّ هنزِّلك آخِر الكّوبْري و إنْتَ عدّي النّاحْيَة التّانْيَة.
I'm sorry, I really don't have any change.	*ma3alíšš ma-3īš fákka, wallāhi.*	معلِشّ معيش فكّة والله.

Asking for Directions في الشّارِع

As a well-known Egyptian proverb goes, اللي يِسْأل مَيْتوهْش. *íIli yísʔal ma-ytúhš.* **He who asks does not get lost.** So it's better to ask for help than wander around aimlessly. Asking shopkeepers or traffic officers for directions is your best bet. You'll find that most Egyptians are happy to stop and give directions. Someone may even take the time to guide you to the place you're trying to find if it's not too far. Rarely will you find someone in such a rush that they'll blow you off with a hasty "I don't know." In fact, people seem to be reluctant to admit when they don't know the way. While you may hear an occasional معْرفْش والله *ma-3ráfš wallāhi* **I really don't know.**, more often than not, people will instead give you the wrong directions... unintentionally, making their best guess, in an optimistic attempt to seem helpful. And if they respond to your request for directions with هُوَّ قالّك فينْ؟ *húwwa ʔállak fēn?* **Did they tell you where it was?**, this is a dead giveaway that they don't actually know where the place you're trying to find is. (See dialogue 6 on p. 24.) In any case, head in the indicated direction, and if in any doubt, ask a second—and even a third—person for directions. After all, it just gives you more practice with Arabic!

Asking for Directions

o أقْرب محطّةْ مِتْرو فيْن الله يِخلّيك[1]؟

◇ هتِمْشي طَوّالي[2] لِحدّ ما تِوْصل لِلْميدان. هتْعدّيه، هتْلاقي في يافْطِةْ مِتْرو، تاني مفْرِق مِ الميدان عَ الشِّمال.

o بِعيد مِن هِنا أَوي يَعْني؟

◇ لا يادوْب[3] عشر دقايِق مشْي.

o Excuse me, where is the nearest subway station?

◇ You'll go straight until you reach the square, cross it and you'll find a "Metro" sign at the second intersection left of the square.

o Is it very far from here?

◇ No, it's just a ten-minute walk.

o *áʔrab maḥáṭṭit mítru fēn allāh yixallīk*[1]*?*

◇ *hatímši ṭawwāli*[2] *li-ḥádd*^{ə} *ma tíwṣal li-lmidān. hat3addī, hatlāʔi fi yáfṭit mítru, tāni máfriʔ mi -lmidān 3a -ššimāl.*

o *bi3īd min hína áwi yá3ni?*

◇ *laʔ, yadōb*[3] *3ášar daʔāyiʔ mašy.*

[1] الله يِخلّيك *allāh yixallīk* literally means 'May God keep you' and can be used in various contexts to mean **excuse me** or **please**, as in this dialogue, or to mean **thank you** when someone pays you a compliment, offers to help, or does you a favor.

[2] = على طول *3ála ṭūl*

[3] = يادوْبك *yadōbak* = مُجرّد *mugárrad* **barely**; مفيش *ma-fīš* **there is not (even)**

Even locals can get lost in a city as big as Cairo. Mostafa tells us about his experience getting lost and trying to ask for directions in the blog series Egyptian Arabic Diaries on the Lingualism website.

2

Asking for Directions

o مِن فضْلك، أَوْصل[1] شارِع الأزْهر إزّاي؟

◇ خُد المِلفّ[2] اللي جايّ أحْسن و اِرْجع، و بعْديْن اِطْلع مِن عَ الكّوبْري شِمال و اِجْوِد[3] يمِين. آخِر نزْلِة الكّوبْري هتْلاقي نفْسك في شارِع الأزْهر.

o Excuse me, how can I get to Al-Azhar Street?

◇ You'd best take the next u-turn and go back the other way, then go up onto the bridge on the left and turn right at the end of the bridge. You'll find yourself on Al-Azhar Street.

o *min fáḍlak, áwṣal[1] šāri3 ilʔázhar izzāy?*

◇ *xud ilmiláff[2] ílli gayy áɦsan w írga3, wi ba3dēn íṭla3 min 3a -kkúbri šimāl w íɦwid[3] yimīn. āxir názlit ikkúbri. hatlāʔi náfsak fi šāri3 ilʔázhar.*

[1] = أروح *arūɦ*

[2] = اليوتيرْن *ilyūtirn*

[3] = اِكْسر *íksar*

Both Google Maps and Apple Maps have streets, major landmarks, and many restaurants and shops mapped out throughout Egypt, especially in Cairo and Alexandria. Even if you prefer to interact with locals to get directions, it may be a good idea to check your map to make sure you're going the right way and get a better idea of how long it might take you to arrive.

Asking for directions

o مطْعم صِدْقي فينْ لَوْ سمحْتي؟

◇ آخِرِ الشّارِع ده هتِكْسر[1] شِمال، تِفْضل ماشي لِحدّ ما تْلاقي جامِع.
هتْلاقي المطْعم في وِشُّه[2] بِالظّبْط.

o ألْف شُكْر.[3]

o Where is the restaurant [called] Sedky, please?

◇ At the end of this street, you'll turn left and keep walking until you find a mosque. You'll find the restaurant right across the street from it.

o Thanks so much!

o *máṭ3am ṣídʔi fēn law samáɧti?*

◇ *āxir iššāri3 da hatíksar*[1] *šimāl, tífḍal māši li-ɧádd*^{ə} *ma tlāʔi gāmi3. hatlāʔi -lmáṭ3am fi wíššu*[2] *bi-ẓẓábṭ.*

o *alf*^{ə} *šukr.*[3]

1 = هتِحْوِد *hatíɧwid*

2 = قُدّامُه *ʔuddāmu* = قُصادُه *ʔuṣāḍu*

3 = ألْف شُكْر *alf*^{ə} *šukr* (lit. a thousand thanks) = مُتْشكِّر جِدّاً *mutšákkir gíddan*

Look for street signs not only on posts but also on corner buildings and fences. The Arabic font may sometimes be ornate and a challenge to read on older signs, but they are often written in English underneath.

4

ASKING FOR DIRECTIONS

○ سلامُ عليْكم. هُوَّ فُنْدُق دهب بِعيد مِن هِنا؟

◇ لا خالِص. هتِدْخُلي تالِت شارِع يمِين في أوِّل شِمال.

○ تمام و بعْديْن؟[1]

◇ هتْلاقيه عَ اليمين. تحْتُه قهْوَة.

○ Hello. Is Dahab hotel far from here?

◇ Not at all. You'll take the third street on the right and then the first one on the left.

○ Okay, and then?

◇ You'll find it on the right. There's a coffee shop downstairs.

○ *salāmu 3alēkam. húwwa fúndu? dáhab bi3īd min hína?*

◇ *la?, xāliṣ. hatidxúli tālit šāri3 yimīn fi áwwil šimāl.*

○ *tamām, wi ba3dēn?*[1]

◇ *hatla?ī 3a -lyimīn. táħtu ?áhwa.*

[1] تمام فيْن في الشّارع؟ *tamām, fēn fi -ššāri3?* **All right, where exactly on that street?**

In addition to numerical addresses, many buildings have names, which locals may more easily recognize. Always be sure to get the building's name when taking down an address.

5

ASKING FOR DIRECTIONS

o أطْلع عَ[1] الحُسينْ إزّاي؟

◇ ارْجعي وَرا شُوَيّة لِحدّ ما تْلاقي متْحف المنْسوجات. اِدْخُلي[2] شِمال و خلّيكي ماشْيَة طَوّالي[3] لِحدّ الآخِر. و اِسْألي مِن هِناك حدّ تاني.

o تمام مُتْشكِّرة أَوي.

o How can I reach Hussein [District/Mosque]?

◇ Go back a bit until you see the textile museum, then go left and keep walking straight until the end [of the street]. Then ask someone else over there.

o Thanks a lot.

o *áṭla3 3a*[1] *-lḫusēn izzāy?*

◇ *irgá3i wára šuwáyya li-ḫádd*ᵊ *ma tlāʔi mátḫaf ilmansugāt. idxúli*[2] *šmāl wi xallīki mášya ṭawwāli*[3] *li-ḫádd ilʔāxir. w isʔáli min hināk ḫadd*ᵊ *tāni.*

o *tamām, mutšakkíra áwi.*

[1] أروح *arūḫ* **I go to;** أَوْصل *áwṣal* **I arrive at, I get to**

[2] = اِحْوِدي *iḫwídi*

[3] = على طول *3ála ṭūl*

6

Asking for Directions

o هُوَّ فيه صالوْن حِلاقة هِنا إسْمُه البرِنْس؟

◇ هُوَّ قالّك فيْن؟[1]

o أنا رايِح بيْت حدّ. قالّي[2] إنُّه في شارِع مُحمّد عبْد العزيز فوْق صالوْن البرِنْس.

◇ آه الشّارِع ده تالِت شارِع على إيدك اليِمين بسّ ارْكِن هِنا في الوَسعة أحْسنك و اِتْمشّاها.

o تمام مُتْشكِّر جِدّاً.

o Is there an barber shop [called] El-Berens around here?

◇ Where were you told it was?

o I'm visiting someone's house over there, and he told me it's at the end of Muhammad Abdel Aziz Street above "El-Berens" barbershop.

◇ Ah, okay. That street is the third one on your right, but you'd better park where there's space here and walk.

o Okay, thank you very much!

o *húwwa fī ṣalōn ḫilāʔa hína ísmu ilbiríns?*

◇ *húwwa ʔállak fēn?*[1]

o *ána rāyiḫ bēt ḫadd. ʔálli*[2] *ínnu f šāri3 muḫámmad 3abd il3azīz, fōʔ ṣalōn ilbiríns.*

◇ *āh, iššāri3 da tālit šāri3 3ála īdak ilyimīn, bass írkin hína fi -lwása3a aḫsának wi -tmaššāha.*

o *tamām, mutšákkir gíddan.*

[1] This is a common question to a question posed by many people when they want to seem helpful by asking for further details even though they have no clue where the place is.

[2] أزور حدّ هِناك قالّي... *azūr ḫaddᵊ hnāk ʔálli...* **I'm visiting someone there who told me...**

○ مِن فضْلك، كُنْت عايِز أَوْصل لِشارِع شِهاب.

◇ هُوَّ بِعيد شُوَيّة. لَوْ هتاخْدُه مشْي ييجي تِلْت ساعة كِده[1].

○ طيِّب، تمام أنا مُمْكِن أتْمشّى.

◇ طيِّب، هتاخُد شِمال في تاني يِمين و تِمْشي على طول لِحدّ ما تِوْصل لِميدان لِبْنان و مِن هِناك اِسْأل تاني.

○ تمام مُتْشكِّر أوي.

◇ بسّ إنْتَ رايِح فيْن في شارِع شِهاب؟ ده شارِع طَويل.

○ رايِح عنْد البنْك الأهْلي.

◇ بسّ لَوْ كِده خلّي بالك. البنْك بِيِقْفل ٣.

○ يا خبر![2] طيِّب لَوْ كِده أرْكب أحْسن بقى يادوْب[3].

◇ لَوْ كِده خُد تاكْسي. مِن هِنا أحْسن حاجة.

○ طيِّب، أدّيله كام لِحدّ هِناك؟

◇ مُمْكِن تِدّيلُه ٢٠ - ٢٥ مِش أكْتر مِن كِده.

○ طيِّب، معلِشّ آخِر سُؤال.

◇ أُؤْمُر![4]

○ فيه مكان هِناك أقْدر أتْغدّى فيه؟ عشان هطْلع مِ البنْك على رمْسيس على طول، حاجِز قطْر السّاعة ٥.

◇ آه شارِع شِهاب كُلُّه مطاعِم و كافيْهات، بسّ أحْسنْلك تُطْلُب بِسُرْعة و تِدْخُل البنْك. على بال ما[5] تِخلّص يِكون الأكْل جِهِز.

○ صحّ كلامك[6]... مُتْشكِّر أوي.

◇ العفو. تِوْصل بِالسّلامة.

○ مُمْكِن بسّ تِشْرح[7] لِلتّاكْسي أقْصر طريق عشان مَيْطوِّليش المسافة و ملْحقْش المعاد؟

◇ أكيد! ثَواني أوَقّفْلك تاكْسي.

○ Excuse me, I wanted to get to Shehab Street.

◇ It's a bit far if you're going on foot. It will take you about 20 minutes.

○ Well, it's okay. I can walk.

◇ Okay, you will take the next street on the left, then the second street on the right, and keep walking straight until you reach Lebanon Square. And from there, ask again.

○ All right, thanks a lot!

◇ But [hold on], where are you going on Shehab Street? It's a really long street.

○ I'm going to the National Bank.

◇ If that's the case, keep in mind that it closes at 3 p.m.

○ Oh my goodness! Then, I'd better take something to barely make it in time.

◇ Yes, if that's the case, take a taxi. That's best from here.

○ Okay, how much shall I give him?

◇ You can give him 20-25 LE but no more than that.

○ All right. One last question, please.

◇ Sure!

○ Is there any place over there I can have lunch at? Because I'll leave the bank and head right to Ramses. I have a train at five.

◇ Yes, Shehab Street is full of restaurants and cafés, but you'd better order something and then go into the bank. By the time you're done, the order will be ready.

○ Yes, you're right! Thanks a lot!

◇ You're welcome. Arrive safely!

○ If you could just please explain to the taxi the shortest way so that he won't take a long way and I miss getting to the bank on time.

◇ Sure! Just a second and I'll stop a taxi for you.

○ *min fáḍlak, kuntᵊ 3āyiz áwṣal li-šāri3 šihāb.*
◇ *húwwa bi3īd šuwáyya. law hatáxdu mašyᵊ yīgi tiltᵊ sā3a kída*[1].
○ *ṭáyyib, tamām ána múmkin atmašša.*
◇ *ṭáyyib, hatāxud šimāl fi tāni yimīn wi tímši 3ála ṭūl li-ɦáddᵊ ma tíwṣal li-midān libnān wi min hināk ísʔal tāni.*
○ *tamām, mutšákkir áwi.*
◇ *bass ínta rāyiɦ fēn fi šāri3 šihāb? da šāri3 ṭawīl.*
○ *rāyiɦ 3and ilbánk ilʔáhli.*
◇ *bassᵊ law kída xálli bālak. ilbánkᵊ biyíʔfal talāta.*
○ *ya xábar!*[2] *ṭáyyib law kída árkab áɦsan báʔa yadōb*[3].
◇ *law kída xud táksi. min hína áɦsan ɦāga.*
○ *ṭáyyib, addīlu kām li-ɦáddᵊ hināk?*
◇ *múmkin tiddīlu 3išrīn, xamsa w 3išrīn, miš áktar min kída.*
○ *ṭáyyib, ma3alíšš āxir suʔāl.*
◇ *úʔmur!*[4]
○ *fī makān hināk áʔdar atɣádda fīʔ 3ašān háṭla3 mi -lbankᵊ 3ála ramsīs 3ála ṭūl, ɦāgiz ʔaṭr issā3a xámsa.*
◇ *āh, šāri3 šihāb kúllu maṭā3im wi kafihāt, bass aɦsánlak túṭlub bi-súr3a wi tídxul ilbánk. 3ála bāl ma*[5] *txállaṣ yikūn ilʔáklᵊ gíhiz.*
○ *ṣaɦɦᵊ kalāmak*[6]*... mutšákkir áwi.*
◇ *il3áfw. tíwṣal bi-ssalāma.*
○ *múmkin bassᵊ ṭíšraɦ*[7] *li-ttáksi áʔṣar ṭarīʔ 3ašān ma-yṭawwilīš ilmasāfa wi ma-lɦáʔš ilma3ād?*
◇ *akīd! sawāni awaʔʔáflak táksi.*

[1] هتِوْصل في حَوالي تِلْت ساعة *hatíwṣal fi ɦawāli tiltᵊ sā3a* **you'll get there in about 20 minutes [1/3 hour]**

[2] = يا نْهار أبْيَض! *ya nhār ábyaḍ!*

[3] لَوْ كِده يادوْب أرْكب حاجة لِهِناك. *law kída yadōb árkab ɦāga l-hināk.* **In that case, I have just enough time if I take [a taxi] there.**

[4] = اِتْفضّل *itfáḍḍal*

[5] = لِحدّ ما *li-ɦáddᵊ ma* **until**

[6] عنْدك حقّ *3ándak ɦaʔʔ* **you're right**; مظْبوط *maẓbūṭ* **exactly**

[7] تِوْصِف *tíwṣif* **(you) describe**

Vocabulary

to go	*rāђ* *míši*	راح مِشي
to turn	*ђáwad* *kásar*	حَوَد كسر
right	*yimīn*	يمِين
left	*šimāl*	شِمال
straight ahead	*ţawwāli*	طوّالي
to park	*rákan*	ركن
street	*šāri3 (šawāri3)*	شارِع (شَوارِع)
sidewalk	*raşīf*	رصيف
square, plaza	*midān*	ميدان
tunnel	*náfaʔ*	نفق
bridge	*kúbri*	كوبْري
bend, turn	*miláff*	مِلفّ
u-turn	*yūtirn*	يوتيرْن
across from it; across the street	*fi wíššu* *ʔuşādu*	في وِشُّه قُصادُه
behind it	*warā*	وَراه
next to it	*gámbu*	جمْبُه
on foot, walking	*mašy*	مشْي

Landmarks

bakery	*xabbāz*	خبّاز
barber	*ḥallāʔ*	حلّاق
butcher's	*gazzār*	جزّار
carpenter's	*naggār*	نجّار
church	*kinīsa*	كِنيسة
confectioner's	*ḥalawāni*	حلَواني
electrician's	*kahrabāʔi*	كهْربائي
fish shop	*sammāk*	سمّاك
fruit seller's	*fakahāni*	فكهاني
gas station	*banzīna*	بنْزينة
hairdresser	*kuwafīr*	كُوافير
mechanic's	*mikanīki*	ميكانيكي
monastery, convent	*dēr*	ديْر
(street) market	*sūʔ*	سوق
(big) mosque	*gāmi3*	جامِع
(small) mosque	*másgid*	مسْجِد
pharmacy	*ṣaydalíyya*	صَيْدلية
poultry butcher	*farárgi*	فرارْجي
restaurant	*máṭ3am (maṭā3im)*	مطْعم (مطاعِم)
(hair) salon	*ṣalōn*	صالوْن
station	*maḥáṭṭa*	محطّة

supermarket	*subirmárkit*	سوبِرْمارْكِت
tailor's	*xayyāṭ*	خيّاط
workshop	*wárša*	وَرْشة

Expressions

Excuse me, where is ___?	*min fáḍlak, fēn ___?*	مِن فضْلك فينْ ___؟
Excuse me, where is the beginning of ___ street?	*law samáħt, húwwa dáxlit šāri3 ___ minēn?*	لَوْ سمحْت هُوَّ دخْلِةْ شارِع ___ مِنينْ؟
How can I get to ___?	*áṭla3 3ála ___ minēn?* *arūħ ___ izzāy?*	أطْلع على ___ مِنينْ؟ أروح ___ إزّاي؟
What is the shortest way to ___?	*áʔṣar ṭarīʔ li-___ izzāy?*	أقْصر طريق لِـ ___ إزّاي؟
Is there a ___ around here?	*ma-fīš ___ ʔuráyyib min hína, min fáḍlak?*	مفيش ___ قُرِّيب مِن هِنا مِن فضْلك؟
Excuse me, what can I take to reach ___?	*law samáħt, árkab ʔē min hína 3ašān arūħ ___?*	لَوْ سمحْت أرْكب أيْه مِن هِنا عشان أروح ___؟
How far is it?	*bi3īda ʔadd^{ə} ʔē?*	بعيدة قدّ أيْه؟
I'm looking for this address.	*ána badáwwar 3ála -l3inwān da.*	أنا بدوّر على العِنْوان ده.

Can you show me on the map?	*tíʔdar tiwarrīni 3ála -lxarīṭa?*	تِقْدر تِوَرّيني على الخريطة؟

◇

Go straight.	*ímši 3ala ṭūl.*	اِمْشي على طول.
Turn right/left.	*íksar/íɦwid/ídxul yimīn/šimāl.*	اِكْسر/اِحْوِد/اِدْخُل يمِين/شِمال.
Go over the bridge and take the second offramp on the right.	*íṭla3 fōʔ ilkúbri wi xud tāni názla 3a -lyimīn.*	اِطْلع فوْق الكوبْري و خُد تاني نازْلة عَ اليمِين.
Go through the tunnel and as soon as you're out, turn onto the third street on the right.	*ínzil innáfaʔ w áwwil ma tíṭla3 íksar tālit šāri3 yimīn.*	اِنْزِل النّفق و أوِّل ما تِطْلع اِكْسر تالِت شارِع يمِين.
You'll find it by the big green sign over there.	*hatlaʔīʔ 3and ilyáfṭa ilxáḍra -kkibīra ílli hināk di.*	هتْلاقية عنْد اليافْطة الخضْرا الكِّبيرة اللي هِناك دي.
I don't know really. You can ask at the shop next to me.	*ma-3ráfšᵊ wallāhi, múmkin tísʔal ilmaɦáll ílli gámbi.*	معْرفْش واللهِ، مُمْكِن تِسْأل المحلّ اللي جمْبي.
I have no idea. I'm not from around here.	*miš 3ārif wallāhi, miš min hína.*	مِش عارِف واللهِ، مِش مِن هِنا.
Where did he tell you exactly?	*húwwa ʔállak fēn bi-ẓẓábṭ?*	هُوَّ قالّك فيْن بِالظّبْط؟

Where do you want to go?	*ínta 3āyiz tirūḫ fēn bi-ẓẓábṭ?*	إنْتَ عايِز تِروح فينْ بِالظّبْط؟
It's ten minutes on foot.	*3ášar daʔāyiʔ mašy.*	عشر دقايِق مشْي.
You're going in the wrong direction.	*ínta māši fi -lʔittigāh ilɣálaṭ.*	إنْتَ ماشي في الاِتِّجاهْ الغلط.

Taking the Subway جُوّه المِتْرو

Cairo has three مِتْرو *mítru* **subway** lines. For only a few Egyptian pounds, you can travel across the city, and even into its suburbs, making it by far the cheapest means of transportation available. By taking the subway, you can also avoid getting stuck in traffic jams and having to negotiate fares with taxi drivers. Although the subway system does not reach all parts of the city, it may get you closer to where you're trying to go, after which you can take a short taxi or bus ride. Using the subway in Cairo is the same as anywhere else in the world. You go into the station, purchase a ticket at any of the ticket windows, feed your ticket into the turnstile (and hold onto your ticket until you exit), find the right platform, and get on the train. Signs above the platforms indicate the direction the train is going by showing the last station on the line. Be sure that you get on in the right direction by double checking on the subway-line maps posted throughout the station and in the subway cars, or, for your convenience, on p. 48.

Figuring out which line to take

o مِن فضْلك، أروح[1] ثكنات المعادي إزّاي؟

◇ هتاخْدي خطّ المرْج - حِلْوان و ترْكبي مِ اتِّجاهْ حِلْوان.

o هِيَّ بِعيدة مِن المعادي؟

◇ لا يادوْب هتْفوتي محطّةْ حدايِق المعادي و المعادي و تِنْزِلي
بعْدها على طول.

o Excuse me, how do I get to Sakanat El-Maadi?

◇ You'll take the Marg-Helwan line in the Helwan direction.

o Is it far from Maadi?

◇ No, you will just pass Hadaye' El-Maadi and El-Maadi and get off right afterward.

o *min fáḍlak, arūḫ*[1] *sakanāt ilma3ādi izzāy?*

◇ *hatáxdi xaṭṭ ilmárg - ḫilwān wi tarkábi mi -ttigāh ḫilwān.*

o *híyya bi3īda min ilma3ādi?*

◇ *laʔ, yadōb hatfūti maḫáṭṭit ḫadāyiʔ ilma3ādi wi -lma3ādi wi tinzíli ba3dáha 3ála ṭūl.*

[1] = أقْدر أروح *áʔdar arūḫ*

The entrances to subway stations are marked with a red letter M on a blue star.

The ticket windows in subway stations are famously great places to get small change.

Trains run every five minutes or so from around 6 a.m. to midnight. Hours of operation are extended during Ramadan.

Al-Shohadaa (formally Mubarak), Attaba, and Sadat are especially crowded stations because they are transfer stations—where two lines meet. So be sure to get on the right line and in the right direction!

2

BUYING TICKETS

o لَوْ سمحْتي، عايْزة تذْكرْتينْ اِتّجاهْ حِلْوان.
◇ هتِنْزِلي محطّةْ أيْه؟
o جامْعِةْ حِلْوان.
◇ يِبْقى كِده ١٤ جنيْه.

o Excuse me, I'd like two tickets for the Helwan direction.
◇ Which station will you get off at?
o Gam'et Helwan.
◇ Then that will be 14 LE.

o *law samáɧti, 3áyza tazkartēn ittigāh ɧilwān.*
◇ *hatinzíli maɧáṭṭit ʔē?*
o *gám3it ɧilwān.*
◇ *yíbʔa kída arba3tāšar ginēh.*

Ticket prices vary depending on the number of stations to your destination. Just say your destination when you buy your ticket.

Line 1 is the oldest (opening in 1987) and longest line, with 35 stations over 27.5 miles (44.3 km). It runs from New El Marg station in the north to Helwan in the south, staying to the east of the Nile river. Most of the line is above ground, only going underground in the city center.

Line 2 was added in the 1990s. It runs 13 miles (21.5 km) from the northern terminus Shubra El-Kheima in the Nile Delta region to El-Mounib station in Giza, crossing the Nile at Gezira Island.

Line 3, at the time of publication of this book, is an ongoing project, with stations currently open from Attaba (where you can transfer to/from line 1) to Nadi El-Shams, near the Cairo International Airport. It is eventually expected to connect the airport to Imbaba and Mohandiseen in Giza.

3

Getting on your train in the right place

○ هُوَّ أنا واقِف هِنا صحّ؟[1]

◇ هُوَّ إنْتَ واقِف عنْد سهْم الرُّكوب اللي عَ الأرْض مظْبوط بسّ العربية غلط.

○ إزّاي؟

◇ بُصّ عَ اليُفط اللي فوْق. هتْلاقيها مِحدِّدة عربِيّات السّيِّدات. دي ممْنوع رِجالة يِرْكبوا فيها.

○ يا راجِل؟[2] طيِّب نُقف فيْن بقى؟

◇ تعالى نِطْلع قُدّام بعْد منْطقِةْ عربيةْ السّيِّدات.

○ Am I standing in the right place?

◇ You're standing by a boarding arrow, which is correct, but by the wrong car.

○ How so?

◇ Look at the signs above. You'll find they show the ladies' cars, in which men are not allowed.

○ Seriously? So where should we stand then?

◇ Let's move up a bit past the area set for the ladies' car.

○ *húww- ána wāʔif hína ṣaḥḥ?*[1]

◇ *húww- ínta wāʔif 3andᵊ sahm irrukūbílli 3a -lʔarḍᵊ maẓbūṭ bass il3arabíyya ɣálaṭ.*

○ *izzāy?*

◇ *buṣṣᵊ 3a -lyúfaṭ ílli fōʔ. hatlaʔīha mḥaddída 3arabiyyāt issayyidāt. di mamnū3 rigāla yirkábu fīha.*

○ *ya rāgil?*[2] *ṭáyyib núʔaf fēn báʔa?*

◇ *ta3āla níṭla3 ʔuddām ba3dᵊ manṭáʔit 3arabīt issayyidāt.*

[1] كِده صحّ؟ *kída ṣaḥḥ?* **Is this right?** / [2] = لا يا شيْخ؟ *lā ya šēx?* = لا بِجدّ؟ *lā, bi-gádd?* = فِعْلاً؟ *fí3lan?* **No way!; Seriously?; Oh, really?**

Offering your seat to someone in need

o اِتْفضّلي حضْرِتك.
◇ مُتْشكِّرة يابْني[1]، مفيش مُشْكِلة[2].
o لا يا حاجّة[3] إزّاي؟[4] أنا نازِل كمان محطِّتيْن و إنْتي شايْلة حاجات. اِتْفضّلي اُقْعُدي مكاني.
◇ ربِّنا يِبارِك فيك[4] يابْني.

o Please! (Have a seat!)
◇ Thank you, young man. That's okay.
o No, no, ma'am. I'm getting off in two stations anyway, and you're carrying some stuff. Please, take my seat.
◇ God bless you, son!

o *itfaḍḍáli ɧaḍrítik.*
◇ *mutšakkíra yábni*[1], *ma-fīš muškíla*[2].
o *la ya ɧágga*[3] *-zzāy?*[4] *ána nāzil kamān maɧaṭṭitēn w ínti šáyla ɧagāt. itfaḍḍáli uʔ3údi makāni.*
◇ *rabbína yibārik fīk*[5] *yábni.*

[1] يابْني *yábni* (lit. my son) is how an older person may address a younger man or boy. To a younger woman or girl, it would be يا بِنْتي *ya bínti* (lit. my daughter).

[2] = مِش مُشْكِلة *miš muškíla;* ملوش لِزوم *ma-lūš lizūm* **there is no need**

[3] حاجّة *ɧágga* **Haji, pilgrim** is a polite form of address to an elderly woman. To an eldery man, it's حاجّ *ɧagg.*

[4] = لا والله أبداً *lā wallāhi ábadan* **No way.** (i.e., I insist.)

[5] = ربِّنا يبارِكْلك *rabbína ybaríklak*

Some older women prefer to ride in the mixed cars rather than the ladies' cars because there is a better chance of being offered a seat.

5

ASKING ABOUT YOUR DESTINATION

o هُوَّ إحْنا فينْ دِلْوَقْتي لَوْ سمحْتي؟

◇ إحْنا لِسّه ماشْيين مِن الشُّهدا و داخْلين على غمْرة.

o طيِّب، فاضِل كِتير[1] على عينْ شمْس؟

◇ آه لِسّه بدْري. ييجي[2] تِسع محطّات كِده بسّ ركِّزي في الخريطة اللي فوْق الباب.

o Where are we now, please?

◇ We've just left Al-Shohadaa and are heading toward Ghamra.

o I see. Are there still [many stations] until Ein Shams?

◇ Yeah, it's still a ways off... around nine more stations. Just examine the map above the door.

o *huwwá -ḫna fēn dilwáʔti, law samáḫti?*

◇ *íḫna líssa mašyīn min iššúhada wi daxlīn 3ála ɣámra.*

o *ṭáyyib, fāḍil kitīr*[1] *3ála 3ēn šams?*

◇ *āh, líssa bádri. yīgi*[2] *tísa3 maḫaṭṭāt kída, bassᵊ rakkízi fi -lxarīṭa -lli fōʔ ilbāb.*

[1] = لِسّه كِتير *líssa ktīr*

[2] = حَوالي *ḫawāli* **around, about**

عربيّات السيِّدات *3arabiyyāt issayyidāt* **ladies' cars**–Two cars (usually the fourth and fifth) of a subway train are reserved for women (and children) only. (Cars marked with green stickers are women-only from 9 a.m. until 9 p.m. only.) This is not for religious reasons, but to help women avoid sexual harassment they might otherwise experience taking public transportation. If you are a man who looks obviously foreign and you unwittingly get on a ladies' car, there is no need to panic. Your fellow female passengers will likely not comment and just assume you were unaware of the rule. Just try to get off at the next station before you are fined.

6

Asking for directions in a subway station

- o لَوْ سمحْت أنا المفْروض هاخُد القطْر. أطْلع عَ المحطّة إزّاي؟
- ◇ لا إنْتَ كِده ماشي غلط. السِّكّة دي اللي طالِع عَ[1] الميدان.
- o أُمّال أمْشي إزّاي كِده؟[2]
- ◇ بُصّ اِرْجع وَرا لِحدّ السّلالِم و اِمْشي وَرا اليُفط اللي مكْتوب عليْها (إلى محطّة القِطار[3]).
- o تمام مُتْشكِّر جِدّاً.

- o Excuse me, I have to take a train. How do I get to the station?
- ◇ No, you're going the wrong way. This way leads up to the square.
- o Then how should I go?
- ◇ Look, go back to where the stairs are and follow the signs that say "Toward the Railway Station."
- o Okay, thanks a lot!

- o *law samáḥt, ána -lmafrūḍ hāxud ilʔáṭr. áṭla3 3a -lmaḥáṭṭa izzāy?*
- ◇ *lā, ínta kída māši ɣálaṭ. issíkka di -lli ṭāli3 3a*[1] *-lmidān.*
- o *ummāl ámši izzāy kída?*[2]
- ◇ *buṣṣ, írga3 wára li-ḥádd issalālim w ímši wára -lyúfaṭ ílli maktūb 3alēha "íla maḥáṭṭat alqiṭār*[3]*".*
- o *tamām, mutšákkir gíddan.*

[1] = بِتْوَدّي عَ/على *bitwáddi 3a-/3ála*

[2] = طب، أمْشي إزّاي؟ *ṭab, ámši -zzāy?*

[3] قِطار *qiṭār* **train** is Modern Standard Arabic, but, of course, this is what you will see written on signs.

The best people to ask for directions are the security guards you will see everywhere in a subway station. They are familiar with all of the lines and exits.

○ مِن فضْلك، أشْترِي التّذاكرِ مِنيْن؟

◇ شِبّاك التّذاكرِ هِناك أهُه. اِمْشي معايا.

○ مُتْشكِّر أَوي. أنا رايِح الملك الصّالح. أحِضّر[1] كام؟

◇ لا دي يادوْب[2] كام محطّة ٣ جِنيْهْ. بسّ اِسْتنّى، أشْترِيلك معايا.

○ مُتْشكِّر جِدّاً.

◇ إنْتَ أوِّل مرّة تاخُد[3] المِترْو؟

○ بِصراحة آه و مِتْلخْبط أَوي.

◇ معلِش هُوَّ في الأوِّل يِلخْبط بسّ طول ما إنْتَ ماشي معَ الخريطة الدُّنْيا تمام[4].

○ آه أنا مِلاحِظ الخريطة في كُلّ حِتّة.[5]

◇ بُصّ يا سيدي، بِتْحُطّ التّذْكرة هِنا تْعدّي و تاخُدْها أوِّل ما تْعدّي مِن النّاحْيَة التّانْيَة.

○ تمام و لَوْ ضاعِت؟[6]

◇ هتِدْفع تاني و إنْتَ خارِج مِن المحطّة اللي نازِل فيها.

○ طيِّب، و أيْه الأسْهُم دي؟

◇ دي أسْهُم عشان تِحدِّد أبْواب النُّزول و الرُّكوب عشان النّاس تِلْحق ترْكب.

○ طيِّب، أنا مِلاحِظ فيه عربِيّات سيِّدات[7]. اِفْرِض معايا عيلْتي؟

◇ دي عربِيّات لِلسّيِّدات بسّ و ممْنوع نِرْكب فيها. بسّ هُمّا أحْرار يِرْكبوا في بِتوعْنا عادي.

○ مْمْم... تمام مُتْشكِّر جِدّاً بِجدّ.

◇ على أيْه بسّ! أهُه جِهْ. يَلّا خلّيك وَرايا[8].

○ يا نْهار أبْيَض![9] ده زحْمة جِدّاً!

◇ آه ما كُلُّه طالع مِن شُغْلُه دِلْوَقْتي.
o و أيْه الرّاجِل ده؟ بيْبيع أيْه؟
◇ ده بِيْبيع كُتَيِّبات. فيه بيّاعين كِتير بِيِطْلعوا بِيبيعوا حاجات لَوْ حابِب تِشْترِي.
o حِلْو واللهِ!
◇ بِالظّبْط. على الأقلّ بِيِشْتغلوا و بِيْدوّروا على رِزْق حلال.

o Excuse me, where can I buy tickets?
◇ The window is just over there. Follow me.
o Thanks a lot. I'm heading to El-Malek El-Saleh. How much should I prepare [to pay]?
◇ It's just a couple of stations away, so it'll be 3 LE. Wait, I'll buy it for you.
o Thank you so much.
◇ Is it your first time taking the subway?
o Actually, yes. And I'm so confused.
◇ It's okay. It's a bit confusing at first, but as long as you're following the maps, you'll be fine.
o Yeah, I've noticed the map is everywhere.
◇ Look, you put the ticket right here, then pass, then take it again as soon as you cross to the other side
o Okay. And what if I lose it?
◇ You'll have to pay again when you exit at the station you're getting off at.
o What about those arrows?
◇ They are arrows [that line up with] the doors for getting on and off so that people can get on in time.
o I see. I notice there are ladies' cars... what if I have my family with me?
◇ Those are only for women, and we're not allowed on them, but they are free to get on "ours."
o Ah, I see. Thanks a lot, really!
◇ Not at all! Here it comes. Follow me.

○ Oh my goodness! It's so crowded!

◇ Yeah, everyone is off work now.

○ What about this man? What is he selling?

◇ He's selling some booklets. There are many vendors that get on and sell stuff if you want to buy.

○ Nice!

◇ Exactly. At least, they are working to earn some legitimate money.

○ *min fáḍlak, aštíri -ttazākir minēn?*

◇ *šibbāk ittazākir hināk ahú. ímši ma3āya.*

○ *mutšákkir áwi. ána rāyiɦ ilmálak iṣṣāliɦ. aɦáḍḍar*[1] *kām?*

◇ *lā, di yadōb*[2] *kām maɦáṭṭa, talāta gnēh. bass istanna, aštirīlak ma3āya.*

○ *mutšákkir gíddan.*

◇ *ínta áwwil márra ṭāxud*[3] *ilmítru?*

○ *bi-ṣarāɦa āh, wi mitláxbaṭ áwi.*

◇ *ma3alíšš, húwwa fi -lʔáwwil yiláxbaṭ bassᵊ ṭūl má-nta māši má3a -lxarīṭa iddúnya tamām*[4].

○ *āh, ána mlāɦiẓ ilxarīṭa fi kullᵊ ɦitta.*[5]

◇ *buṣṣᵊ ya sīdi, bitɦúṭṭ ittazkára hína t3áddi wi taxúdha áwwil ma t3áddi min innáɦya ittánya.*

○ *tamām, wi law ḍā3it?*[6]

◇ *hatídfa3 tāni w ínta xārig min ilmaɦáṭṭa ílli nāzil fīha.*

○ *ṭáyyib, w ʔē ilʔáshum di?*

◇ *di áshum 3ašān tiɦáddid abwāb innuzūl wi -rrukūb 3ašān innās tílɦaʔ tírkab.*

○ *ṭáyyib, ána mlāɦiẓ fī 3arabiyyāt ṣayyidāt*[7]. *ífriḍ ma3āya 3ílti?*

◇ *di 3arabiyyāt li-ssayyidāt bass, wi mamnū3 nírkab fīha. bassᵊ húmma aɦrār yirkábu fi bitú3na 3ādi.*

○ *mmm... tamām mutšákkir gíddan bi-gádd.*

◇ *3ála ʔē bass! ahú gih. yálla xallīk warāya*[8].

○ *ya nhār ábyaḍ!*[9] *da záɦma gíddan!*

◇ *āh, ma kúllu ṭāli3 min šúɣlu dilwáʔti.*

○ *wi ʔē -rrāgil da? biybī3 ʔē?*

◇ *da biybī3 kutayyibāt. fī bayya3īn kitīr biyiṭlá3u yibī3u ɦagāt law ɦābib tištíri.*

○ *ɦilwᵊ wallāhi!*

◇ *bi-ẓẓábṭ. 3ála -lʔaʔállᵊ biyištáɣalu wi biydawwáru 3ála rizʔᵊ ɦalāl.*

[1] = أجهِّز agáhhiz

[2] = دوْل بسّ dōl bass

[3] = ترْكب tírkab

[4] مِش هتتوه miš hattūh **you won't get lost**

[5] كُلّ حِتّة فيها خرايِط. *kullᵊ ḫitta fīha xarāyiṭ.* = الدُّنْيا كُلّها خرايِط. *iddúnya kulláha xarāyiṭ.* **There are maps everywhere.**

[6] = و لَوْ وِقْعِت؟ *wi law wíʔ3it?*

[7] سيِّدات *sayyidāt* is actually a Modern Standard Arabic word. It is always used to refer to the ladies' car, but in other contexts, Egyptians use the word سِتّات to mean **ladies**.

[8] = تعالى وَرايا *ta3āla warāya*

[9] = يا خبر أبْيَض! *ya xábar ábyaḍ!* = يا لهْوي! *ya láhwi!* = يانْهاري *ya nhāri!*

You may see vendors walking through the subway cars selling their wares. This is common, and it is fine to buy from them.

You may also see people begging on subway cars. Know that the majority of them are frauds (pretending to be blind, etc.) and have made a profession out of begging, often earning more in a month than the average civil servant would. Some carry babies and bring children with them to garner sympathy. Never give them money. The children are often kidnapped, mistreated, and mercilessly used as props. (See book 2, p. 216 for more on dealing with beggars.)

The subway is nearly always crowded, especially the ladies' cars. When your station is coming up, start getting ready by getting as close to the door as you can. To make your way through the crowd, ask people standing in your way in a loud voice: نازْلين المحطّة الجّايّة يا جماعة؟ *nazlīn ilmaháṭṭa -ggáyya ya gamā3a?* **Is everyone getting off at the next station?** (It sounds more polite in Arabic!) Hearing this question, anyone who isn't getting off will move to the side to let you get closer to the door. When exiting, move fast because the doors close quickly, and others will be pushing their way out right behind you.

Vocabulary

subway, metro (UK: underground)	*mítru*	مِتْرو
to take the subway	*xad/ríkib mítru*	خد/رِكِب مِتْرو
car, carriage	*3arabíyya*	عربية
door	*bāb (abwāb)*	باب (أبْواب)
seat	*kúrsi (karāsi)*	كُرْسي (كراسي)
station	*maɦáṭṭa*	محطّة
to change trains (to another line)	*báddil maɦaṭṭāt*	بدِّل محطّات
(subway) line	*xaṭṭ*	خطّ
direction	*ittigāh*	اِتِّجاهْ
map	*xarīṭa (xarāyiṭ)*	خريطة (خرايِط)
sign	*yáfṭa (yúfaṭ)*	يافْطة (يُفط)
ticket	*tazkára (tazākir)*	تذْكرة (تذاكِر)
ticket window	*šibbāk ittazākir*	شِبّاك التّذاكِر
stairs	*síllim*	سِلِّم
platform	*raṣīf*	رصيف
arrow	*sahm (áshum)*	سهْم (أسْهُم)
exit	*xurūg*	خُروج
entrance	*duxūl*	دُخول
boarding, getting on	*rukūb*	رُكوب
to get on; to ride	*ríkib*	رِكِب

alighting, getting off	*nuzūl*	نُزول
to get off	*nízil*	نِزِل
seller	*bayyā3*	بيّاع
beggar	*šaḫḫāt*	شحّات
security	*amn*	أمْن
officer	*3askári*	عسْكري
police officer	*ẓābiṭ*	ظابِط

Expressions

Where is the ticket window, please?	*šibbāk ittazākir fēn?*	شِبّاك التّذاكِر فينْ؟
Excuse me, I want a ticket to ___.	*min fáḍlak, 3āyiz tazkára li-___.*	مِن فضْلك، عايِز تذْكرة لِـ ___.
I'm sorry, my ticket is gone/lost.	*ma3alíšš, tazkárti wíʔ3it.*	معلِشّ تذْكرْتي وِقْعِت.
How much is it to ___?	*bi-kām li-ḫádd^{ə} ___?*	بِكام لِحدّ ___؟
Where can I take the subway to go to ___?	*árkab li-___ minēn?*	أرْكب لِـ ___ مِنينْ؟
Excuse me, can I get by? I'm getting off at the next station.	*ba3d íznak múmkin a3áddi 3ašān nāzil ilmaḫáṭṭa iggáyya.*	بعْد إذْنك مُمْكِن أعدّي عشان نازِل المحطّة الجّايّة.
Where is the exit, please?	*ilxurūg minēn law samáḫt?*	الخُروج مِنينْ لَوْ سمحْت؟

◇

Transfer at ___ and take the ___ direction.	*báddil fi -___ w írkab xaṭṭᵊ ___.*	بدِّل في ___ و اِرْكب خطّ ___.
This car is for ladies only.	*il3arabíyya di li-ssayyidāt bass.*	العربية دي لِلسّيِّدات بسّ.
You're on the wrong train. Get off and take the opposite direction.	*ínta rākib ɣálaṭ. ínzil w írkab 3aks ilʔittigāh.*	إنْتَ راكِب غلط. اِنْزِل و اِرْكب عكْس الاِتِّجاهْ.

Cairo Subway System: The Metro

Line 1

1 New El-Marg المرج الجديدة
2 El-Marg المرج
3 Ezbet El-Nakhl عزبة النخل
4 Ain Shams عين شمس
5 El-Matareyya المطرية
6 Helmeyet El-Zaitoun حلمية الزيتون
7 Hadayeq El-Zaitoun حدائق الزيتون
8 Saray El-Qobba ساراي القبة
9 Hammamat El-Qobba حمامات القبة
10 Kobri El-Qobba كوبري القبة
11 Manshiet El-Sadr منشية الصدر
12 El-Demerdash الدمرداش
13 Ghamra غمرة
14 Al-Shohadaa الشهداء
15 Orabi عرابي
16 Nasser جمال عبدالناصر
17 Sadat السادات
18 Saad Zaghloul سعد زغلول
19 Al-Sayeda Zeinab السيدة زينب
20 El-Malek El-Saleh الملك الصالح
21 Mar Girgis مار جرجس
22 El-Zahraa' الزهراء
23 Dar El-Salam دار السلام
24 Hadayek El-Maadi حدائق المعادي
25 Maadi المعادي
26 Sakanat El-Maadi ثكنات المعادي
27 Tora El-Balad طرة البلد
28 Kozzika كوتسيكا
29 Tora El-Asmant طرة الأسمنت
30 El-Maasara المعصرة
31 Hadayek Helwan حدائق حلوان
32 Wadi Hof وادي حوف
33 Helwan University جامعة حلوان
34 Ain Helwan عين حلوان
35 Helwan حلوان

Line 2

1 Shubra El-Kheima شبرا الخيمة

2 Kolleyyet El-Zeraa كلية الزراعة

3 Mezallat المظلات

4 Khalafawy الخلفاوي

5 St. Teresa سانتا تريزا

6 Rod El-Farag روض الفرج

7 Masarra مسرة

8 Al-Shohadaa الشهداء

9 Attaba العتبة

10 Mohamed Naguib محمد نجيب

11 Sadat السادات

12 Opera الأوبرا

13 Dokki الدقي

14 El Bohoth البحوث

15 Cairo University جامعة القاهرة

16 Faisal فيصل

17 Giza الجيزة

18 Omm El-Masryeen أم المصريين

19 Sakiat Mekky ساقية مكي

20 El-Mounib المنيب

Line 3

1 Cairo University جامعة القاهرة

2 Bulaq El-Dakroor بولاق الدكرور

3 Gamaat El Dowal Al-Arabiya جامعة الدول العربية

4 Wadi El-Nil وادي النيل

5 El-Tawfikeya التوفيقية

6 Rod El-Farag Axis محور روض الفرج

7 Ring Road الطريق الدائري

8 El-Kawmeya Al-Arabiya القومية العربية

9 El-Bohy البوهي

10 Imbaba إمبابة

11 Sudan St. السودان

12 Kit Kat الكيت كات

13 Zamalek الزمالك

14 Maspero ماسبيرو

15 Nasser جمال عبدالناصر

16 Attaba العتبة

17 Bab El-Shaaria باب الشعرية

18 El-Geish الجيش

19 Abdou Pasha عبدة باشا

20 Abbassiya العباسية

21 Fair Zone أرض المعارض

22 Stadium الإستاد

23 Koleyet El-Banat كلية البنات

24 Al-Ahram الأهرام

25 Haroun هارون

26 Heliopolis Square ميدان هليوبوليس

27 Alf Maskan ألف مسكن

28 Nadi El-Shams نادي الشمس

29 El-Nozha 1 النزهة ١

30 El-Nozha 2 النزهة ٢

31 Keba' قباء

32 Omar Ibn El-Khattab عمر بن الخطاب

33 El-Herafyeen الحرفيين

34 Assalam السلام

35 Ahmed Galal أحمد جلال

36 Airport المطار

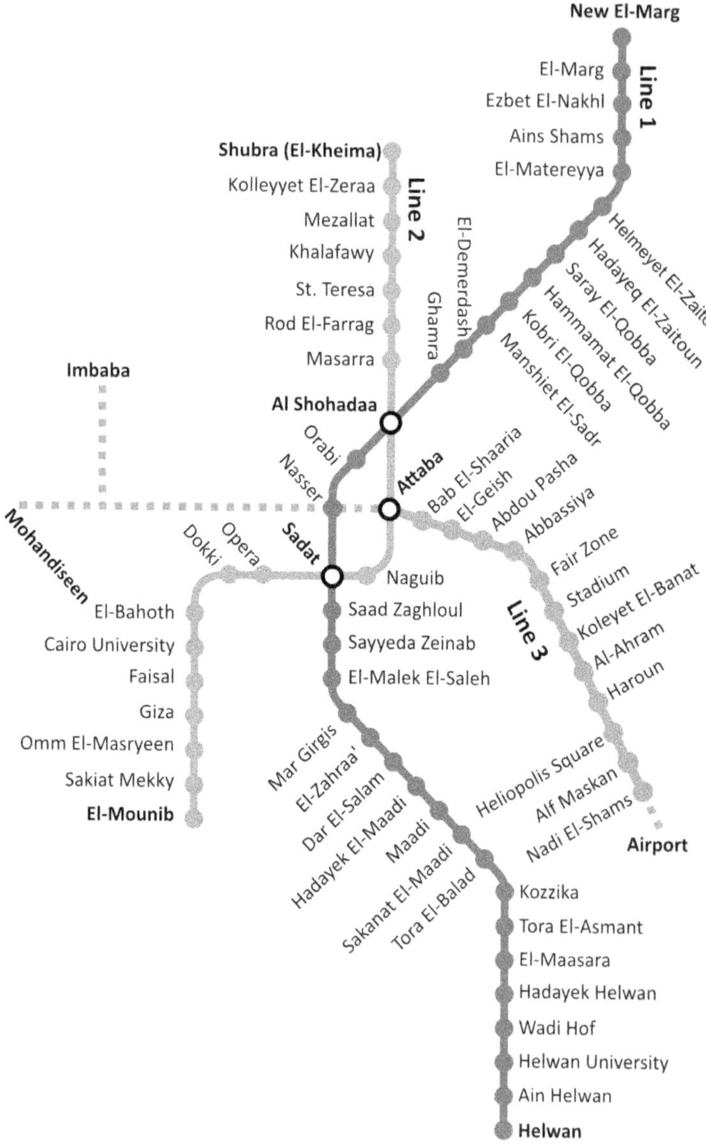

New El-Marg
El-Marg
Ezbet El-Nakhl
Ains Shams
El-Matereyya
Line 1
Helmeyet El-Zaitoun
Hadayeq El-Zaitoun
Saray El-Qobba
Hammamat El-Qobba
Kobri El-Qobba
Manshiet El-Sadr
El-Demerdash
Ghamra
Shubra (El-Kheima)
Kolleyyet El-Zeraa
Mezallat
Khalafawy
St. Teresa
Rod El-Farrag
Masarra
Line 2
Imbaba
Al Shohadaa
Orabi
Nasser
Attaba
Bab El-Shaaria
El-Geish
Abdou Pasha
Abbassiya
Fair Zone
Stadium
Koleyet El-Banat
Al-Ahram
Haroun
Line 3
Heliopolis Square
Alf Maskan
Nadi El-Shams
Airport
Mohandiseen
Dokki
Opera
Sadat
Naguib
Saad Zaghloul
Sayyeda Zeinab
El-Malek El-Saleh
El-Bahoth
Cairo University
Faisal
Giza
Omm El-Masryeen
Sakiat Mekky
El-Mounib
Mar Girgis
El-Zahraa'
Dar El-Salam
Hadayek El-Maadi
Maadi
Sakanat El-Maadi
Tora El-Balad
Kozzika
Tora El-Asmant
El-Maasara
Hadayek Helwan
Wadi Hof
Helwan University
Ain Helwan
Helwan

Taking a Microbus في الميكْروباص

The idea of taking a ميكْروباص *mikrubāṣ* **microbus** can at first seem daunting to a newcomer. It requires being quick, getting in and out to let others by, having the correct change, as well as some mathematical skills in case you're lucky enough to gather fares from other passengers. But once you learn the system, you'll find microbuses to be a convenient and efficient way to commute. Microbuses don't have predetermined stops as buses do. They do follow a set route but stop only when flagged down. And when you're approaching your destination, use a nice, loud voice to tell the driver هنْزِل هِنا! *hánzil hína!* **I'll get out here!** In this chapter, you'll learn how to find the right microbus, be part of the system of passing fares forward and passing change back, as well as communicate with your fellow passengers and the driver to ensure you have a successful microbus journey.

Finding your microbus at the station

○ مِن فضْلك، لَوْ عايْزة أروح المُهنْدِسين أرْكب أيْه؟[1]

◇ العربِيّات اللي واقْفة هِناك دي. اِرْكبي واحْدة بِتْحمِّل.

(after reaching the microbus)

○ بِترْوح المُهنْدِسين دي لَوْ سمحْت؟

◇ أَيْوَه اِرْكبي هِنا.

○ Excuse me, if I want to get to Mohandeseen, what [microbus] should I take?

◇ Those microbuses over there. Get on one that is boarding.

(after reaching the microbus)

○ Excuse me, does this go to Mohandeseen?

◇ Yes, get in.

○ *min fáḍlak, law 3áyza arūḥ ilmuhandisīn, árkab ʔē?*[1]

◇ *il3arabiyyāt ílli wáʔfa hinēk di. irkábi wáḥda bitḥámmil.*

(after reaching the microbus)

○ *bitrūḥ ilmuhandisīn di law samáḥt?*

◇ *áywa, irkábi hína.*

[1] = أرْكب أيْه لِلمُهنْدِسين؟ *árkab ʔē li-lmuhandisīn?*

Egyptians have a number of ways to refer to a ميكْروباص *mikrubāṣ* **microbus**. The brand name سوزوكي *suzūki* **Suzuki** is synonymous with microbus, as many microbuses are 6-seat Suzuki models. You may also hear تُنّاية *tunnāya*. In Cairo, where many older-model microbuses are **Volkswagen**, a shortened form فيلوكْس *vilúks* is generically used. عربية *3arabíyya* **car** is also understood in context to mean microbus. Alexandrians say مشْروع *mašrū3* (lit. undertaking) and, less commonly, زئْردة *zaʔráda*.

2

DEALING WITH OTHER PASSENGERS

o مِن فضْلك، مُمْكِن أعدّي؟[1]

◇ آه اِتْفضّلي، ثَواني أنْزِلّك أحْسن.

o حضْرِتك واخِد كُرْسِيينْ؟

◇ لا مُؤاخْذة معلِشّ... اِتْفضّلي.

o أسْتأْذِنك بسّ تِفْتح الشِّبّاك عشان النّفس.

◇ ماشي بسّ مِش هفْتحُه أَوي[2] عشان الدُّنْيا ساقْعة.

o Excuse me, can I get by?

◇ Yes, go ahead. Hold on, it's better if I get off first [to let you on].

o Are you paying for two seats?

◇ Pardon me. Here you go.

o Excuse me, can you open the window for some [fresh] air?

◇ Sure, but I won't open it a lot because it's cold.

o *min fáḍlak, múmkin a3áddi?*[1]

◇ *āh, itfaḍḍáli, sawāni anzíllik áɧsan.*

o *ɧaḍrítak wāxid kursiyēn?*

◇ *la mu?áxza ma3alíšš... itfaḍḍáli.*

o *asta?zínak bass*ᵊ *tíftaɧ iššibbāk 3ašān innáfas.*

◇ *māši bass*ᵊ *miš haftáɧu áwi*[2] *3ašān iddúnya sá?3a.*

[1] بعْد إذْنك لَوْ سمحْت! *ba3d*ᵊ *íznak, law samáɧt!* **Excuse me, please!**

[2] هفْتحُه حِتّة صُغيرّة *haftáɧu ɧitta ṣɣayyára* **I'll open it a little bit**

It's always recommended to get in crowded microbuses with mixed genders (i.e., not completely empty or with only male passengers), especially for women, in order to avoid any potential harassment or scams).

3

ASKING A FELLOW PASSENGER ABOUT THE FARE

o الأُجْرة كام مِن فضْلك؟

◇ نازِل فينْ؟

o ميدان لِبْنان.

◇ يِبْقى ٣ جِنيْهْ.

o طب، أدْفع لِمين؟

◇ اِدّيها لِلْلي قُدّامك أَوْ هات أنا هلِمّ الصّفّ بِتاعْنا.

- o How much is the fare, please?
- ◇ Where will you get off?
- o Lebanon Square.
- ◇ Then it's 3 LE.
- o I see. Who should I pay?
- ◇ Give it to the person [sitting] in front of you. Or, hand it to me and I'll collect [the fares for] our row.

- o *ilʔúgra kām, min fáḍlak?*
- ◇ *nāzil fēn?*
- o *midān libnān.*
- ◇ *yíbʔa talāta gnēh.*
- o *ṭab, ádfa3 li-mīn?*
- ◇ *iddīha li-lli ʔuddāmak aw hāt ána halímm iṣṣáffᵊ btá3na.*

When you get in the microbus, you can hand your fare to the driver or sit down and pass it to someone sitting in front of you. And If you're taking a microbus from a station where they begin their journeys, you'll need to ask where the vehicles for your destination are parked and then find the one that is leaving next. Generally, the driver will wait until the seats fill up with passengers before setting off. There is no scheduled departure time.

4

PASSING UP YOUR FARE TO THE DRIVER

o اِتْنينْ مِن خمْسة طَوابِق.
◇ كِده ليكو باقي؟
o معْرفْش الأُجْرة كام.
◇ لِحدّ الطَّوابِق كام ياسْطى[1]؟
◇ اِتْنينْ جِنيْهْ و نُصّ.
◇ تمام كِده ملْكوش باقي.

o Two (seats) from five (LE) for Tawabe'!
◇ [Do you need] any change back?
o I don't know the fare.
◇ Driver, how much is it to Tawabe'?
◇ Two and a half [LE].
◇ Okay, so no change for you then.

o *itnēn min xámsa ṭawābiʔ.*
◇ *kída līku bāʔi?*
o *ma-3ráfš ilʔúgra kām.*
◇ *li-ḥádd iṭṭawābiʔ kām yásṭa[1]?*
◇ *itnēn ginēh wi nuṣṣ.*
◇ *tamām, kída ma-lkūš bāʔi.*

[1] ياسْطى *yásṭa* is the polite form of address for a (micro)bus driver. It is a contraction of the words يا أُسْطى *ya úsṭa.*

In the first line of the dialogue, the speaker is handing a five-pound bill to the woman sitting in front of him. He is letting her know that he's passing up two fares for the destination Tawabe'. It turns out that five pounds is the right amount for two passengers, so she won't be passing back any change to him.

Keep in mind that where you sit on the microbus will affect how active you will need to be in passing fares up and change back.

5

Telling the Driver Where You Want to Get Out

o مِن فضْلك، ياسْطى نزِّلْني أقْرب حاجة لِلْمُعِزّ.[1]

◇ هنزِّلك عنْد الأزْهر و هتْعدّي النّاحْيَة التّانْيَة مِن النّفق.

o بِعيد ياسْطى ده؟

◇ لا ده خطْوِتيْن.

o تمام بسّ متِنْسانيش الله يِكْرِمك.

◇ عينيّا.[2]

o Excuse me, driver, let me out at the nearest place to Muizz Street.

◇ I'll drop you off near Al-Azhar [Mosque] and you'll just have to cross [the street] via the tunnel (pedestrian underpass).

o Is it very far?

◇ No, it's a few steps.

o Okay, just don't forget about me, please.

◇ My pleasure!

o *min fáḏlak, yásṭa nazzílni áʔrab ḥāga li-lmu3ízz*[1].

◇ *hanazzílak 3and ilʔázhar wi hat3áddi -nnáḥya ittánya min innáfaʔ.*

o *bi3īd yásṭa da?*

◇ *lā, da xaṭwitēn.*

o *tamām, bassᵊ ma-tinsanīš allāh yikrímak.*

◇ *3ináyya.*[2]

[1] عايِز أنْزِل قُرْب المُعِزّ. *3āyiz ánzil ʔurb ilmu3ízz.* **I want to get out near Muizz Street.**

[2] = مِن عينيّا *min 3ináyya* (lit. (from) my eyes), a common and folksy affirmative response to a request.

Swvl (www.swvl.com) is an Egyptian startup, basically the Uber of microbuses. Through their app, you can book fixed-rate shared rides on existing routes. Careem has a similar service.

6

GETTING CHANGE BACK FROM COLLECTED FARES

o كِده وَرا خلاص.
◇ ملْكوش باقي؟
o آه باقي بسّ ٣ جِنيْه.
◇ تمام اِتْفضّل جِنيْه يِبْقالْكُم اِتْنين.

(talking to the row in front of her)

◇ كِده السِّتّة اللي وَرا بسّ باقيلْنا[1] ٥ جِنيْه فكّة[2].

o This takes care of the back row.
◇ No change for you?
o We just need 3 LE back.
◇ Okay, here's 1 LE. And you still have 2 [LE] coming.

(talking to the row in front of her)

◇ Okay, this is for the six of us. We need 5 LE in change.[2]

o *kída wára xalāṣ.*
◇ *ma-lkūš bāʔi?*
o *āh, bāʔi bassᵊ talāta gnēh.*
◇ *tamām, itfáḍḍal ginēh, yibʔálkum itnēn.*

(talking to the row in front of her)

◇ *kída -ssítta -lli wára bassᵊ baʔílna[1] xámsa gnēh fákka[2].*

[1] = فاضِلّنا *faḍillína* / [2] i.e., five one-pound coins to distribute among those still waiting on change

If you want to relax during your microbus ride, sit next to a window on the left side of the vehicle. You'll mostly avoid having to pass money along and won't have to get in and out, as you will if you sit in one of the folding seats on the right, to let people by. If you sit next to the sliding door, you will have the temporary job of helping to open and close it again for other passengers. And if you have large bags, sit in the row behind the driver, as it has more space.

Extended Dialogue

○ لَوْ عايْزة أروح شارِع مُراد أرْكب أيْه؟

◇ اِرْكبي الفيلوكْس[1] اللي وَرا دي.

(approaches microbus)

○ رايِح شارِع مُراد ده ياسْطى؟

◇ آه إن شاء الله.

(gets on microbus)

○ طب، كُنْت عايْزة أنْزِل عنْد محطِّةْ السّوبر جيْت الله يِكْرِمك.

◇ ماشي. فكّريني و إحْنا نازْلين مِن الكّوبْري.

○ شُكْراً ياسْطى. كام الأُجْرة لِحدّ هِناك بقى؟

◇ اِتْنيْن و نُصّ.

○ اِتْفضّل.

◇ معكيش[2] فكّة؟

○ لا ياسْطى معيش[3].

◇ طب، اِسْتنّي أمّا حدّ يِرْكب بقى تاخْدي بقية أُجْرِتِك.

○ ماشي ياسْطى. أقولّك خلّيهُم كُرْسِيين أحْسن.[4]

◇ تمام زيّ ما تْحِبّي. خُدي الباقي بقى.

○ شُكْراً ياسْطى.

(a while later)

○ لِسّه كِتير[5] عَ المحطّة؟

◇ خلاص أهُه، داخْلين عليْها. بُصّي هتِنْزِلي و تْعدّي النّاحْيَة التّانْيَة.

○ تمام ياسْطى، هنْزِل هِنا.

○ If I want to get to Mourad Street, what [microbus] should I take?

◇ Get in that "Volkswagen"[1] back there.

(approaches microbus)

- ○ Is this going to Mourad Street, sir?
- ◇ Yes, God willing.

(gets on microbus)

- ○ Okay, I'd like to get out near the Superjet station, please.
- ◇ All right, just remind me once we get off the bridge.
- ○ Thank you, driver. How much is the fare there?
- ◇ Two and a half [LE].
- ○ Here you are.
- ◇ You don't have anything smaller?
- ○ No, sir. I don't.
- ◇ Okay. Wait until someone else gets on to get your change.
- ○ Okay, sir. You know what? Make it two seats.[4] That would be better.
- ◇ All right. Whatever you want. Here's your change then.
- ○ Thank you, driver.

(a while later)

- ○ Is it still a ways to the station?
- ◇ We're almost there. You're going to get out and cross the street.
- ○ Okay, driver. I'll get out here.

- ○ *law 3áyza -rūḫ šāri3 murād, árkab ʔē?*
- ◇ *irkábi -lvilúks*[1] *ílli wára di.*

(approaches microbus)

- ○ *rāyiḫ šāri3 murād da yásṭa?*
- ◇ *āh, in šāʔ allāh.*

(gets on microbus)

- ○ *ṭab, kuntᵊ 3áyz- ánzil 3andᵊ maḫáṭṭit issūbar žēt allāh yikrímak.*
- ◇ *māši. fakkarīni w íḫna nazlīn min ikkúbri.*
- ○ *šúkran yásṭa. kām ilʔúgra li-ḫáddᵊ hināk báʔa?*
- ◇ *itnēn wi nuṣṣ.*
- ○ *itfáḍḍal.*
- ◇ *ma-3akīš*[2] *fákka?*

○ *lā, yásṭa ma-3īš*[3].
◇ *ṭab, istánni ámma ḥaddᵊ yírkab báʔa táxdi baʔīt ugrítik.*
○ *māši yásṭa. aʔúllak xallīhum kursiyīn áḥsan.*[4]
◇ *tamām, zayyᵊ ma tḥíbbi. xúdi -lbāʔi báʔa.*
○ *šúkran yásṭa.*

(a while later)

○ *líssa ktīr*[5] *3a -lmaḥáṭṭa?*
◇ *xalāṣ ahú, daxlīn 3alēha. búṣṣi hatinzíli wi t3áddi -nnáḥya ittánya.*
○ *tamām, yásṭa, hánzil hína.*

1 فيلوكْس *vilúks* is a shortened form of Volkswagen, which has come into common usage, especially in Cairo, to refer to microbuses in general. In Cairo, people also just say عربية *3arabíyya* for a microbus.

2 معكيش *ma3akīš* is a contraction of مفيش معاكي *mafīš ma3āki.*

3 معيش *ma3īš* < مفيش معايا *mafīš ma3āya.*

4 Some people prefer to pay for two seats even if they will only use one. A woman may do this to avoid potential sexual harassment or when the only available seats are next to the driver.

5 = لِسّه بدْري *líssa bádri*

Microbuses don't display signs showing their destination. So how do you know if a microbus is going your way? You need to use coded hand gestures. If your hand signal matches the route and the microbus has a free seat, the driver will pull over for you. There's a whole system here. A "peace sign" indicates the 7th District (Nasser City), logically, as this looks like the Arabic numeral 7 (٧). A flat hand turned sideways intuitively means "end of the street", for shorter rides. If you're not sure of the hand signal, stop a passing microbus and quickly ask if they're going to your destination. Learn more about how to use microbuses and learn the hand signals in Maissara's article with photos and video on the Lingualism blog at **www.lingualism.com/microbus**

The folding chair is notoriously the worst seat on the microbus. Try to avoid it, especially if you have a long way to go. Not only will you have to get up repeatedly to let people by, but it's also small and uncomfortable. The folding back of the chair isn't as sturdy, so if you lean back, the person behind you might complain you are hurting their legs.

Some drivers may claim that they do not have small change even when they do in an attempt to get out of having to give you change. It is better to have the exact fare ready to avoid problems such as this.

Vocabulary

microbus	*mikrubāṣ*	ميكْروباص
microbus station (where they load and start their trips)	*máwʔaf*	مَوْقف
to load up (with passengers)	*ḥámmil*	حمِّل
seat	*kúrsi*	كُرْسي
double seat, bench	*kánaba*	كنبة
flip-down seat	*kúrsi ʔallāb*	كُرْسي قلّاب
two front seats (next to the driver)	*kursiyēn ʔuddām*	كُرْسِيينْ قُدّام
hand signal	*išāra* *3alāma*	إشارة علامة
to make a hand signal	*šāwir*	شاوِر

Also, see the vocabulary section for **Taking a Taxi** starting on p. 13.

Expressions

○

Does this go to ___?	*biyrūḫ ___ da?*	بِيْروح ___ ده؟
What's the hand signal for ___?	*law 3āyiz arūḫ ___, ašāwir izzāy?*	لَوْ عايِز أروح ___ أشاوِر إزّاي؟
(paying) I don't have anything smaller.	*ma-3īš fákka.*	معيش فكّة.
(waiting on change) I have three pounds coming back.	*kída baʔīli talāta gnēh yásṭa.*	كِده باقيلي ٣ جِنيْهْ ياسْطى.
One [seat paying] from five [LE]!	*wāḫid min xámsa.*	واحِد مِن خمْسة.
Three [seats] from ten [LE]!	*talāta min 3ášara.*	تلاتة مِن عشرة.
All the seats at the back are done (paying)	*kída kúllu wára xalāṣ.*	كِده كُلُّه وَرا خلاص.
Drop me off at the nearest place to ___.	*nazzílni áʔrab ḫítta li-___.*	نزِّلْني أقْرب حِتّة لِـ ___.
I want to get out at ___.	*3āyiz ánzil 3and ___.*	عايِز أنْزِل عنْد ___.
I want to get out. [lit. On the side (of the road), driver!]	*3ála gambᵊ yásṭa.*	على جمْب ياسْطى.
Any place here.	*ayyᵊ ḫítta hína.*	أيّ حِتّة هِنا.
Drop me off by the tunnel.	*innáfaʔ ma3āk yásṭa.*	النّفق معاك ياسْطى.

◇

We're still taking passengers. Get in.	*da líssa biyḫámmil, írkab hína.*	ده لِسّه بِيْحمِّل، اِرْكب هِنا.

One more passenger, then we'll set off.	*bāʔi náfar wi níṭla3.*	باقي نفر و نِطْلع.
Collect the fare in one go.[1]	*límmu -lʔúgra márra wáḥda.*	لِمّوا الأُجْرة مرّة واحْدة.
Close door gently when you get out.	*bi-rrāḥa 3a -lbāb w ínta nāzil.*	بِالرّاحة عَ الباب و إنْتَ نازِل.

[1] The driver might say this if he wants to save himself the hassle of making change for each passenger individually.

Taking a Train في القطر

القطْر *ilʔáṭr* **the train** is, arguably, the most comfortable way to travel between القاهِرة *ilqāhíra* **Cairo**, إسْكِنْدِرية *iskindiríyya* **Alexandria**, بور سعيد *būr sa3īd* **Port Said**, السُّويْس *issuwēs* **Suez**, الأُقْصر *ilʔúʔṣur* **Luxor**, and أسْوان *aswān* **Aswan**. Other options are to fly, drive, or take a bus. But nothing beats the atmosphere of the train. Sit back and enjoy observing snippets of Egyptian life pass by outside the train's windows—small towns, green fields, palm trees along the Nile, and desert landscapes. Get up to stretch your legs and use the restroom as needed. Absorb yourself in a good book. Buy snacks and drinks from a passing cart. Of course, you'll also be enjoying air-conditioning, provided you are in درجة أولة *dáraga ūla* **first class** or درجة تانْيَة *dáraga tánya* **second class.** درجة تالْتة *dáraga tálta* **third class** is not recommended—crowded, uncomfortable bench seats, and possibly lots of stares... as you'll be the only foreigner on the train. Between Alexandria and Cairo, the express train that only makes one stop along the way is called أسْباني *asbāni* **Spanish**; the توربيني *turbīni* makes a couple stops, while the فرنْساوي *faransāwi* **French** train is a bit less comfortable and makes more stops. Sleeper trains are available from Cairo to مرْسى مطْروح *mársa maṭrūḥ* **Marsa Matruh** and Upper Egypt.

Buying a ticket at the train station

○ لَوْ سمحْت فيه قطْر مُباشِر لِإسْكِنْدِرية السّاعة ٨ بِاللّيْل؟
◇ لا فيه السّاعة ٧، درجة أولى ١٥٠، و تانْيَة ٧٠.
○ طيِّب، و بِيوْصل خِلال قدّ أيْه؟
◇ ساعتيْن، ساعتيْن و نُصّ بِالكِتير.
○ تمام، عايِز تذْكرْتيْن جمْب بعْض لَوْ سمحْت يوْم الجُمْعة.

○ Excuse me, is there an express train to Alexandria at 8 p.m.?
◇ No, but there is a one at 7 p.m. First class is 150 LE and second class is 70 LE.
○ And how long does it take to reach there?
◇ Two hours, two and a half hours at most.
○ Okay, I want two tickets next to each other for Friday.

○ *law samáḫt, fī ʔaṭrᵊ mubāšir l-iskindiríyya issā3a tamánya bi-llēl?*
◇ *laʔ, fī -ssā3a sáb3a, dáraga ūla míyya wi xamsīn, wi tánya sab3īn.*
○ *ṭáyyib, wi byíwṣal xilāl ʔaddᵊ ʔē?*
◇ *sa3atēn, sa3atēn wi nuṣṣᵊ bi-kkitīr.*
○ *tamām, 3āyiz tazkartēn gambᵊ ba3ḍᵊ law samáḫtᵊ yōm iggúm3a.*

You can purchase اِتِّجاهْ واحِد *ittigāh wāḫid* **one-way** or رايِح جايّ *rāyiḫ gayy* **round-trip** tickets at the train station before departure. You can also buy tickets online at **enr.gov.eg** (without www) or, even better, by using the ENR app, which has the icon. In the app, you can learn details about train schedules, available seats, journey times, the number of stops, etc. You can purchase your tickets up to 15 days in advance and cancel them for a refund to your credit card up to 48 hours in advance.

2

FINDING YOUR TRAIN IN THE STATION

○ لَوْ سمحْت هُوَّ قطْر ٩٢٧ رصيف رقم كام؟

◇ رصيف رقم ٤.

○ طيِّب... ده أروحْلُه إزّاي؟[1]

◇ هتِنْزِل مِن النّفق ده و اِطْلع السِّلِّم اللي مكْتوب عليْه (إلى رصيف رقم ٤).

○ Excuse me, which platform for train number 927?

◇ Platform 4.

○ And how do I reach it?

◇ You go down this tunnel and take the stairs where it says "to Platform number 4."

○ *law samáḫt, húwwa ʔaṭr tusu3míyya sáb3a wi 3išrīn raṣīf ráqam kām?*

◇ *raṣīf ráqam arbá3a.*

○ *ṭáyyib... da arúḫlu izzāy?*[1]

◇ *hatínzil min innáfaʔ da w íṭla3 issíllim ílli maktūb 3alē "íla raṣīf ráqam arbá3a".*

[1] = أروحْلُه مِنينْ؟ *arúḫlu minēn?*

For a sleeper train to Luxor, Aswan, or Marsa Matruh, you can book your tickets online (www.wataniasleepingtrains.com). Note that there are different rules and prices for foreigners. You can also book through a travel agent, but with an additional fee. It is possible to get a ticket for a sleeper train at the train station, provided there are vacancies, but you must pay in dollars and have exact change (or pay by credit card).

3

MAKING SURE YOU ARE ON THE RIGHT TRAIN

o مِن فضْلك، شوف التّذْكرة دي كِده. أنا كِده في القطْر المظْبوط؟

◇ أَيْوَه مظْبوط[1]. بسّ دي عربية رقم ١ و إنْتي عربيِّتِك رقم ٦.

o طب، لَوْ نزِلْت مِش مُمْكِن يِتْحرّك؟[2]

◇ لِسّه ٥ دقايِق على بال ما يِتْحرّك و بعْد كِده اِبْقي اُقفي عنْد اليافْطة اللي عليْها رقم العربية.

o Excuse me, could you check this ticket and let me know if I'm on the right train?

◇ Yes, it's correct. But this is car number 1, and yours is number 6.

o But if I get out, is there a chance it will start moving?

◇ No, there are still five minutes until it departs. But for future reference, always wait at the sign with your car number.

o *min fádlak, šūf ittazkára di kída. ána kída fi -lʔaṭr ilmazbūṭ?*

◇ *áywa, mazbūṭ*[1]*. bass*[ə] *di 3arabíyya ráqam wāḫid w ínti 3arabītik ráqam sítta.*

o *ṭab, law nizílt, miš múmkin yitḫárrak?*[2]

◇ *líssa xámas daʔāyiʔ 3ála bāl ma yitḫárrak wi ba3d*[ə] *kída íbʔi uʔáfi 3and ilyáfṭa ílli 3alēha ráqam il3arabíyya.*

1 = صحّ *ṣaḫḫ* = تمام كِده *tamām kída*

2 طب مُمْكِن أنْزِل دِلْوَقْتي؟ وَلّا هَيِتْحرّك؟ *ṭab, múmkin ánzil dilwáʔti? wálla hayitḫárrak?* **Well, can I get off now? Or will it start moving?**

4

Buying a Ticket on the Train

◇ التّذاكِر؟

○ أنا ملْحِقْتِش أجيب تذْكرة. يِنْفع أشْترِي دِلْوَقْتي؟

◇ آه التّذْكرة بِـ٧٠ بسّ أحْسن اِشْترِيها قبْل معادْها عشان مُمْكِن متْلاقيش.

○ أنا كُنْت خايْفة أتْطوّق[1] فِعْلاً بسّ الحمْدُ لله القطْر النّهارْده فيه كراسي فاضْيَة.

◇ Tickets?

○ I didn't have time to buy a ticket. Can I buy a one now?

◇ Yes, the ticket is for 70 LE, but it is better to buy it prior to the trip because sometimes you might not find any [free seats].

○ As a matter of fact, I was worried I might have to pay a fine[1], but thank God, today there are empty seats.

◇ *ittazākir?*

○ *ána ma-lḫíʔtiš agīb tazkára. yínfa3 aštíri dilwáʔti?*

◇ *āh, ittazkára b-sab3īn, bassᵊ áḫsan ištirīha ʔablᵊ ma3ádha 3ašān múmkin ma-tlaʔīš.*

○ *ána kuntᵊ xáyfa attáwwaʔ[1] fí3lan bass ilḫámdu li-llāh, ilʔáṭr innahárda fī karāsi fáḍya.*

[1] Until recently, you could simply buy a ticket on the train and pay a nominal fine. But now, penalties have been increased substantially, creating an incentive to always buy your ticket before boarding. The fine is 30 LE for first class and 20 LE for second class. Also, if you don't buy a ticket in advance, you might not get a seat on the train. Even if you find empty seats, they may be reserved for passengers who get on at subsequent stations.

5

FINDING YOUR SEAT

◇ مِن فضْلك، حضْرتك قاعِد في الكُّرْسي الغلط.

o ليْه حضْرِتك؟ أنا رقم ٣٧، قاعِد مظْبوط يَعْني.

◇ بسّ حضْرِتك ٣٧ ده اللي في الممرّ مِش اللي جمْب الشِّبّاك.

o مين اللي قال كِده؟

◇ مكْتوب أهُه فوْق الكّراسي.

o لا مُؤاخْذة، مأخدْتِش بالي، معلِشّ. اِتْفضّل حضْرِتك.

◇ Excuse me, you're sitting in the wrong seat.

o How come? Mine is 37, so I'm sitting in the right place.

◇ But 37 is an aisle seat, not next to the window.

o Who says?

◇ It is written here above the chairs!

o Oh, excuse me! I didn't notice. My mistake. There you are.

◇ *min fáḍlak, ɧaḍrítak ʔā3id fi -kkúrsi -lɣálaṭ.*

o *lē ɧaḍrítak? ána ráqam sáb3a wi talatīn. ʔā3id maẓbūṭ yá3ni.*

◇ *bassᵊ ɧaḍrítak sáb3a wi talatīn da -lli fi -lmamárr, miš ílli gamb iššibbāk.*

o *mīn ílli ʔāl kída?*

◇ *maktūb ahú fōʔ ikkarāsi.*

o *la muʔáxza, ma-ʔaxádtiš bāli, ma3alíšš. itfáḍḍal ɧaḍrítak.*

Save your ticket even after you get off the train, as inspectors in the station sometimes check passengers getting off trains.

An alternative to traveling by train is to take an intercity bus. The most well-known bus companies are Superjet (www.superjet.com.eg), Gobus (go-bus.com –without www), and Blue Bus (www.bluebus.com.eg).

6

Asking about your stop

○ معلِشّ كُنْت عايْزة أنْزِل طنْطا.

◇ لِسّه بدْري. متِقْلقيش. القطْر ده محطّات.

○ طيِّب، مُمْكِن لمّا تيجي محطِّةْ طنْطا حضْرتك تِقوليلي؟

◇ حاضِر مِن عينيّا[1]، بسّ لَوْ عايْزة تِنامي دِلْوَقْتي بِراحْتِك[2]. قُدّامِك ييجي ساعة مثلاً.

○ Excuse me, I wanted to get off in Tanta.

◇ There's still a ways to go. Don't worry, this train stops at stations.

○ Can you please let me know when we get to Tanta station?

◇ Sure, my pleasure. If you want to sleep now, go ahead. You still have an hour or so.

○ *ma3alíšš, kuntᵊ 3áyza ánzil ṭánṭa.*

◇ *líssa bádri. ma-tiʔlaʔīš. ilʔáṭrᵊ da maḫaṭṭāt.*

○ *ṭáyyib, múmkin lámma tīgi maḫáṭṭit ṭánṭa ḫaḍrítak tiʔulīli?*

◇ *ḫāḍir min 3ináyya*[1]*, bassᵊ law 3áyza tnāmi dilwáʔti, bi-ráḫtik*[2]*. ʔuddāmik yīgi sā3a másalan.*

[1] Some people say مِن العينْ دي قبْل العينْ دي. *min il3ēn di ʔabl il3ēn di.* (lit. from this eye before this eye)

[2] بِراحْتك! *bi-ráḫtak!* **At your leisure!**; **Take your time!**; **No rush!**

○ لَوْ سمحْت أَسْتأْذِنك بسّ الشّنْطة عشان أقْعُد.

◇ آه معلِشّ اِتْفضّل.

○ هُوَّ أنا قاعِد كِده مظْبوط في مكاني؟

◇ آه مظْبوط بسّ كُرْسي حضْرِتك جمْب الشِّبّاك. لَوْ حابِب تِبدِّل مفيش مُشْكِلة.

○ لا خلّيني كِده أقْرب لِلْحمّام أحْسن بسّ معْرِفْش ليْه مقْفول[1].

◇ ما هُوَّ بيِفْتح أوِّل ما القطْر يِبْدأ يِتْحرّك و يِتْقِفِل لمّا القطْر يِكون واقِف.

○ طيِّب، لَوْ حابِب[2] أطْلُب حاجة؟ فيه كافيتيرْيا مثلاً؟

◇ فيه كافيتيرْيا بعْدِنا بِعربيتيْن و كِده كِده[3] فيه واحِد بِيْعدّي بِأيّ مشاريب أَوْ سنْدوِتْشات.

○ طيِّب، حِلْو أوي[4].

◇ و في المحطّات فيه ناس بِتِطْلع تِبيع جرايِد و حاجات حِلْوَة كمان.

○ بِالمُناسْبة صحيح أنا نازِل محطِّةْ دهْشور. متِعْرفْش دي قُدّامْها قدّ أيْه؟

◇ مِش عارِف والله بِالظّبْط[5] بسّ مُمْكِن تِسْأل المُفتِّش لمّا يِعدّي[6].

(ticket inspector comes by)

◇ التّذاكِر!

◇ أهُه المُفتِّش جه. اِسْألُه.

○ باقي على محطِّةْ دهْشور قدّ أيْه مِن فضْلك؟

◇ لِسّه حَوالي نُصّ ساعة، متِقْلقْش.

○ تمام مُتْشكِّر جِدّاً.

◇ اِتْفضّل التّذْكرة. تِوْصل بِالسّلامة إن شاء الله.

- o Excuse me, can you move your bag, so that I can sit down?
- ◇ Yeah, sure. There you go.
- o Am I sitting in the right seat?
- ◇ Yes, but your seat is next to the window. If you want to switch, it's no problem at all.
- o No, it's okay. This way, I'm closer to the toilet, but I don't know why it is closed.
- ◇ It opens once the train starts moving and is closed when it stops.
- o What about if I want to order something? Is there a café or something?
- ◇ There is a café two cars ahead, and someone will come by anyway with drinks or sandwiches.
- o Okay, great!
- ◇ Also, at the stations, some sellers pass by with newspapers and snacks.
- o Speaking of which, I'll be getting off at Dahshour Station. Do you know how much further it is?
- ◇ I really don't know exactly, but you can ask the inspector when he comes by.

(ticket inspector comes by)

- ◇ Tickets!
- ◇ Here's the inspector. You can ask him.
- o Excuse me, how much further to Dahshour station?
- ◇ 30 more minutes. Don't worry.
- o Okay, thanks a lot.
- ◇ Here's your ticket. May you arrive safely, God willing.

- o *law samáɧt, astaʔzínak bass iššánʈa 3ašān áʔ3ud.*
- ◇ *āh, ma3alíšš, itfáɖɖal.*
- o *húww- ána ʔā3id kída maʐbūʈ fi makāni?*
- ◇ *āh, maʐbūʈ, bassᵊ kúrsi ɧaɖrítak gamb iššibbāk. law ɧābib tibáddil ma-fīš muškíla.*
- o *lā, xallīni kída áʔrab li-lɧammām áɧsan bassᵊ ma-3ráfšᵊ lē maʔfūl*[1]*.*
- ◇ *ma húwwa byíftaɧ áwwil ma -lʔaʈrᵊ yíbdaʔ yitɧárrak wi yitʔífil lámma -lʔaʈrᵊ ykūn wāʔif.*

○ *ţáyyib, law ђābib[2] áţlub ђāga? fī kafitírya másalan?*
◇ *fī kafitírya ba3dína bi-3arabitēn wi kída kída[3] fī wāђid biy3áddi bi-ayyᵊ mašarīb aw sandiwitšāt.*
○ *ţáyyib, ђilw áwi[4].*
◇ *wi fi -lmaђaţţāt fī nās bitíţla3 tibī3 garāyid wi ђagāt ђílwa kamān.*
○ *bi-lmunásba şaђīђ. ána nāzil maђáţţit dahšūr. ma-ti3ráfšᵊ di ʔuddámha ʔaddᵊ ʔē?*
◇ *miš 3ārif wallāhi bi-ẓẓábţᵊ[5] bassᵊ múmkin tísʔal ilmufáttiš lámma yi3áddi[6].*

(ticket inspector comes by)

◇ *ittazākir!*
◇ *ahú ilmufáttiš gih. isʔálu.*
○ *bāʔi 3ála maђáţţit dahšūr ʔaddᵊ ʔē, min fáḑlak?*
◇ *líssa ђawāli nuşşᵊ sā3a, ma-tiʔláʔš.*
○ *tamām, mutšákkir gíddan.*
◇ *itfáḑḑal ittazkára. tíwşal bi-ssalāma in šāʔ allāh.*

[1] هُوَّ مقْفول ليْه؟ *húwwa maʔfūl lē?* **Why is it closed?**

[2] = لَوْ عايْز *law 3āyiz* / [3] = و عُموماً *wi 3umūman* / [4] = جميل جِدّاً *gamīl gíddan* /

[5] = بِالتّحْديد *bi-ttaђdīd* / [6] = يمُرّ *yimúrr*

Vocabulary

station	*maђáţţa*	محطّة
ticket	*tazkára (tazākir)*	تذْكرة (تذاكِر)
ticket window	*šibbāk tazākir*	شِبّاك تذاكِر
stairs	*síllim*	سِلِّم
tunnel	*náfaʔ*	نفق
platform	*raşīf*	رصيف
sign	*yáfţa*	يافْطة
train	*ʔaţr*	قطْر

sleeper train	*ʔaṭrᵊ nōm*	قطْر نوْم
train car, carriage, wagon	*3arabíyya*	عربية
car number	*ráqam il3arabíyya*	رقم العربية
seat	*kúrsi (karāsi)*	كُرْسي (كراسي)
seat number	*ráqam ikkúrsi*	رقم الكُّرْسي
window	*šibbāk*	شِبّاك
express, direct	*mubāšir*	مُباشِر
non-express train, slow train	*marākiz*	مراكِز
first class	*dáraga ūla*	درجة أولى
second class	*dáraga tánya*	درجة تانْيَة
air-conditioned	*mukáyyaf*	مُكيّف
inspector	*mufáttiš*	مُفتِّش
fine	*taṭwīʔ* *ɣarāma*	تطْويق غرامة
to be fined	*itṭáwwaʔ*	اِتْطوّق

Expressions

○

I'd like to buy two tickets for an express train to Alexandria.	*kuntᵊ 3āyziz aštíri tazkartēn mubāšir iskindiríyya.*	كُنْت عايِز أشْترِي تذْكرْتين مُباشِر إسْكِنْدِرية.

How much is a first-class sleeping cabin?	*ʔaṭr innōm dáraga ūla sí3ru kām?*	قطْر النّوْم درجة أولى سِعْرُه كام؟
Excuse me, can I switch seats with you so we can sit next to each other?	*ma3alíšš^ə múmkin abáddil ilkúrsi 3ašān núʔ3ud gamb^ə ba3ḍ?*	معلِشّ مُمْكِن أبدِّل الكُرْسي عشان نُقْعُد جمْب بعْض؟
Excuse me, can I turn the seat around? I feel dizzy.	*astaʔzínak halíff ilkúrsi bass^ə 3ašān badūx.*	أسْتأْذِنك هلِفّ الكُرْسي بسّ عشان بدوخ.
Can you help me get my luggage down [from the rack]?	*múmkin tisa3ídni anázzil iššánṭa?*	مُمْكِن تِساعِدْني أنزِّل الشّنْطة؟
Excuse me, I want to hang this bag up [on the wall hook].	*min fáḍlak, 3āyiz a3állaʔ iššánṭa di.*	مِن فضْلك عايِز أعلّق الشّنْطة دي.
Excuse me while I just put my bag on the overhead rack.	*min fáḍlak, bass aḫúṭṭ iššánṭa fōʔ.*	مِن فضْلك بسّ أحُطّ الشّنْطة فوْق.
How much longer to ___ station?	*bāʔi ʔadd^ə ʔē 3ála maḫáṭṭit ___?*	باقي قدّ أيْه على محطِّةْ ___؟

◇

The date on this ticket is not correct.	*ittazkára di taríxha miš maẓbūṭ.*	التّذْكرة دي تاريخْها مِش مظْبوط.

At the Airport في المطار

مطار القاهِرة الدَّوْلي *maṭār ilqāhíra -ddáwli* **Cairo International Airport** (CAI) is one of the largest and busiest airports in Africa and the Middle East. The setup of the airport and procedures are all fairly standard and will seem familiar. Note, however, that you will need a فيزا *vīza* **visa** to enter the country. Nationals of some 40 countries, including the USA, the UK, Canada, Australia, and the EU can get tourist visas upon arrival (or online in advance). Before you reach passport control, you can purchase your visa from any of the bank counters. At the time of publication of this book, a tourist visa is $25. You will need exact change and cannot pay by credit card. Once you make your way through passport control and collect your luggage, you'll find yourself, very suddenly, in the bustle of the real Egypt... with taxi drivers surrounding you like a swarm of bees. Know that you won't get a great fare from the airport. Most drivers will insist on a flat fare rather than turn on their meter. (See **Taking a Taxi** starting on p. 1 for tips and phrases for negotiating with taxi drivers.) But taxis are not your only option. Uber and other rideshare services are available from the airport. There are also limousine buses that will get you downtown, from where you can take a shorter, cheaper taxi ride. And eventually, line 3 of the Cairo Metro (subway) will reach the airport.

Going through Security

◇ الموبايْل و اللّابْتوْب في الصّينية[1] و نِعدّي.

o تمام كِده؟

◇ معلِشّ ارْجع تاني كِده و اِقْلع الجّزْمة و عدّي.

◇ Cellphone and laptop on the tray and pass through.

o Am I all right?

◇ Sorry, go back and take off your shoes and pass through again.

◇ *ilmubāyl wi -llaptōp fi -ṣṣiníyya[1] wi n3áddi.*

o *tamām kída?*

◇ *ma3alíšš, írga3 tāni kída w íʔla3 iggázma wi 3áddi.*

[1] عَ السّيرْ *3a -ssēr* **on the conveyor belt**

2

CHECKING IN

◇ تِحِبّ كُرْسي جمْب الشِّبّاك وَلّا في الممرّ؟
○ لا جمْب الشِّبّاك مِن فضْلِك.
◇ طيِّب، مِش هَيِنْفع البرْطمان ده يِطْلع عَ الطّيّارة.
○ بسّ ده مِش سَوايِل. ده برْطمان مِربىّ.
◇ معلِشّ، برْضُه مِش هَيِنْفع[1].

◇ Would you like a window or aisle seat?
○ A window seat, please.
◇ Okay. But that jar cannot be taken as carry-on.
○ It's not liquid; it's just jam.
◇ You still can't take it.

◇ *tiђíbbᵊ kúrsi gamb iššibbāk wálla fi -lmamárr?*
○ *lā, gamb iššibbāk, min fáḍlik.*
◇ *ṭáyyib, miš hayínfa3 ilbarṭamān da yíṭla3 3a -ṭṭayyāra.*
○ *bassᵊ da miš sawāyil. da barṭamān mirábba.*
◇ *ma3alíšš, bárḍu miš hayínfa3*[1].

[1] = مَيِنْفعْش *ma-yinfá3š*

3

CHECKING IN BAGGAGE

◇ الشّنْطة دي وَزْنها ٢٩ كيلو[1]. مِش هَينْفع تِطْلع كِده.

o طيِّب حضْرتِك، مجاتْش مِن ٧ كيلو يَعْني. مِش أزْمة[2].

◇ بقول لِحضْرتِك مِش هَينْفع. حاوِل تِقسِّمْها[3] على شنْطِتيْن.

o بسّ الشّنْطة التّانْيَة صُغيّرة زيّ ما إنْتي شايْفة.

◇ اِرْجع وَرا و ظبّطْهُم و قسِّمْهُم تاني و اِرْجعْلي[4].

◇ This suitcase is 29 kilograms and cannot be loaded this way.

o Okay, ma'am, it's only 7 kilograms over. No big deal.

◇ I'm telling you, it's not possible. Try to divide it into two suitcases.

o But the other one is too small, as you can see.

◇ Take a step back, adjust and redistribute them, then come back again.

◇ *iššánṭa di waznáha tís3a w 3išrīn kīlu[1]. miš hayínfa3 títla3 kída.*

o *ṭáyyib, ħadrítik, ma-gátšᵊ min sáb3a kīlu yá3ni. miš ázma[2].*

◇ *baʔūl li-ħadrítak, miš hayínfa3. ħāwil tiʔassímha[3] 3ála šanṭitēn.*

o *bass iššánṭa -ttánya ṣɣayyára zayyᵊ má-nti šáyfa.*

◇ *írga3 wára wi ẓabbáṭhum wi ʔassímhum tāni w irgá3li[4].*

[1] وَزْنها زِيادة ٧ كيلو. *waznáha ziyāda sáb3a kīlu.* **It's seven kilograms over(weight).**

[2] = مِش قِصّة *miš qíṣṣa*

[3] = تِوَزّعْها *tiwazzá3ha*

[4] ظبّط الشّنْطِتيْن بِالأَوْزان بقى و اِرْجعْلي تاني. *ẓábbaṭ iššanṭitēn bi-lʔawzān báʔa w irgá3li tāni.* **Adjust the weight of the two bags and then come back to see me.**

Getting in line

o مِن فضْلِك، مُمْكِن تِقوليلي لَوْ أنا واقْفة[1] في الطّابور المظْبوط.

◇ حضْرِتك طَيَران داخِلي وَلّا خارِجي؟

o لا مِسافْرة لِمطار شرْم الشّيْخ.

◇ لا حضْرِتِك تُقفي في الطّابور اللي هِناك. اللي إحْنا فيه ده لِلرّحلات الخارِجية.

o Excuse me, can you tell me if I'm standing in the right line.

◇ Is your flight domestic or international?

o I'm traveling to Sharm El-Sheikh.

◇ In that case, you should stand in that line over there. This one is for international flights.

o *min fáḍlik, múmkin tiʔulīli law ána wáʔfa*[1] *fi -ṭṭabūr ilmaẓbūṭ.*

◇ *ḫaḍrítik ṭayarān daxíli wálla xarígi?*

o *laʔ, misáfra l-maṭār šarm iššēx.*

◇ *laʔ, ḫaḍrítik túʔafi fi -ṭṭabūr ílli hināk. íll- íḫna fī da li-rraḫalāt ilxarigíyya.*

[1] = إذا كُنْت واقْفة *íza kunt^{ə} wáʔfa*

5

At passport control

◇ باسْبوْرك مِن فضْلك.

o اِتْفضّل.

◇ بسّ شكْلك مُخْتلِف خالِص[1].

o حلقْت دقْني مِش أكْتر[2].

◇ تمام. الباسْبوْر اِتْختم كِده. رِحْلة سعيدة[3].

◇ Your passport, please.

o Here you are.

◇ But you look so different.

o I've shaved my beard. That's all.

◇ Okay, here's your stamped passport. Have a good trip!

◇ *paspōrak min fáḍlak.*

o *itfáḍḍal.*

◇ *bassᵊ šáklak muxtálif xāliṣ*[1].

o *ḫaláʔtᵊ dáʔni miš áktar*[2].

◇ *tamām. ilpaspōr itxátam kída. ríḫla sa3īda*[3].

[1] = مِتْغيرّ أَوي *mityáyyar áwi*

[2] = بسّ *bass*

[3] The response can be الله يِخلّيك *allāh yixallīk,* or simply شُكْراً *šúkran* or مُتْشكِّر جِدّاً *mutšákkir gíddan.*

6

FINDING YOUR GATE

o أَوْصل بوّابة رقم ٥٠٤ إزّاي؟[1]

◇ خلّيك ماشي على طول في تالِت يمين.

o تمام مُتْشكِّر جِدّاً.

◇ العفْو بسّ اِنْجِز بقى[2] عشان تِلْحق.

o How can I reach gate number 504?

◇ Keep walking and take the third right.

o Okay, thanks a lot.

◇ You're welcome. But hurry up to make it [in time].

o *áwṣal bawwāba ráqam xumsumíyya w arbá3a izzāy*[1]*?*

◇ *xallīk māši 3ála ṭūl, fi tālit yimīn.*

o *tamām, mutšákkir gíddan.*

◇ *il3áfw, bass íngiz báʔa*[2] *3ašān tílḥaʔ.*

[1] = هِيَّ بَوّابة رقم ــ منِيْن؟ *híyya bawwāba ráqam ___ minēn?*

[2] = بِسُرْعة بسّ *bi-súr3a bass* = يَلّا بْسُرْعة *yálla b-súr3a* **quickly**

Extended Dialogue

◇ حضْرِتِك أوِّل مرّة تِنْزِلي مطار القاهِرة؟

o لا أنا بسافِر مِنُّه و بنْزِل عليْه كِتير.

◇ شكْلِك بِتْسافْري مصْر كِتير.

o أنا اصْلاً مُقيمة هِنا كام سنة و برْجع بلدي في الأجازات بسّ.

◇ حِلْو جِدّاً. يُسْتحْسِن[1] تُرْبُطي الحِزام عشان خلاص الطّيّارة نازْلة المطار.[2]

o اِتْفضّل لِبان[3] لَوْ عايِز.

◇ مُتْشكِّر جِدّاً[4]. هنِحْتاجُه فِعْلاً.

(plane lands)

◇ حمْدِلْله عَ السّلامة.

o الله يِسلِّمك.

◇ تِحِبّي أساعْدِك في الشُّنط؟

o مُتْشكِّرة جِدّاً

(They disembark together and wait for their luggage at baggage claim.)

o أيْه ده خلاص كِده مفيش شُنط تانْيَة؟[5]

◇ لا... كِده أنا ناقِصْلي[6] شنْطة مجتْش عَ الطّيّارة.

o و أنا كمان نفْس الكّلام[7].

◇ طب، تعالي وَرايا[8]... بِتِحْصل معايا على طول[9].

o هنِعْمِل أيْه[10] دِلْوَقْتي؟

◇ هنرْوح لِشِبّاك المفْقودات و نِبلّغ عن مُواصفات الشُّنط. ساعات[11] بِتوْصل في الطّيّارة اللي بعْدها.

o يا ريْت فِعْلاً.[12]

◇ ربِّنا يِسهِّل.[12] خلّينا نِبلّغ الأوِّل و بعْديْن نِشوف.

◇ Is this your first time landing at Cairo airport?
o No, I travel to and from it a lot.
◇ Looks like you travel to Egypt a lot
o I've actually been living here for a few years, and I just go back home on vacations.
◇ Very nice. You'd better fasten your belt. The plane is starting its descent to the airport.
o Would you like some gum?
◇ Thank you. We probably need it.

(plane lands)

◇ Thank God you arrived safely!
o Bless you!
◇ Would you like any help with the luggage?
o Thank you so much.

(They disembark together and wait for their luggage at baggage claim.)

o What!? No more suitcases?
◇ Nope... And I still have one suitcase that [apparently] wasn't on the plane.
o Same for me.
◇ All right, follow me. This always happens to me.
o What shall we do now?
◇ We'll go to the lost luggage window and report them. Sometimes they'll arrive on the next plane.
o I hope so!
◇ Hopefully! Let's report it first and see what happens.

◇ *ɧaɖrítik áwwil márra tinzíli maʈār ilqāhíra?*
o *laʔ, ána basāfir mínnu wi bánzil 3alē ktīr.*
◇ *šáklik bitsáfri maʂrᵊ ktīr.*
o *ána áʂlan muqīma hína kām sána wi bárga3 báladi fi -lʔagazāt bass.*
◇ *ɧilwᵊ gíddan. yusʈáɧsin*[1] *turbúʈi -lɧizām 3ašān xalāʂ iʈʈayyāra názla -lmaʈār.*[2]
o *itfáɖɖal libān*[3]*, law 3āyiz.*
◇ *mutšákkir gíddan*[4]*. haniɧtāgu fí3lan.*

(plane lands)

◇ *ɧamdílla 3a -ssalāma.*
o *allāh yisallímak.*

◇ *tiḫíbbi asá3dik fi -ššúnaṭ?*
○ *mutšakkíra gíddan*
(They disembark together and wait for their luggage at baggage claim.)
○ *ʔē da xalāṣ kída ma-fīš šúnaṭ tánya?*[5]
◇ *laʔ... kída ána naʔíṣli*[6] *šánṭa ma-gátšᵊ 3a -ṭṭayyāra.*
○ *w ána kamān nafṣ ikkalām*[7].
◇ *ṭab, ta3āli warāya*[8]*... bitíḫṣal ma3āya 3ála ṭūl*[9].
○ *haní3mil ʔē*[10] *dilwáʔti?*
◇ *hanrūḫ li-šibbāk ilmafqudāt wi nibállaɣ 3an muwaṣafāt iššúnaṭ. ṣa3āt*[11] *bitíwṣal fi -ṭṭayyāra ílli ba3dáha.*
○ *ya rēt fí3lan*[12].
◇ *rabbína yisáhhil*[12]. *xallīna nbállaɣ ilʔáwwil wi ba3dēn nišūf.*

[1] = يا ريْت *ya rēt*

[2] طب، يَلّا نِرْبُط الحِزام لأحْسن قرّبْنا نِنْزِل. *ṭab, yálla nírbuṭ ilḫizām láḫsan, ʔarrábna nínzil.* **Well, let's buckle up. We're about to land.**

[3] (Alexandrian) مسْتيكة *mastīka*

[4] تِسْلمي معايا. *tislámi, ma3āya.* **Thanks, but I have some (already).**

[5] دي كُلّ الشُنط؟ *di kull iššúnaṭ?* **Are these all the bags?**

[6] = فاضِلّي *faḍílli*

[7] = زيّك *záyyak* **like you**

[8] تعالي معايا *ta3āli ma3āya* **come with me**

[9] = دايْماً *dáyman*

[10] = هنِتْصرّف ازّاي؟ *hanitṣárraf izzāy?*

[11] = أحْياناً *aḫyānan*

[12] = يا مُسهِّل! *ya musáhhil* (lit. O facilitator! (invocation of God)) = إن شاء الله خيْر! *in šāʔ allāh xēr*

Vocabulary

airport	*maṭār*	مطار
hall	*ṣāla*	صالة
arrivals	*wuṣūl*	وُصول
departure	*muɣádra*	مُغادْرة
ticket	*tazkára (tazākir)*	تذْكرة (تذاكِر)
airline	*šírkit ṭayarān*	شِرْكِةْ طيَران
worker	*3āmil*	عامِل
suitcase	*šánṭa, šánṭit issáfar*	شنْطة، شنْطِةْ السّفر
luggage	*šúnaṭ (issáfar)*	شُنَط (السّفر)
luggage cart	*3arabīt šúnaṭ*	عربيةْ شُنط
wrapping (suitcases with silicon wrap)	*taɣlīf*	تغْليف
weight	*wazn*	وَزْن
over the weight limit	*wazn^ə ziyāda*	وَزْن زِيادة
forbidden	*mamnū3*	ممْنوع
liquids	*sawāyil*	سَوايِل
blade	*āla ḫádda*	آلة حادّة
conveyor belt; baggage carousel	*sēr*	سيرْ
passport control	*gawazāt*	جَوازات
stamp	*xitm (axtām)*	خِتْم (أخْتام)
officer	*ẓābiṭ*	ظابِط

inspection, search	*taftīš*	تفْتيش
body search	*taftīš zāti*	تفْتيش ذاتي
fine	*ɣarāma*	غرامة
shuttle bus	[shuttle] *bāṣ*	شاتل باص
gate	*bawwāba*	بوّابة
plane	*ṭayyāra*	طيّارة
boarding	[boarding]	بوْرْدينْج
window	*šibbāk*	شِبّاك
corridor	*mamárr*	ممرّ
take-off	*iʔlā3*	إقْلاع
landing	*hubūṭ*	هُبوط
belt	*ɦizām*	حِزام
to fasten	*rábaṭ*	ربط
flight attendant	*muḍīf*	مُضيف
pilot	*ṭayyār*	طيّار
captain	*kábtin*	كابْتِن
trip, flight	*ríɦla*	رِحْلة
transit	*tiránzit*	تِرانْزيت
to arrive	*wáṣal*	وَصل
to travel	*sāfir*	سافِر

Expressions

○

I would like to wrap this suitcase [in silicon wrap].	*3āyiz aɣállif iššánţa di, min fáḑlak.*	عايِز أغلِّف الشّنْطة دي مِن فضْلك.
Excuse me. This suitcase is heavy. Can you put it on the conveyor belt for me?	*ma3alíšš iššánţa tʔīla. múmkin tiħuţţahāli 3a -ssēr?*	معلِشّ الشّنْطة تِقيلة. مُمْكِن تِحُطّهالي عَ السّيرْ؟
There's a suitcase that hasn't arrived.	*fī šánţa ma-waşalítš.*	فيه شنْطة مَوَصلِتْش.

◇

Jacket and shoes in the tray, please.	*ilgázma wi -žžākit 3a -şşiníyya.*	الجزْمة و الجّاكيت عَ الصّينية.
Raise your arms, please.	*írfa3 idēk, min fáḑlak.*	اِرْفع إيديْك مِن فضْلك.
Could you take off your belt?	*múmkin tíʔla3 ilħizām?*	مُمْكِن تِقْلع الحِزام؟
Chicken or beef?	*firāx wálla láħma?*	فِراخ وَلّا لحْمة؟
Cola or juice?	*kōka wálla 3aşīr?*	كوْكا وَلّا عصير؟
What does the suitcase look like?	*muwaşafāt iššánţa ʔē?*	مُواصفات الشّنْطة أيْه؟

At a Restaurant في المطْعم

Restaurants vary in the levels of service. Some are fancy, air-conditioned establishments with waiters in uniforms that can even take your order using a tablet, while others are basic—just on a sidewalk on the side of the street but have a more local, friendly atmosphere. As with everything in Egypt, بقْشيش *baʔšīš* **tips** are expected. There isn't a set percentage to tip, as in the US. The custom is to give your waiter a few pounds extra for service directly. Or sometimes you'll see a tip box by the cashier. At nicer restaurants, taxes and service charges are usually added to the bill, and these can add 20-25% to the prices on the menu. Tips are still expected in addition to their charges. Egyptian Arabic has borrowed the French word garçon to mean **waiter**: جارْسوْن *garsōn*. The plural is جارْسونات *garsunāt*. The word for **waitress** is جارسوْنة *garsōna*. While these words designate the profession, they are not used to get your server's attention. Instead, Egyptians tend to call out لَوْ سمحْت! *law samáḥt!* or, in more casual restaurants, يا ريِّس! *ya ráyyis!*, and in fancier restaurants يا مِترْ! *ya mitr!*

Ordering food

o عايِز طبق فول بِالطّحينة و طبق شكْشوكة.

◇ مِش عايِز طعْمية[1] معاهُم؟

o لا بسّ عايِز بابا غنوج في السّلطات[2].

◇ مِن عينيّا.

o I'd like an order of ful with tahini and an order of shakshouka.

◇ You don't want falafel with it?

o No, but I'd like some baba ghanoush as one of the side salads.

◇ Coming right up!

o *3āyiz ṭába? fūl bi-ṭṭaḥīna wi ṭába? šakšūka.*

◇ *miš 3āyiz ṭa3míyya*[1] *ma3āhum?*

o *la?, bass^ə 3āyiz bāba ɣanūg fi -ssalaṭāt*[2].

◇ *min 3ináyya.*

[1] (Alexandrian) فلافِل *falāfil*

[2] (lit. among the salads.) Egyptian restaurants usually offer a couple of mini-salad side dishes alongside the main dish. You can request your favorites.

Ful (also spelled foul) and falafel make up the traditional Egyptian breakfast, especially on Fridays when families have time to eat together. Other common foods at the breakfast table are بيْض مقْلي *bēḍ má?li* **fried eggs**, جِبْنة *gíbna* **cheese**, بطاطِس مِحمّرة *baṭāṭis miḥammára* **fried potatoes**, بِتِنْجان مقْلي *bitingān má?li* **fried eggplant** or بِتِنْجان مِخلِّل *bitingān mixállil* **pickled eggplant**, and طرْشي *ṭárši* / مِخلِّل *mixállil* **pickled vegetables**.

2

Ordering food

◇ تُؤْمُروا بِأيْه يا بشَوات[1]؟

o بُصّ[2] يا مُعلِّم[3]، عايْزين ٢٥ سنْدِوِتْش كِبْدة.

◇ السّنْدِوِتْش نُصّيْن. كِده هَيِبْقى ٥٠ سنْدِوِتْش. و معاهُم فِلْفِل و طحينة.

o حِلْو جِدّاً! اِلْحقْنا بقى عشان واقْعين[4].

◇ What would you like to order, gentlemen?

o Listen, boss, we want 25 liver sandwiches.

◇ Each sandwich is two halves, so it will be a total of 50 halves, with pepper and tahini.

o Perfect! Save us quickly because we are starving!

◇ *tuʔmúru b-ʔē ya bašawāt*[1]*?*

o *buṣṣ*[ə] [2] *ya mu3állim*[3]*, 3ayzīn xámsa w 3išrīn sandiwítš*[ə] *kíbda.*

◇ *issandiwítš*[ə] *nuṣṣēn. kída hayíbʔa xamsīn sandiwítš. wi ma3āhum fílfil wi ṭaḥīna.*

o *ḥilw*[ə] *gíddan! ilḥáʔna báʔa 3ašān waʔ3īn*[4]*.*

[1] بشَوات *bašawāt* is the plural of باشا *bāša* **Pasha**, a formal title used until the 1950s. Nowadays, it is usually used by waiters, doormen, etc. as a friendly way of addressing someone respectfully.

[2] بُصّ *buṣṣ* is literally "**Look, ...**" but this literal translation sounds aggressive in English. It is better left untranslated and thought of as a filler or opener for statements.

[3] يا مِعلِّم *ya mi3állim* (lit. teacher) is another example of a friendly form of address.

[4] ميِّتين مِن الجّوع *mayyitīn min iggū3* **dying of hunger**

3

ORDERING FOOD

○ عايْزين سنْدِوِتْشين مُخّ و طبقينْ فتِّةْ كَوارِع.
◇ فيه طرْب حِلْو أَوي. تِحِبّ تِجرّب؟
○ لا لا مليش فيه خالِص، بسّ مُمْكِن تِنزِّلْنا على جمْب نُصّ كباب و كُفْتة.
◇ مِن عينيّا[1]!

○ We'd like two brain sandwiches and two orders of fattah kawara.
◇ There is also some really nice tarb. Would you like to try?
○ No, I don't care for that, but you can add half a kilo of kebab and kofta as a side dish.
◇ My pleasure!

○ *3ayzīn sandiwitšēn muxx, wi ṭabaʔēn fáttit kawāri3.*
◇ *fī ṭarbᵊ ħilw áwi. tiħíbbᵊ tgárrab?*
○ *lā lā, ma-līš fī xāliṣ, bassᵊ múmkin tinazzílna 3ála gambᵊ nuṣṣᵊ kabāb wi kúfta.*
◇ *min 3ináyya[1]!*

[1] مِن عينيّا *min 3ináyya* (lit. from my eyes) is one of many ways to respond to a request or order. You may also hear تحْت أمْرك *taħtᵊ ámrak* **under your order** or اللي إنْتَ عايْزُه *ill- ínta 3áyzu* **whatever you want**.

This dialogue takes place in a مسْمط *másmaṭ,* which is a kind of restaurant that specializes in meat and organs, such as كِبْدة *kíbda* **liver**, سُجُق *súguʔ* **sausage**, مُخّ *muxx* **brains**, كَوارِع *kawāri3* **cow's trotters**, كِرْشة *kírša* **tripe**, مُمْبار *mumbār* **intestines**, لِسان *lisān* **tongue**, and لحْمِةْ راس *láħmit rās* **beef head meat**. Al-Hussein district of Cairo is known for having many of these restaurants, which are often extensions of butcher shops. (See also **At the Butcher's**, book 2, p. 16.)

Ordering food

o مِن فضْلك، عايْزة اِتْنين كُشري وَسط.

◇ ماشي تِجِبّي معاه بصل زِيادة أَوْ حُمُّص زِيادة.

o لا زوِّد[1] البصل في الاِتْنيْن و عايْزين شطّة.

◇ اللي إنْتي عايْزاه![2]

o I'd like two medium [orders of] koshary, please.

◇ Sure, would you like some extra fried onions or extra hummus with it?

o Just add extra onions on both, and we want hot pepper sauce.

◇ As you wish!

o *min fáḍlak, 3áyza -tnēn kúšari wásaṭ.*

◇ *māši tiɦíbbi ma3ā báṣal ziyāda aw ɦúmmuṣ ziyāda.*

o *laʔ, záwwid*[1] *ilbáṣal fi -lʔitnēn wi 3ayzīn šáṭṭa.*

◇ *íll- ínti 3ayzā!*[2]

1 = كتّر *káttar*

2 = زيّ ما انْتي عايْزة *zayyᵊ má-nti 3áyza*

At koshary restaurants, you may hear some people tell the waiter عايِز طبق كِمالة. *3āyiz ṭábaʔ kimāla.* **I'd like an additional small koshary**. People order a كِمالة *kimāla* when they still feel hungry but, at the same time, don't need another full portion.

Some famous koshary restaurants in Cairo are أبو طارِق *ábu ṭāriʔ* **Abou Tarek** and كُشري التّحْرير *kúšari -ttaɦrīr* **Koshary El-Tahrir**.

5

Ordering food

◇ اِتْفضّلي المنْيو يافنْدِم.

o لَوْ سمحْت كُنْت عايْزة اِتْنينْ بيتْزا سْتافْت كْراسْت تْشيكِن بارْبيكْيو.

◇ الحجْم أيْه يافنْدِم؟

o الاِتْنينْ وَسط بسّ سْتافْت كْراسْت و عايْزين طبق سلطة.

◇ تِحِبّوا أيّ حاجة تِشْربوها معَ البيتْزا؟

o لَوْ فيه بيبْسي دايِت يارِيْت[1].

◇ Here's the menu, miss!

o I'd like to order two barbecue chicken stuffed crust pizzas, please.

◇ And what size, ma'am?

o Two mediums but stuffed crust, and we want one salad.

◇ Would you like anything to drink with the pizza?

o If you have Diet Pepsi, that would be great.

◇ *itfaḍḍáli -lmínyu yafándim.*

o *law samáɦtᵊ kuntᵊ 3áyza itnēn pítza* [stuffed crust chicken barbecue].

◇ *ilɦágmᵊ ʔē yafándim?*

o *ilʔitnēn wásaṭ bassᵊ* [stuffed crust], *wi 3ayzīn ṭábaʔ sálaṭa.*

◇ *tiɦíbbu ayyᵊ ɦāga tišrabūha má3a -lpítza?*

o *law fī pípsi dāyit yarēt*[1].

[1] = يِبْقى تمام *yíbʔa tamām*

6

Getting the Bill

o لَوْ سمحْت كُنْت عايْزة التّْشيْك[1]!

◇ اِتْفضّلي يافنْدِم. يا ربّ يِكون الأكْل عجبْكُم.

o آه الأكْل عنْدُكُم لطيف أوي بسّ الفِرِنْش فْرايْز[2] المرّة اللي فاتِت كانِت أحْلى.

o Excuse me! I'd like the check!

◇ Here you are! I hope you liked the food.

o Yes, your food here is really nice, but last time the French fries were much better.

o *law samáħt, kuntᵊ 3áyza -l[check]!*

◇ *itfaḍḍáli yafándim. ya rabbᵊ ykūn ilʔáklᵊ 3agábkum.*

o *āh, ilʔáklᵊ 3andúkum laṭīf áwi, bass ilfirínšᵊ frāyz[2] ilmárra -lli fātit kānit áħla.*

[1] = الحِساب *ilħisāb*

[2] البطاطِس المِحمّرة *ilbaṭāṭis ilmiħammára*

On any given workday in the morning, you can find people gathered around a عربيةْ فول *3arabīt fūl*, a colorful cart selling ful and falafel for much cheaper than in restaurants. These are popular with both blue- and white-collar workers, who will stand there eating their breakfast on their way to work. Although the food is generally delicious and the experience is fun, these carts are not always sanitary and are known to be a frequent culprit of upset stomachs.

Extended Dialogue

○ لَوْ سمحْت كُنْت عايْزة أعْرف مِنْيو الفِطار لِسّه مَوْجود وَلّا خِلِص؟

◇ لا لِسّه مَوْجود[1] يافنْدِم لِحدّ السّاعة ١.

○ طب، حِلْو أَوي. فيه فول؟

◇ فيه يافنْدِم.

○ خلاص، عايْزين فول و بيْض سْبانيش و جِبْنة بِالطّماطِم.

◇ مِش حابّين تِشْربوا حاجة معاه؟

○ لا خلّينا بعْد الفِطار أحْسن.

◇ تمام يافنْدِم، تحْت أمْرِك.

○ فيه بان كيْك؟

◇ آه فيه يافنْدِم.

○ تمام عايْزين اِتْنيْن.

◇ عسل وَلّا نْيوتيلّا؟

○ لا سيرب أَوْ عسل عادي.

(30 minutes later)

◇ تِحِبّوا تِشْربوا حاجة دِلْوَقْتي؟

○ آه لَوْ سمحْت، عايْزة واحِد كابُتْشينو ميدْيام و واحِد شاي بِلبن.

◇ تِحِبّي أيّ إضافات على الكّابُتْشينو؟

○ لا شُكْراً بسّ مُمْكِن تِجيبْلِنا الحِساب عشان قرّبْنا نِمْشي.

(10 minutes later)

○ مِن فضْلك، فيه غلْطة في الحِساب.[2]

◇ خيْر يافنْدِم، فيْن بِالظّبْط؟

○ مكْتوب إنِّنا اخدْنا مشْروب معَ الفِطار غيْر المشْروبات اللي خدْناها بعْد كِده.

◇ آه هِيَّ فِعْلاً بِتِبْقى ضِمْن مِنْيو الفِطار.
o طيِّب، ليْه مَوَضّحْتِش ده لينا مِن الأوِّل؟[3]
◇ أنا آسِف يافنْدِم. حصل خيْر. عُموماً اِدّيني خمس دقايِق أظبّط الرّيسيت.

o Excuse me, I'd like to know if the breakfast menu is still available or is it over?
◇ No, it's still available until 1 p.m.
o Okay, great. Do you have ful?
◇ Yes, we do.
o Okay, we'd like some ful, a spinach omelet, and white cheese with tomatoes.
◇ Would you like something to drink with it?
o No, maybe after breakfast.
◇ Certainly. As you wish.
o Are there any pancakes?
◇ Yes, miss, there are.
o Okay, we would like two [orders].
◇ With honey or Nutella?
o Just syrup or honey.

(30 minutes later)

o Would you like something to drink now?
◇ Yes, please. We would like one medium cappuccino and one tea with milk.
o Would you like to add any flavors to the cappuccino?
◇ No, thanks. We just need the check because we are going to leave soon.

(10 minutes later)

o Excuse me, there is a mistake on the check.
◇ What is it? Where exactly?
o It says that we ordered some drinks with the breakfast besides those we ordered later.

◇ Yeah! Because they're already included in the breakfast set.

○ Why didn't you clarify this in the first place?

◇ I'm sorry, miss. It's all right. Just give me five minutes and I'll correct the check.

○ *law samáɧt, kunt^{ə} 3áyza á3raf mínyu -lfiţār líssa mawgūd wálla xíliṣ?*

◇ *laʔ, líssa mawgūd*[1] *yafándim li-ɧádd issā3a wáɧda.*

○ *ţab, ɧilw áwi. fī fūl?*

◇ *fī yafándim.*

○ *xalāṣ, 3ayzīn fūl wi bēḍ* [spinach] *wi gíbna bi-ţţamāţim.*

◇ *miš ɧabbīn tišrábu ɧāga ma3ā?*

○ *laʔ, xallīna ba3d ilfiţār áɧsan.*

◇ *tamām, yafándim, taɧt^{ə} ámrik.*

○ *fī pān kēk?*

◇ *āh, fī yafándim.*

○ *tamām, 3ayzīn itnēn.*

◇ *3ásal wálla nyutīla?*

○ *laʔ, sírab aw 3ásal 3ādi.*

(30 minutes later)

◇ *tiɧíbbu tišrábu ɧāga dilwáʔti?*

○ *āh, law samáɧt, 3áyza wāɧid kabutšīnu mídyam wi wāɧid šāy bi-lában.*

◇ *tiɧíbbi ayy^{ə} iḍafāt 3ála -kkabutšīnu?*

○ *laʔ, šúkran bass^{ə} múmkin tigiblína -lɧisāb 3ašān ʔarrábna nímši.*

(10 minutes later)

○ *min fáḍlak, fī ɣálţa fi -lɧisāb.*[2]

◇ *xēr yafándim, fēn bi-ẓẓábţ?*

○ *maktūb innína axádna mašrūb má3a -lfiţār ɣēr ilmašrubāt ílli xadnāha ba3d^{ə} kída.*

◇ *āh, híyya fí3lan bitíbʔa ḍimn^{ə} mínyu -lfiţār.*

○ *ţáyyib, lē ma-waḍḍáɧtiš da līna min ilʔáwwil?*[3]

◇ *ána āsif yafándim. ɧáṣal xēr. 3umūman iddīni xámas daʔāyiʔ, aẓábbaţ irrisīt.*

[1] = متاح *mutāɧ* = مُتَوَفِّر *mutawáffir*

[2] = فيه حاجة غلط في الحِساب. *fī ɧāga ɣálaţ fi -lɧisāb.* = الحِساب مِش مظْبوط. *ilɧisāb miš maẓbūţ.*

[3] ليْه مقُلْتِش كِده مِن الأوِّل؟ *lē ma-ʔúltiš kída min ilʔáwwil.* **Why didn't you say so in the first place?**

Vocabulary

restaurant	*máṭ3am (maṭā3im)*	مطْعم (مطاعِم)
butcher's restaurant	*másmaṭ*	مسْمط
kiosk, stand	*kušk (kišāk)*	كُشْك (كِشاك)
waiter	*garsōn (garsunāt)*	جرْسوْن (جرْسُنات)
waitress	*garsōna*	جرْسوْنة
cook	*ṭabbāx*	طبّاخ
menu; set meal	*mínyu*	مِنْيو
check, bill	*ḥisāb* *fatūra*	حِساب فاتورة
order	*ōrdar*	أوْرْدر
mistake	*ɣálṭa*	غلْطة
pizza	*pítza*	بيتْزا
hamburger	*hambúrgar*	هامْبُرْجر
French fries	*baṭāṭis*	بطاطِس
salad	*sálaṭa*	سلطة
cheese	*gíbna*	جِبْنة
ketchup	*kátšab*	كاتْشب
mayonnaise	*mayunēz*	مايونيْز
grilled chicken	*firāx mašwíyya*	فِراخ مشْوية

fried fish	*sámak máʔli*	سمك مقْلي
grilled fish	*sámak mášwi*	سمك مشْوي
shrimp	*gambári*	جمْبري
lobster	*istakōza*	إسْتاكوْزا
crab	*kabúrya*	كابورْيا
meatballs	*kúfta*	كُفْتة
kebab (grilled meat on a skewer)	*kabāb*	كباب
hawashi (pita stuffed with minced meat or sausage)	*ḩawáwši*	حَواوْشي
liver	*kíbda*	كِبْدة
koshary (bowl of rice, macaroni, lentils, tomato sauce, hummus, and fried onions)	*kúšari*	كُشري
ful (mashed fava beans)	*fūl*	فول
falafel (fried fava bean paste)	*ţa3míyya*	طعْمية
falafel (Alexandrian)	*falāfil*	فلافِل
bissara (dip made from fava beans)	*bişāra*	بِصارة
shakshouka (eggs poached in tomato sauce with onions)	*šakšūka*	شكْشوكة
kawary (cow's trotters)	*kawāri3*	كَوارِع
fattah (meat soup with rice and crispy flatbread)	*fátta*	فتّة

tarb (meat wrapped in fats)	*ţarb*	طرْب
(fried) brains	*muxx*	مُخّ
tahini	*ţaђīna*	طحينة
baba ghanoush (pureed grilled eggplant)	*bāba ɣanūg*	بابا غنوج
pickled vegetables	*mixállil*	مِخلِّل
tea	*šāy*	شاي
coffee	*ʔáhwa*	قهْوَة
juice	*3aşīr*	عصير
Pepsi	*pípsi*	بيبْسي

Expressions

◇

I'd like a table for five, please.	*law samáђtᵊ 3āyiz tarabēza tikáffi xámas ašxāş/afrād.*	لَوْ سمحْت عايِز ترابيْزة تِكفّي ٥ أشْخاص/أفْراد.
Could I reserve a table for 5 p.m.?	*múmkin áђgiz tarabēza li-ssā3a xámsa?*	مُمْكِن أحْجِز ترابيْزة لِلسّاعة ٥؟
Waiter!	*law samáђt!*	لَوْ سمحْت!
Can I have the pizza without mushrooms?	*múmkin pítza bassᵊ min ɣēr mášrum?*	مُمْكِن بيتْزا بسّ مِن غيْر مشْروم؟

The food is cold. Could you please reheat it?	*ilʔáklᵊ bārid áwi. múmkin tisaxxánu tāni ma3alíšš?*	الأكْل بارِد أَوي. مُمْكِن تِسخّنُه تاني معلِشّ؟
I would like to order another plate of tahini.	*3āyiz azáwwid ṭábaʔ ṭaɦīna kamān.*	عايِز أزوِّد طبق طحينة كمان.
Can I have extra bread?	*múmkin 3ēš ziyāda?*	مُمْكِن عيْش زِيادة؟
Excuse me, these pickles are off/spoiled.	*law samáɦt ilmixállil da ɦamḍān.*	لَوْ سمحْت المِخلِّل ده حمْضان.
Check, please!	*ilɦisāb law samáɦt!*	الحِساب لَوْ سمحْت!
Excuse me, there is a mistake on the check.	*law samáɦt, fī ɣálṭa fi -lɦisāb.*	لَوْ سمحْت فيه غلْطة في الحِساب.
Do you take credit cards?	*fī vīza?*	فيه فيزا؟
Could you put it on this card?	*múmkin tísɦab min ilkártᵊ da?*	مُمْكِن تِسْحب مِن الكارْت ده؟

At the Coffee House عَ القَهْوَة

The قَهْوَة *ʔáhwa* **coffee house** is the quintessential hang-out for Egyptian men. You will rarely find yourself more than a minute's walk from the next coffee house. Some are holes in the wall; others are spacious establishments, sprawling onto the sidewalks, and even taking over entire alleys in the evening. At coffee houses, you will see Egyptian men, young and old alike, reading newspapers, watching soccer matches on TV, playing backgammon, cards, or dominoes, or just chatting with friends and strangers all while enjoying tea, Turkish coffee, or other beverages... and occasionally while smoking shisha. Although women may not be openly welcome at many neighborhood coffee houses, you will notice some Egyptian women (mostly accompanied by men) in coffee houses downtown and in more middle-class neighborhoods. Tourists, however, are always welcome. It's Egyptian hospitality.

Asking about Available Beverages

○ لَوْ سمحْت.

◇ اُؤْمُر يا أُسْتاذ.

○ عنْدُكُم أيْه مشْروبات؟

◇ فيه شاي و قِهْوَة[1] و سحْلب و يَنْسون و نِعْناع و حِلْبة و البارِد فيه عصايِر و حاجة ساقْعة و فيه شيشِةْ قصّ و سلّوم و فَواكِهْ.

○ تمام طب دِقيقة و هقولّك.

○ Waiter!

◇ Yes sir, how can I help you?

○ What drinks do you have?

◇ We have tea, coffee, sahlep, anise, mint, fenugreek, and for cold drinks, we have juice and soft drinks. And we have qas, salloum, and fruit-flavored shishas.

○ Okay, give me a minute, please.

○ *law samáɧt.*

◇ *úʔmur ya ustāz.*

○ *3andúkum ʔē mašrubāt?*

◇ *fī šāy wi ʔáhwa[1] wi sáɧlab wi yansūn wi ni3nā3 wi ɧílba, wi -lbārid fī 3aşāyir wi ɧāga sáʔ3a, wi fī šīšit ʔaşş, wi sallūm wi fawākih.*

○ *tamām, ţab diʔīʔa wi haʔúllak.*

[1] In an Egyptian coffee house, قهْوَة *ʔáhwa* is understood to be قهْوَة تُرْكي *ʔáhwa túrki* **Turkish coffee**, not brewed coffee.

2

ORDERING TEA

o لَوْ سمحْت كُنْت عايِز شاي.

◇ شايَك أيْه؟

o سُكّر برّه.

◇ فتْلة وَلّا كُشري؟[1]

o فتْلة.

o Excuse me, I'd like some tea.
◇ How sweet [would you like] your tea?
o Sugar on the side.
◇ Do you want a tea bag or with tea leaves?
o A tea bag.

o *law samáħtᵊ kuntᵊ 3āyiz šāy.*
◇ *šāyak ʔē?*
o *súkkar bárra.*
◇ *fátla wálla kúšari?*[1]
o *fátla.*

[1] When you order tea, you can specify that you want شاي فتْلة *šāy fátla,* made with tea bags, or شاي كُشري *šāy kúšari,* with loose tea leaves in a pot which you pour through a sieve into your cup.

Don't confuse قهْوَة *ʔáhwa* **coffee house** with كافيْه *kafēh* **café**. The former is the traditional Egyptian establishment with a very بلدي *báladi* **local** atmosphere and very affordable prices for all, while the latter is the Western style café with espresso drinks, frappés, and other fancy drinks, cakes, salads, WiFi, and so on... and fancy prices to match.

Hesham tells us more about the Egyptian coffee house on the Lingualism blog at www.lingualism.com/ahwa .

3

Ordering coffee

o لَوْ سمحْت كُنْت عايِز قهْوَة تُرْكي.
◇ سادة وَلّا عَ ريحة وَلّا زِيادة؟
o زِيادة.

o Excuse me, I'd like some Turkish coffee.
◇ Plain, a little sweet, or very sweet?
o Very sweet.

o *law samáħt, kuntᵊ 3āyiz ʔáhwa túrki.*
◇ *sāda wálla 3a rīħa wálla ziyāda?*
o *ziyāda.*

Sugar is added to Turkish coffee as it is being boiled. Specify the level of sweetness when ordering:

سادة *sāda* (lit. plain) **no sugar**

عَ ريحة *3a rīħa* or على ريحة *3ála rīħa* (lit. with a whiff) **with very little sugar**

مظْبوط *mazbūt* (lit. correct) **medium-sweet**

(سُكّر) زِيادة *súkkar ziyāda* (lit. excess (sugar)) **extra sweet**

The Egyptian coffee house has a history of being the meeting place for figures from science, literature, and art. The Nobel prize-winning author Naguib Mahfouz is widely known to have spent a lot of time in coffee houses, where he wrote some of his best novels. He frequented the famous قهْوِة الفيشاوي *ʔáhwit ilfišāwi* **El Fishawy Café** in Khan El Khalili, Cairo.

ORDERING SAHLEP

○ لَوْ سمحْت عنْدُكُم ميلْك شيْك؟
◇ لا لِلْأسف مفيش بسّ فيه عنْدِنا سحْلب[1].
○ طب، تمام. هات سحْلب.

○ Excuse me do you have milkshakes?
◇ Sorry, we don't. But we have sahlep.
○ Okay, give me a sahlep.

○ *law samáɦt, 3andúkum milk šēk?*
◇ *la?, li-l?ásaf, ma-fīš, bassᵊ fī 3andína sáɦlab[1].*
○ *ṭab, tamām. hāt sáɦlab.*

[1] سحْلب *sáɦlab* is a hot tapioca drink popular in the winter. It has pine nuts, chocolate, shredded coconut, vanilla, cinnamon, and is topped with crushed pistachios and raisins.

5

Ordering Shisha

○ لَوْ سمحْت كُنْت عايز شيشة.

◇ فيه عنْدِنا شيشة قصّ[1] و سلّوم[2] و فَواكِهْ.

○ فَواكِهْ أيْه عنْدُكُم ؟

◇ فيه تُفّاح و عِنب و توت أزْرق و نِعْناع.

○ تمام هاتْلي تُفّاح.

○ Excuse me, I'd like a shisha.
◇ What kind? We have qass[1], salloum[2] and fruit flavors.
○ What fruit flavors do you have?
◇ We have apple, grape, blueberry, and mint.
○ All right, give me apple.

○ *law samáḥt, kunt^{ə} 3āyiz šīša.*
◇ *fī 3andína šīša ʔaṣṣ*[1]*, wi sallūm*[2]*, wi fawākih.*
○ *fawākih ʔē 3andúkum?*
◇ *fī tuffāḥ wi 3ínab wi tūt ázraʔ wi ni3nā3.*
○ *tamām, hátli tuffāḥ.*

[1] قصّ *ʔaṣṣ* is a very strong, unflavored tobacco.

[2] سلّوم *sallūm* is tobacco mixed with molasses and dates.

Smoking shisha is harmful to your health. The dialogues and vocabulary for smoking shisha are only included for educational purposes, but we do not advocate smoking. All of the commonly known dangers in regards to nicotine addiction and the cancer-causing properties of tobacco also hold true for the shisha. The water may cool the smoke, making it less irritating, but it does not filter out harmful chemicals. The sweet flavors can also make you feel like smoking shisha is milder than smoking cigarettes. But in actuality, when you smoke shisha for one hour, the volume of smoke inhaled is equivalent to that of over 100 cigarettes! Furthermore, sharing a shisha mouthpiece can spread disease.

6

Refreshing your shisha

o لَوْ سمحْت عايز وِلْعة[1].

◇ حاضِر جايّ.

o لَوْ سمحْت غيّر الحجر[2].

o Excuse me, I want fresh embers.
◇ Coming right up.
o Excuse me, I want a new shisha bowl.

o *law samáɦt, 3āyiz wíl3a*[1].
◇ *ɦāḍir gayy.*
o *law samáɦt, ɣáyyar ilɦágar*[2].

[1] وِلْعة *wíl3a* **embers/coal** keep the smoke coming. When the shisha seems to be dying out, you can ask for more embers if the waiter isn't already tending to the embers periodically. You can specify if you prefer سماسِم *samāsim* **small pieces of coal** (which burn slowly) or فحْم حرْق *faɦmᵊ ɦar?* **large pieces of coal** (which make the tobacco burn stronger but faster).

[2] حجر *ɦágar* (lit. stone) **shisha bowl** is the ceramic piece holding the packed tobacco in tin foil. When you order a second shisha bowl, you will be charged extra.

7

Starting a game of backgammon

◇ مساء الخيْر.
○ مساء الخيْر.
◇ تِعْرف تِلْعب طاوْلة؟
○ آه أعْرف.
◇ مُمْكِن ألْعب معاك[1]؟
○ طبْعاً اِتْفضّل.

(to waiter)

◇ لَوْ سمحْت كُنْت عايِز طاوْلة.

◇ Good evening!
○ Good evening!
◇ Do you know how to play backgammon?
○ Yes, I do.
◇ Can I play with you?
○ Sure, have a seat.

(to waiter)

◇ Excuse me, I want a backgammon set.

◇ *masāʔ ilxēr.*
○ *masāʔ ilxēr.*
◇ *tí3raf tíl3ab ţáwla?*
○ *āh, á3raf.*
◇ *múmkin ál3ab ma3āk*[1]*?*
○ *ţáb3an, itfáḑḑal.*

(to waiter)

◇ *law samáɧt, kuntᵊ 3āyiz ţáwla.*

[1] نِلْعب سَوا *níl3ab sáwa* **we play together**

8

Settling the Bill

o لَوْ سمحْت حِسابك كام؟

◇ خلّي عنّك[1].

o الله يِخلّيك[2].

◇ ٤٦ جِنيْه.

o خُد ٥٠ و خلّي الباقي.

o Excuse me, how much do I owe you?

◇ Don't worry about it[1].

o Thank you.

◇ 46 pounds.

o Here's 50. Keep the change.

o *law samáħt, ħisābak kām?*

◇ *xálli 3ánnak*[1].

o *allāh yixallīk*[2].

◇ *sítta w arbi3īn ginēh.*

o *xud xamsīn wi xálli -lbāʔi.*

[1] خلّي عنّك *xálli 3ánnak* **keep it**, خلّيها عليْنا المرّة دي *xallīha 3alēna -lmarrā-di* **it's on us this time**, and وَلا أيّ حاجة خالِص *wála ayyᵊ ħāga xāliṣ* **it's nothing at all** are not to be taken literally. Your waiter does expect you to settle your bill. This is just a set expression to show hospitality. After saying thank you, you may need to ask for the bill a second time.

[2] = شُكْراً *šúkran*

Extended Dialogue

○ تعالى نُقْعُد هِناك. فيه تربيْزة فاضْيَة.

◇ تمام.

(to waiter)

○ لَوْ سمحْت!

◇ تحْت أمْرك.

○ هاتْلِنا اِتْنينْ قهْوَة، واحْدة زِيادة لِيّا و إنْتَ يا مْحمّد؟

◇ لا أنا هاتْلي شاي مظْبوط.

◇ تمام جايّ حالاً.

○ بقولّك أيْه نِشيِّش[1]؟

◇ أكيد ليْه لأ[2]؟

(waiter brings drinks)

◇ هاتْلِنا اِتْنينْ شيشة معاك.

◇ عايِزْهُم أيْه؟

◇ هاتْها تُفّاح.

○ أنا عايِزْها قصّ.

(later, after they've been smoking a while)

◇ لَوْ سمحْت وِلْعة مِن فضْلك.

◇ حالاً.

○ و معاك مبْسم جِديد عشان اِتْكسر.

◇ مِن عينيّا.

(a while later)

○ حِسابك كام؟

○ خلّي عليْنا المرّة دي.

○ الله يِخلّيك شُكْراً.

◇ حِسابك كام بِجدّ؟

◇ ٤٦ جِنيْه.

◇ خلاص تمام أنا قُمْت بِالواجِب.

○ لا أبداً، ده دوْري[3]. كِفايَة إنّك دفعْت حقّ الأكْل بدْري.

◇ اِتْفضّل و خلّي الباقي عشانك.

◇ نوّرْتونا[4] و خلّينا نْشوفْكُم.

○ طبْعاً شُكْراً.

◇ سلامُ عليْكو.

◇ وَعليْكُم السّلام.

○ Let's sit over here. There's a free table.

◇ Okay.

(to waiter)

○ Waiter!

◇ How can I help you?

○ We'd like two Turkish coffees, please. Sweet for me. And you, Mohamed?

◇ Oh, actually, bring me a tea, medium sweet.

◇ All right, coming right up.

○ Should we get shishas?

◇ Sure, why not?

(waiter brings drinks)

◇ We'll take two shishas, too.

◇ What kind?

◇ Apple for me.

○ And I want qass.

(later, after they've been smoking a while)

◇ Waiter, could we change out the coals on our shishas?

◇ Right away.

- ○ And a new mouthpiece for me, please. This one is broken.
- ◇ At your service.

(a while later)

- ○ How much do we owe?
- ◇ It's okay this time.
- ○ God save you, thanks.
- ◇ How much do we owe really?
- ◇ 46 pounds.
- ◇ Let me pay this time.
- ○ No way, buddy. It's my treat! You paid for our lunch earlier.
- ◇ Here you are. Keep the change.
- ◇ We are blessed and we looking forward to seeing you again.
- ○ Of course, thanks.
- ◇ Goodbye!
- ◇ Goodbye!

- ○ *ta3āla núʔ3ud hināk. fī tarabēza fáḍya.*
- ◇ *tamām.*

(to waiter)

- ○ *law samáɧt!*
- ◇ *taɧtᵊ ámrak.*
- ○ *hatlína itnēn ʔáhwa, wáɧda ziyāda líyya w ínta ya mɧámmad?*
- ◇ *laʔ, ána hátli šāy maẓbūṭ.*
- ◇ *tamām, gayyᵊ ɧālan.*
- ○ *baʔúllak ʔē, nišáyyiš*[1]*?*
- ◇ *akīd lē laʔ*[2]*?*

(waiter brings drinks)

- ◇ *hatlína -tnēn šīša ma3āk.*
- ◇ *3ayízhum ʔē?*
- ◇ *hátha tuffāɧ.*
- ○ *ána 3ayízha ʔaṣṣ.*

(later, after they've been smoking a while)

- ◇ *law samáɧt, wíl3a, min fáḍlak.*
- ◇ *ɧālan.*

○ *wi ma3āk mábsam gidīd 3ašān itkásar.*
◇ *min 3ináyya.*

(a while later)

○ *ḫisābak kām?*
◇ *xálli 3alēna -lmarrā-di.*
○ *allāh yixallīk, šúkran.*
◇ *ḫisābak kām bi-gádd?*
◇ *sítta w arbi3īn ginēh.*
◇ *xalāṣ tamām, ána ʔumtᵊ bi-lwāgib.*
○ *laʔ, ábadan. da dōri*[3]*. kifāya ínnak dafá3tᵊ ḫaʔʔ ilʔáklᵊ bádri.*
◇ *itfáḍḍal, wi xálli -lbāʔi 3ašānak.*
◇ *nawwartūna*[4] *wi xallīna nšúfkum.*
○ *ṭáb3an, šúkran.*
◇ *salāmu 3alēku.*
◇ *wi 3alēkum issalām.*

[1] = نِشْرب شيشة *níšrab šīša*

[2] و مالُه؟ *wi mālu?* **What of it?**

[3] خلاص تمام، أنا قُمْت بِالواجِب. *xalāṣ tamām, ána ʔumtᵊ bi-lwāgib.* = خلاص تمام، المرّة دي عليّا. *xalāṣ tamām, ilmarrā-di 3aláyya.* **It's okay. It's on me this time.**

[4] = شرّفْتونا *šarraftūna*

Vocabulary

coffee house	*ʔáhwa (ʔahāwi)*	قهْوَة (قهاوي)
Turkish coffee	*ʔáhwa (túrki)*	قهْوَة (تُرْكي)
coffee house waiter	*ʔahwági*	قهْوَجي
drink, beverage	*mašrūb*	مشْروب
hot	*suxn*	سُخْن
cold	*sāʔi3*	ساقع
sahlep	*sáɦlab*	سحْلب
karkadeh (hibiscus drink)	*karkadēh*	كرْكديْه
tea	*šāy*	شاي
mint	*ni3nā3*	نِعْناع
anise, aniseed	*yansūn*	يَنْسون
fenugreek	*ɦílba*	حِلْبة
sugar	*súkkar*	سُكّر
cinnamon	*ʔírfa*	قِرْفة
fruit(s)	*fawākih*	فَواكِهْ
shisha, hookah, waterpipe	*šīša*	شيشة
to smoke a shisha	*šáyyiš* *šírib šīša*	شيِّش شِرِب شيشة
flavor	*nákha* *ṭa3m*	نكْهة طعْم

apple	*tuffāḫ*	تُفّاح
grape	*3ínab*	عِنب
blueberry	*tūt ázra?*	توت أزْرق
coal, embers	*wíl3a*	وِلْعة
shisha bowl (lit. stone; small clay bowl with tobacco)	*ḫágar*	حجر
shisha mouthpiece	*mábsam iššīša*	مبْسم الشّيشة
cigarette	*sigāra (sagāyir)*	سِجارة (سجايِر)
to smoke	*dáxxan*	دخّن
smoking	*tadxīn*	تدْخين
backgammon	*ṭáwla*	طاوْلة
chess	*iššaṭráng*	الشّطْرنْج
cards	*kutšīna*	كوتْشينة
tarneeb (cardgame similar to Whist)	*ṭarnīb*	طرْنيب
dominoes	*dumīnu*	دوْمينو

Expressions

○

Where's the restroom?	*fēn ilḫammām*	فينْ الحمّام؟
(Do you want) a hot or cold drink?	*suxn^{ə} wálla bārid?*	سُخْن وَلّا بارِد؟

Sorry, I can’t read well. Can you tell me what you have?	*ma3alíšš ána miš 3ārif áʔra. múmkin tiʔūlli 3andúkum ʔē?*	معلِشّ أنا مِش عارِف أقْرا. مُمْكِن تِقولّي عنْدُكُم أيْه؟
We’d like two shishas.	*ínzil šištēn.*	اِنْزِل شيشْتيْن.
Can I have another mouthpiece (for my shisha)?	*múmkin tigíbli mábsam tāni má3a -ššīša?*	مُمْكِن تِجيبْلي مبْسم تاني معَ الشّيشة؟
No, thank you. I don’t smoke	*laʔ, šúkran miš badáxxan.*	لا شُكْراً مِش بدخّن.
Do you have a lighter?	*ma3āk walā3a?*	معاك وَلاعة؟
	◇	
The menu is on the sign.	*ilmašrubāt maktūba 3ála -llōḫa.*	المشْروبات مكْتوبة على اللّوْحة.

Making Small Talk   كلام في أيّ حِتّة

The majority of Egyptians are outgoing and welcoming of foreigners in their country. You are seen as a guest in their country, which elicits a sense of hospitality among Egyptians. Don't be surprised if you are asked questions which may, to you, seem a bit too personal for someone you've just met. *Are you married? Why not? What's your religion? How much do you earn?* They're not trying to pry or be rude. This is the way Egyptians get to know each other. They routinely share their religious views, tell about their work, and family (marital status, children, etc.). Politics, however, is typically avoided until you get to know someone well. And they're especially curious about foreigners. At the end of the day, all friends were once strangers, and it is through these casual encounters that people get to know and learn about each other and become friends. In this chapter, you'll learn how to answer personal questions and also what to say if you would rather avoid answering without seeming impolite.

Where are you from?

◇ إنْتَ بتِعْرف عربي كُوَيِّس أَوي.[1] إنْتَ منينْ؟

o مُتْشكّر أَوي. أنا مِن الصّين بسّ بدْرِس عربي هِنا.

◇ You know Arabic very well. Where are you from?

o Thank you! I'm from China, but I'm studying Arabic here.

◇ *ínta btí3raf 3árabi kuwáyyis áwi.*[1] *ínta mnēn?*

o *mutšákkir áwi. ána min iṣṣīn bassᵊ bádris 3árabi hína.*

[1] العربي بِتاعك كُوَيِّس أَوي. *il3árabi btá3ak kuwáyyis áwi.* **Your Arabic is really good.**

Be aware (and skeptical) of people who seem unusually eager to engage with you, especially if they walk up to you out of the blue. Frauds might try to befriend you but have ulterior motives. Use your best judgment, but be very skeptical if someone tries to get you to follow them to a second location soon after meeting you.

2

WHY ARE YOU IN EGYPT?

◇ و أيْه اللي جابِك مصْر بقى؟

o بشْتغل هِنا مُدرِّسة في مدْرسة تبع السِّفارة.

◇ ممْم... و هتْكمِّلي في مصْر؟[1]

o لا يادوْب مُدِّةْ العقْد بسّ و أرْجع بلدي تاني.

◇ And what brought you here to Egypt?

o I'm working here as a teacher in a school attached to the consulate.

◇ Hmm... and will you continue living in Egypt?

o No, just for the duration of the contract, and then I'm going back home again

◇ *wi ʔē ílli gābik maṣrᵊ báʔa?*

o *baštáɣal hína mudarrísa f madrása tába3 issifāra.*

◇ *mmm... wi hatkammíli f maṣr?*[1]

o *laʔ, yadōb múddit il3áʔdᵊ bass, w árga3 báladi tāni.*

[1] هتِسْتمِرّي *hatistamírri* = هتِفْضلي *hatifḍáli;* و ناوْيَة تِكمِّلي في مصْر؟ *wi náwya tkammíli f maṣr?* **Do you intend to stay in Egypt?**

The majority of Egyptians are conservative when dealing with the opposite gender. When you become friends, you can shake hands with the opposite gender, but no hugging or kissing on the cheeks. On the contrary, when becoming friends with someone of the same gender, you can greet them by kissing on both cheeks and a handshake or by adding a hug if you are already close.

3

Where do you live?

◇ و عايِش[1] هِنا لِوَحْدك؟

o لا عايِش في سكن مع اِتْنينْ كمان[2].

◇ ساكْنين فينْ[3] بقى؟

o في مصْر القديمة.

◇ زُرْت الأهْرامات بقى؟

o آه و رِكِبْت الجّمل كمان.

◇ And are you living by yourself here?
o No, I'm sharing a place with two other people.
◇ Where are you staying/living then?
o In Old Cairo.
◇ And have you visited the Pyramids?
o Yes, and I even rode a camel!

◇ *wi 3āyiš hína l-wáḥdak?*
o *laʔ, 3āyiš[1] fi sákan má3a itnēn kamān[2].*
◇ *saknīn fēn[3] báʔa?*
o *fi maṣr ilʔadīma.*
◇ *zurt ilʔahramāt báʔa?*
o *āh, wi rikíbt iggámal kamān.*

[1] = قاعِد *ʔā3id*

[2] سكن مُشْترك *sákan muštárak* **shared accommodation**

[3] قاعْدين فينْ؟ *ʔá3dīn fēn?*

Are you married?

◇ بِتِعْمِلي أيْه هِنا في مصْر؟

o أنا مِتْجوِّزة و عايْشة هِنا معَ جوْزي.

◇ جوْزِك مصْري بقى على كِده؟

o آه مصْري و كُنّا عايْشين في أسْبانْيا بسّ رِجِعْنا مصْر.

◇ و مبْسوطة[1] في مصْر؟

o الحمْدُ لله... يَعْني لِسّه بتْعوِّد[2].

◇ What are you doing here in Egypt?

o I'm married and living here with my husband.

◇ Your husband must be Egyptian then.

o Yes, he is. We used to live in Spain, but we came back to Egypt.

◇ Are you happy in Egypt?

o Praise God... I'm still getting used to it.

◇ *biti3míli ʔē hína f maṣr?*

o *ána mitgawwíza wi 3áyša hína má3a gōzi.*

◇ *gōzik máṣri báʔa 3ála kída?*

o *āh, máṣri wi kúnna 3ayšīn fi asbánya bassᵊ rigí3na maṣr.*

◇ *wi mabsūṭa*[1] *f maṣr?*

o *ilḫámdu li-llāh... yá3ni líssa bat3áwwid*[2].

1 مِرْتاحة *mirtāḫa* **at ease, content**

2 = بتْأقْلِم *batʔáqlim*

5

What is your religion?

◇ و عايِز تِزور الجّامع ده ليْه بقى؟ إنْتَ مُسْلِم؟

○ لا مِش مُسْلِم بسّ بحِبّ اتْفرّج و أزور الأماكِن الأثرية و بحِبّ أتْعرّف على الدِّيانات التّانْيَة.

◇ أمّال إنْتَ أيْه بقى؟ مسيحي؟[1]

○ أُسْرِتي مسيحية[2] بسّ أنا مِش مُتديِّن أوي.

◇ And why do you want to visit this mosque? Are you a Muslim?

○ No, but I like visiting and seeing archeological sites, and I like getting to know other religions, as well.

◇ Then what are you? Christian?

○ My family is, but I'm not that religious.

◇ *wi 3āyiz tizūr iggāmi3 da lē báʔa? ínta múslim?*

○ *laʔ, miš múslim, bassᵊ baḫíbb atfárrag w azūr ilʔamākin ilʔasaríyya wi baḫíbb at3árraf 3ála -ddiyanāt ittánya.*

◇ *ummāl ínta ʔē báʔa? masīḫi?*[1]

○ *usríti masiḫíyya*[2] *bass ána miš mutadáyyin áwi.*

[1] دِيانْتك أيْه؟ *diyántak ʔē?* **What's your religion?**

[2] عيْلْتي مسيحية. *3ílti masiḫíyya.* **My family is Christian.**; مَوْلود مسيحي. *mawlūd masīḫi.* **I was born into a Christian family.**

6

Do you have children?

◇ طيِّب، و عنْدِك أَوْلاد بقى؟

○ آه عنْدي وَلد دُكْتوْر في هامْبُرْج و بِنْت بِتِدْرِس في لنْدن.

◇ مجِبْتيهُمْش معاكي ليْه طيِّب؟[1]

○ لا هُمّا ليهُم حَياتْهُم و مشْغولين خلاص لكِن أنا جايّة معَ جوْزي نِتْفسّح.

◇ And do you have children?

○ Yes, I have a son living in Hamburg, and a daughter studying in London.

◇ Why didn't you bring them over with you then?

○ No, they have their own lives now and are too busy. I came with my husband for a tour.

◇ *ṭáyyib, wi 3ándik awlād báʔa?*

○ *āh, 3ándi wálad duktōr fi hámburg, wi bintᵊ btídris fi lándan.*

◇ *ma-gibtīhumšᵊ ma3āki lē ṭáyyib?*[1]

○ *lā, húmma līhum ḥayáthum wi mašɣulīn xalāṣ, lākin ána gáyya má3a gōzi nitfássaḥ.*

[1] مجوش معاكي ليْه؟ *ma-gūš ma3āki lē?* **Why didn't they come with you?**

◇ إسْمك أيْه بقى؟

○ أليكْس و إنْتَ؟

◇ أنا إسْمي محْمود. و بِتِشْتغل[1] أيْه بقى هِنا؟

○ أنا مُهنْدِس في شِركْةْ بترْوْل امْريكية، شغّالين هِنا في الصّحْرا الغرْبية.

◇ أُمّال أيْه اللي جابك هِنا؟[2]

○ لا واخِد أجازة[3]، قُلْت اتْفسّح في الويك اِنْد

◇ طيِّب، و اِشْمعْنى مُجمّع الأدْيان اللي عايِز تِروحُه؟

○ قالولي فيه كنايِس و معابِد قديمة كِتير مُمْكِن أشوفْها.

◇ آه و قُريِّب مِنْها جامِع عمْرو بْن العاص، أوِّل جامِع اِتْبنّى في مصْر[4] برْضُه.

○ حِلْو أَوي... طيِّب فيه اماكِن أيْه تاني أقْدر أزورْها؟ أنا قاعِد بِالظّبْط يومينْ كمان.

◇ تِقْدر تِروح المتْحف المصْري و الأهْرامات.

○ لا دوْل رُحْتهُم زمان أوِّل ما عِشْت[5] هِنا.

◇ طيِّب، زُرْت المُعِزّ و الحُسينْ؟

○ لا لِسّه مرُحْتُهُمْش.

◇ لا دوْل لازِم تِزورْهُم. هَيِعْجِبوك أَوي. و المُعِزّ كُلُّه[6] جَوامِع و أماكِن أثرية. تِحِسُّه[7] متْحف مفْتوح كِده.

○ جميل جِدّاً! أنا رُحْت خان الخليلي مرّة.

◇ ما هُوَّ مِش بِعيد عن[8] المُعِزّ. إنْتَ دِيانْتك أيْه بقى؟

○ معلِشّ[9] دي مسْألة شخْصية[10].

◇ لا مُؤاخْذة، أنا بسّ بدرْدِش[11]. طيِّب مِتْجوِّز؟

o لا مِش مِتْجوِّز.

◇ ليْه كِده بسّ؟

o آهُه بقى... نصيب زيّ ما بِتْقولوا.

◇ لا بسّ إنْتَ العربي بِتاعك لِبْلِب.[12]

o ربِّنا يِخلّيك تِسْلم. ما أنا اِتْعلِّمْت كِتير قبْل ما آجي و لمّا عِشْت هِنا العربي بِتاعي اِتْحسِّن[13] كِتير.[14]

◇ What's your name?

o Alex. And yours?

◇ My name is Mahmoud. And what do you do here?

o I'm an engineer at an American petroleum company. We're working in the Western Desert.

◇ And what brought you here?

o I'm taking a vacation, so I thought of touring around on the weekend.

◇ I see, and why [did you choose] the Religious Campus to visit?

o They told me there are many ancient churches and temples I can visit.

◇ True, and nearby there's also the mosque of Amr ibn al-As, the very first mosque established in Egypt.

o Very nice. What other places can I visit? I'm staying here for two days.

◇ You can go to the Egyptian Museum and to the Pyramids.

o No, I went to those a long time ago when I first came to live here.

◇ All right. Have you been to Hussein and Muizz?

o No, I haven't been there yet.

◇ Well, these you have to visit! You'll like them a lot, and Muizz Street is full of historical mosques and sites. You feel like it's an open museum.

o Very nice! I have been to Khan El-Khalili once.

◇ It's not that far from Muizz. What's your religion, by the way?

○ Sorry, that's a personal matter.

◇ Pardon me. I'm just making conversation. Are you married then?

○ No, I'm not married.

◇ Why not?

○ Hmm... well, destined, as you guys say.

◇ You know what, your Arabic is so fluent!

○ Thank you! I studied a lot before I came [to Egypt], and after I moved here, it improved a lot.

◇ ísmak ʔē báʔa?

○ [Alex], w ínta?

◇ ána -smi maḫmūd. wi btištáɣal[1] ʔē báʔa hína?

○ ána muhándis fi šírkit batrōl amrikíyya, šaɣɣalīn hína fi -ṣṣáḫra -lɣarbíyya.

◇ ummāl ʔē ílli gābak hína?[2]

○ laʔ, wāxid agāza[3], ʔult atfássaḫ fi -lwīk ind

◇ ṭáyyib, w išmá3na mugámma3 ilʔadyān ílli 3āyiz tirūḫu?

○ ʔalūli fī kanāyis wi ma3ābid ʔadīma ktīr múmkin ašúfha.

◇ āh, wi ʔuráyyib mínha gāmi3 3ámru bn il3āṣ, áwwil gāmi3 itbánna f maṣr^{ə} [4] bárḍu.

○ ḫilw áwi... ṭáyyib fī amākin ʔē tāni áʔdar azúrha? ána ʔā3id bi-ẓẓábṭ^{ə} yumēn kamān.

◇ tíʔdar tirūḫ ilmátḫaf ilmáṣri wi -lʔahramāt.

○ laʔ, dōl ruḫtúhum zamān áwwil ma 3išt^{ə} [5] hína.

◇ ṭáyyib, zurt ilmu3ízz^{ə} wi -lḫusēn?

○ lā, líssa ma-ruḫtuhúmš.

◇ lā, dōl lāzim tizúrhum. hayi3gibūk áwi. wi -lmu3ízz^{ə} kúllu[6] gawāmi3 w amākin asaríyya. tiḫíssu[7] mátḫaf maftūḫ kída.

○ gamīl gíddan! ána ruḫt^{ə} xān ilxalīli márra.

◇ ma húwwa miš bi3īd 3an[8] ilmu3ízz. ínta diyántak ʔē báʔa?

○ ma3alíšš[9], di masʔála šaxṣíyya[10].

◇ la muʔáxza, ána bass^{ə} badárdiš[11]. ṭáyyib mitgáwwiz?

○ laʔ, miš mitgáwwiz.

◇ lē kída bass?

○ áhu báʔa... naṣīb zayy^{ə} ma bitʔūlu.

◇ lā, bass ínta -l3árabi bitā3ak líblib.[12]

○ *rabbína yxallīk, tíslam. m- ána -t3allímtᵊ ktīr ʔablᵊ m- ági wi lámma 3ištᵊ hína -l3árabi bitā3i -tḫássin*[13] *kitīr.*[14]

1 = شغّال *šaɣɣāl*

2 أُمّال بِتِعْمِل أيْه هِنا؟ *ummāl bití3mil ʔē hína?* **What are you doing here?**

3 = عنْدي اجازة *3ándi agāza* = نازِل اجازة *nāzil agāza*

4 أقْدم جامع في مصْر *áʔdam gāmi3 fi maṣr* **the oldest mosque in Egypt**

5 = نقلْت *naʔált*

6 ملْيان *malyān* **full of**

7 = تِحِسّ إنُّه *tiḫíss ínnu*

8 قُريِّب مِن *ʔuráyyib min* **close to, near**

9 اُعْذُرْني *u3zúrni* = سامِحْني *samíḫni*

10 ده سُؤال شخْصي *da suʔāl šáxṣi*

11 بتْكلِّم معاك. *batkállim ma3āk.* **I'm talking to you.;** بتْعرّف عليْك. *bat3árraf 3alēk.* **I'm getting to know you.**

12 إنْتَ بربنْط في العربي. *ínta barabánṭ fi -l3árabi.* **You're fluent in Arabic.**

13 = بقى أحْسن *báʔa áḫsan*

14 لا ده أنا لِسّه بحاوِل كِده. *laʔ, d- ána líssa baḫāwil kída.* **No, I'm just trying my best.**

Vocabulary

to chat, have a conversation	*dárdiš*	دَرْدِش
conversation	*dardáša*	دَرْدشة
chatting	*raɣy*	رَغْي
talk	*kalām*	كلام
question	*suʔāl*	سُؤال
answer	*igāba*	إجابة
reason	*sábab*	سبب
friendship	*ṣuḫubíyya*	صُحوبية
getting to know one another	*ta3āruf*	تعارُف
married	*mitgáwwiz*	مِتْجوِّز
single (male)	*á3zab*	أعْزب
single (female)	*ānisa*	آنِسة
madam, ma'am (married woman)	*madām*	مدام
ma'am, Ms. (formal when you do not know if she's married or not)	*ustāza*	أُسْتاذة
sir, Mr.	*ustāz*	أُسْتاذ
my husband	*gōzi*	جوْزي
my wife	*mirāti*	مِراتي
my wife	*ilmadām*	المدام
child	*wálad (wilād)*	وَلد (وِلاد)

son	*ibn*	إِبْن
daughter	*bint (banāt)*	بِنْت (بنات)
Muslim	*múslim*	مُسْلِم
Christian	*masīḫi*	مسيحي
Jewish	*yahūdi*	يَهودي
religious	*mutadáyyin*	مُتديِّن
non-religious	*miš mutadáyyin*	مِش مُتديِّن
mosque	*gāmi3*	جامِع
church	*kinīsa*	كِنيسة
temple, synagogue	*má3bad*	معْبد

Expressions

○

Cairo is really crowded but beautiful.	*ilqāhíra záḫma áwi bassᵊ gamīla.*	القاهِرة زحْمة أَوي بسّ جميلة.
I'd rather not say.	*miš ḫābib aʔūl ma3alíšš.*	مِش حابِب أقول معلِشّ.
That's personal.	*di ḫāga šaxṣíyya.*	دي حاجة شخْصية.

◇

Do you like Cairo?	*wi bitḫíbb ilqāhíra?*	و بِتْحِبّ القاهِرة؟
You have to try the Cairene koshary.	*lāzim tigárrab ilkúšari -lmáṣri.*	لازِم تِجرّب الكُشري المصْري.
Have you tried ful?	*ṭáyyib, akáltᵊ fūl?*	طيِّب، أكلْت فول؟

Have you tried sugarcane juice?	*garrábtᵊ 3aṣīr ilʔáṣab?*	جرّبْت عصير القصب؟
You have to come over.	*lāzim titfáḍḍal ma3āya.*	لازِم تِتْفضّل معايا.
Wait I'll show you myself. What is keeping me busy anyway!	*istanna, awarrīk binắfsi. ána warāya ʔē yá3ni?*	اِسْتنّى، أوَرّيك بِنفْسي. أنا وَرايا أيْه يَعْني؟
You have to take your kids to the Pyramids	*lāzim tiwáddi wilādak ilʔahramāt.*	لازِم تِوَدّي وِلادك الأهْرامات.
How much do you spend on rent?	*wi bitídfa3 kām fi -lʔigār?*	و بِتِدْفع كام في الإيجار؟
How much do you earn (a month)?	*wi bitíʔbaḍ/bití3mil/ bitíksab kām (fi -ššahr)?*	و بِتِقْبض/بِتِعْمِل/ بِتِكْسب كام (في الشّهْر)؟

Visiting Someone's Home في زِيارة

Exchanging visits is very common among friends, or even friends of friends and new acquaintances. Egyptians might invite you over to lunch or dinner, or just for a cup of tea. When invited to have a meal at someone's home, cultural norms dictate that you should bring a dessert or fruit with you. Your host will make some remarks insisting that you didn't need to trouble yourself, but these are just pleasantries; you really should always bring something with you. Soon after arriving, your host will offer you something to drink: تِشْرب أيْه؟ *tíšrab ʔē?* **What would you like to drink?** It is customary to politely decline at first: لا معْلِشّ، وَلا حاجة. *lā, ma3líšš, wála ḫāga.* **No, it's okay. Nothing.** But your host will insist, and you should eventually accept. They will feel offended if you didn't at least have a drink at their place. If you have no preference for a drink, say طيِّب ماشي، أيّ حاجة *ṭáyyib māši, ayyᵊ ḫāga.* **All right then, anything is fine.** It's important to keep this in mind when you have company over, as well. Your Egyptian guests will be taken aback if you simply accept that they aren't thirsty at face value and don't offer a second time.

Accepting an Invitation

◇ بقولّك أيْه، أنا عازْمك[1] عَ الغدا عنْدي الأُسْبوع الجّاي.

○ ربِّنا يِخلّيك تِسْلم.

◇ شوف يِناسْبك يوْم أيْه[2] و قولّي[3].

○ التّلات هَيِبْقى مُناسِب[4].

◇ تمام و أنا كمان فاضي. خلاص هسْتنّاك السّاعة ٤ نِتْغدّى سَوا[5].

◇ Hey, I'd like to invite you to lunch at my place next week.

○ Bless you! Thanks!

◇ Check which day suits you and let me know.

○ I think Tuesday would be okay.

◇ Okay, I'm free on that day too, so I'll wait for you at 4 p.m. to have lunch together.

◇ *baʔúllak ʔē, ána 3ázmak*[1] *3a -lɣáda 3ándi -lʔusbū3 iggáyy.*

○ *rabbína yxallīk, tíslam.*

◇ *šūf yinásbak yōm ʔē*[2] *wi ʔúlli*[3]*.*

○ *ittalāt hayíbʔa munāsib*[4]*.*

◇ *tamām, w ána kamān fāḍi. xalāṣ, hastannāk issā3a arbá3a, nitɣádda sáwa*[5]*.*

[1] إنْتَ معْزوم عنْدي. *ínta ma3zūm 3ándi.* **You're invited.**

[2] = شوف أيْه اليوْم المُناسِب *šúf ʔē -lyōm ilmunāsib* / [3] = عرّفْني *3arráfni* = بلّغْني *balláɣni* / [4] كُوَيِّس *kuwáyyis* / [5] = معَ بعْض *má3a ba3ḍ*

Check with your host if it's a mixed gathering or not. The cultural boundaries between genders vary from one family to another. I was once invited to my teacher's home for dinner. I expected to having dinner with his wife and children, but it turned out he was very conservative. His wife made dinner for us, but I never even met her. She and the children ate in the kitchen while I ate alone with my teacher in the dining room.

2

Arriving at Someone's Home

◇ يا أهْلاً وَ سهْلاً[1]. حمْدِلْله عَ السّلامة.
○ الله يِسلِّمك.
◇ اِتْفضّل. متِقْلعْش الجِّزْمة[2]، زيّ ما إنْتَ.
○ كُوَيِّس إنّك بعتِّلي اللّوكيْشِن، سهِّل عليّا كِتير.
◇ طب، الحمْدُ لله. و العِنْوان مَيْتوهْش كمان.

◇ Welcome, welcome! Thank God you arrived safely!
○ God bless you.
◇ Come in. Don't take your shoes off. You're fine as you are.
○ It's good you sent me the location. That made it much easier.
◇ Cool, thanks to God. And the address is easy, too.

◇ *ya áhlan wa sáhlan*[1]*. ɦamdílla 3a -ssalāma.*
○ *allāh yisallímak.*
◇ *itfáḍḍal. ma-ti?lá3š iggázma*[2]*, zayyᵊ má-nta.*
○ *kuwáyyis ínnak ba3attíli -llukēšin, sáhhil 3aláyya ktīr.*
◇ *ṭab, ilɦámdu li-llāh. wi -l3inwān ma-ytúhšᵊ kamān.*

[1] = يا مرْحب يا مرْحب! *ya márɦab ya márɦab!*, to which the response is مرْحب بيك! *márɦab bīk.*

[2] والله ما إنْتَ قالع *wallāhi má-nta ?āli3*

Some homes have a "no shoes in the house" policy, while others don't. It is best to start removing your shoes. If your hosts don't mind you keeping your shoes on, they will tell you not to bother, as in this dialogue.

Before offering sweets to children, it's best to check with their parents whether they are allowed to have them.

3

Sitting down to eat

◇ اِتْفضّلي عَ السُّفْرة.

○ أيْه ده كُلُّه بسّ؟ تِسْلم إيديْكي.

◇ أنا عملْت أيْه[1] يا بِنْتي[2]؟ دي كُلّها حاجات بسيطة. يَلّا بِسْمِ الله[3].

○ تعبْتي نفْسِك بِجدّ.[4]

◇ Come to the dining table.

○ What is all this? Bless your hands!

◇ What did I do, girl? It's all simple stuff. Come on. In the name of God.

○ You've really worn yourself out.

◇ *itfaḍḍáli 3a -ssúfra.*

○ *ʔē da kúllu bass? tíslam idēki.*

◇ *ána 3amált ʔē*[1] *ya bínti*[2]*? di kulláha ḫagāt basīṭa. yálla bi-smí-lla*[3].

○ *ta3ábti náfsik bi-gádd.*[4]

[1] = هُوَّ أنا عملْت حاجة؟ *huww- ána 3amáltᵊ ḫāga?*

[2] يا بِنْتي! *ya bínti!* **Girl!** can be used to address someone younger or the same age in a friendly way, or when joking or angry. يا سِتّي *ya sítti,* on the other hand, which means **my lady** can be said to someone the same age or older (or rarely someone younger). For men, we have يابْني *yábni* and يا سيدي *ya sīdi,* respectively.

[3] a statement made by the host to invite the guest to start eating; = يَلّا مِدّي إيدِك *yálla míddi īdik.*

[4] a statement to show gratitude for effort = لا إزّاي بقى؟ *lā, izzāy báʔa?* **No, come on!** (i.e., it's not just simple stuff)

It is always courteous to offer to help with bringing out dishes, clearing the table, and even doing the dishes after the meal. The host, however, will strongly refuse to let you do anything.

Finishing the meal

o تِسْلم إيدك. بِجدّ الأكْل رَوْعة. دايْماً عامِر.[1]

◇ إنْتَ مكلْتِش حاجة على فِكْرة.[2]

o مكلْتِش أيْه بسّ ده أنا خلاص على آخِري. سُفْرة دايْمة.[3]

◇ بِالهنا و الشِّفا[4] يا حبيبي. بِتِعْمِل أيْه بسّ؟ سيب كُلّ حاجة، أنا هلِمّ السُّفْرة.

o Bless your hands, really. The food is amazing! May it always be blessed.

◇ You barely ate anything!

o I didn't eat anything?! I'm stuffed. An enduring dining table![3]

◇ I hope you enjoyed the food. What are you doing? Leave everything as it is. I'll clear the table.

o *tíslam īdak. bi-gádd il?ákl^{ə} ráw3a. dáyman 3āmir*[1].

◇ *ínta ma-káltiš ḫāga 3ála fíkra.*[2]

o *ma-káltiš ?ē bass? da -na xalāṣ 3ála āxiri. súfra dáyma.*[3]

◇ *bi-lhána wi -ššífa*[4] *ya ḫabībi. bití3mil ?ē bass? sīb kull^{ə} ḫāga, ána halímm issúfra.*

[1] You can respond with يِدوْم عِزّك. *yidōm 3ízzak.*

[2] = إنْتَ مكلْتِش خالِص. *ínta ma-káltiš xāliṣ.*

[3] This is a formulaic expression, as are those in the first line of the dialogue, all to show gratitude to your host for the meal.

[4] The response is الله يهنّيك. *allāh yihannīk.*

One thing to keep in mind, as a guest, is to ask for permission before moving to the kitchen or going to the bathroom. It's not appropriate to look around other rooms even if just out of curiosity. As welcoming as people can be, they are also quite private and have boundaries. Of course, this changes if you are close friends with your host and have been given carte blanche to make yourself at home.

5

VISITING A SICK FRIEND

○ حمْدِلله عَ السّلامة يا وَحْش.[1]

◇ الله يِسلّمِك يا ربّ.

○ أوّل ما عِرِفْنا إنّك طِلِعْت مِن المُسْتشْفى قُلْنا لازِم نيجي نِتْطمّن عليْك.

◇ تِسْلموا يا ربّ! بِسّ أيْه اللي إنْتو جايْبينه ده؟[2] تعبْتوا نفْسُكو.[3]

○ تعب أيْه بسّ؟ دي حاجة بسيطة.[4] المُهِمّ تِشِدّ حيلك[5] و تِطمّنّا عليْك.

○ Thank God you're okay, my brave friend.

◇ God bless you!

○ The moment we knew you were out of the hospital, we thought we should come and check on you.

◇ Bless you! And what's this you've brought? You shouldn't have [gone to the trouble]!

○ What trouble? It's nothing really. What's important is that you get back your strength and let us hear good news about you.

○ *ħamdílla 3a -ssalāma ya waħš*[1].

◇ *allāh yisallímik ya rabb.*

○ *áwwil ma 3irífna ínnak ṭilí3tᵊ min ilmustášfa ʔúlna lāzim nīgi nitṭámmin 3alēk.*

◇ *tislámu ya rabb! bass ʔē ílli íntu gaybīnu da?*[2] *ta3ábtu nafsúku.*[3]

○ *tá3ab ʔē bass? di ħāga basīṭa.*[4] *ilmuhímmᵊ tšíddᵊ ħīlak*[5] *wi tiṭammínna 3alēk.*

[1] يا وَحْش *ya waħš* **monster** and يا بطل *ya báṭal* **hero** are friendly ways of telling a man that he made it or survived. / [2] بسّ ليْه كلّفْتوا نفْسُكو كِده؟ *bassᵊ lē kallíftu nafsúku kída?* **Why did you put yourself to so much trouble?** / [3] مكانْش لُه لِزوم واللهِ التّعب ده. *ma-kánšᵊ lū lizūm wallāhi -ttá3ab da.* **There was no need for all this trouble.** / [4] لا تعب وَلا حاجة. *la tá3ab wála ħāga* **No trouble at all.**; تعبك راحة يا عمّ. *tá3ab rāħa ya 3amm.* **The effort is a pleasure, buddy.** / [5] = تِقوم بِالسّلامة *tiʔūm bi-ssalāma*

Appropriate gifts: flowers, chocolates, or fruit; and for children, toys.

Making your "escape"

o طيِّب، أنا يادوْب ألْحق أمْشي بقى.

◇ ما إنْتي لِسّه قاعْدة[1] يا بِنْتي. وَراكي أيْه؟

o لا واللهِ كِفايَة كِده بقى. أنا سهرْتِك أساساً.

◇ سهّرْتيني أيْه بسّ؟ ده إنْتي نوّرْتيني واللهِ و كانِت زِيارة جميلة.

o تِسْلمي[2] يا حبيبْتي. و المرّة الجّايّة عنْدي[3] إن شاء الله.

o Well, it's about time I get going.
◇ But you just got here. What do you have to do?
o No, but seriously it's enough. I've kept you up late.
◇ What are you talking about? Your visit has made me happy. It was a really nice visit.
o Bless you, dear. Next time, at my place, God willing.

o *ṭáyyib, ána yadōb álḫaʔ ámši báʔa.*
◇ *má-nti líssa ʔá3da*[1] *ya bínti. warāki ʔē.*
o *lā, wallāhi kifāya kída báʔa. ána sahhártik asāsan.*
◇ *sahhartīni ʔē bass? da -nti nawwartīni wallāhi, wi kānit ziyāra gamīla.*
o *tislámi*[2] *ya ḫabíbti. wi -lmárra iggáyya 3ándi*[3] *in šāʔ allāh.*

[1] a statement to insist on the guest staying longer, whether sincere or just social convention; خلّيكي كمان شُوَيّة. *xallīki kamān šuwáyya.* **Stay a bit longer.** / [2] = دايْماً مفْتوح بِحِسِّك *dáyman maftūḫ bi-ḫíssik* / [3] = و لازِم تِشرّفيني *wi lāzim tišarrafīni*

The title of this dialogue is tongue-in-cheek, but there are, again, some cultural pleasantries expected when announcing that you are ready to leave. Your Egyptian host will automatically insist that it's so early or that you stay longer. Although Egyptians tend to socialize later into the evening than Americans, they may, in fact, be ready to call it a night, too, and are just trying to be polite. Don't let your host "strong-arm" you into staying too late. You'll have to insist that you be going when you think appropriate.

◇ أهْلاً وَ سهْلاً. وَصلْتي بِسُرْعة[1].

○ آه الحمْدُ لله الطّريق كان حِلْو[2]. و اِفْتكرْت العِنْوان مِ المرّة اللي فاتِت.

◇ طب، كُوَيِّس إنِّك منْسيتيش. يَلّا بينا بقى الأكْل لِسّه طافْيَة عليْه[3].

○ طيِّب، حُطّي[4] ده في التّلاجة بقى.

◇ يا نْهار ابْيَض! ليْه يا بِنْتي الهبل ده؟[5]

○ هبل أيْه بسّ يا بِنْتي؟[6] دي حاجة بسيطة نِحلّي بيها.

◇ ميرْسي يا حبيبْتي، تِسْلم إيدِك.

○ تِسْلم إيدك إنْتي. آجي أساعْدِك في حاجة؟

◇ لا كُلّ حاجة جاهْزة. يَلّا اُدْخُلي اِغْسِلي إيدِك و تعالي عَ السُّفْرة.

(guest comes to the dining table)

○ الله الله الله... أيْه الشُّغْل العالي ده بسّ؟[7]

◇ دي اقلّ حاجة عنْدي يا بِنْتي.[8]

○ مِش كُنّا عملْناها ديش بارْتي أحْسن بدل ما تعبْتي نفْسِك كِده؟

◇ يا شيْخة روحي كِده. إنْتي بتِعْرفي تِطْبُخي أساساً. خلّي الطّابِق مِسْتور.[9]

○ ماشي! خلّيكي فاكْرة أنا عرضْت خدماتي و إنْتي اللي رفضْتي.

◇ طب، يَلّا بقى مِدّي إيدِك و كُلي قبْل ما الأكْل يِبرْد. تِحِبّي اغْرفْلِك أيْه؟

○ لا متِتْعِبيش نفْسِك. أنا هتْعامِل.

◇ طيِّب، البيْت بيْتِك بقى، و عيْشي حَياتِك[10]. أنا مِش هعْزِم.

(after finishing the meal)

○ بِجدّ تِسْلم إيديْكي و عينيْكي. الأكْل تُحْفة.

◇ بِالهنا و الشِّفا يا حبيبْتي. يَلّا نِعْمِل دوْر شاي و ناكُل الحِلْو معاه بقى.

o لا ده أنا يادوْب ألْحق معاد الدُّكْتوْر.

◇ إنْتي جايّة تاكْلي و تمِشْي؟ ما بلاش غلاسه![11] هعْمِل الشّاي بِسُرْعة.

o طيِّب، ماشي هقْعُد شُوَيّة كمان بسّ مِش هقْدر أتْأخّر جامِد.

◇ متِقْلقيش.[12] يادوْب هعلّق عَ الشّاي على بال ما تِغْسِلي إيدِك.

◇ Welcome! You got here fast!

o Yeah, thank God, the roads were good, and I remembered the address from last time.

◇ Well, that's good you didn't forget it. Come on then. The food is ready. I just took it off the stove.

o Okay, put this in the refrigerator then.

◇ Oh my! You shouldn't have!

o What do you mean! It's something simple we'll have for dessert.

◇ Thank you, dear! Bless your hands!

o Bless *your* hands! Shall I help you with anything?

◇ No, everything is ready. Go wash your hands, then come to the dining table.

(guest comes to the dining table)

o Wow!! What's all this top-quality work?

◇ It's the least I could do, hun!

o Wouldn't it have been better if we had made it a potluck instead of you wearing yourself out like this?

◇ Yeah right! Like you even know how to cook! Keep that on the down low!

o Okay! Just remember that I offered my services and you rejected them.

◇ Come on then. Get your hands moving and eat before it gets cold. What items shall I dish out for you?

o No, don't trouble yourself. I'll do it myself.

◇ Okay, make yourself at home. I won't offer.

(after finishing the meal)

○ Really, bless your hands and eyes! The food was amazing!

◇ My pleasure, dear! Let's have some tea and eat the dessert with it.

○ No, it's just about time for me to get to my doctor's appointment.

◇ So you're eating and running? Don't be ridiculous! I'll make the tea quickly.

○ All right, I'll stay a bit, but I can't be too late.

◇ Don't worry. I'll make the tea while you go wash your hands.

◇ *áhlan wa sáhlan. waṣálti b-súr3a*[1].

○ *āh, ilħámdu li-llāh, iţţarīʔ kān ħilw*[2]. *wi -ftakárt il3inwān mi -lmárra ílli fātit.*

◇ *ţab, kuwáyyis ínnik ma-nsitīš. yálla bīna báʔa, ilʔaklᵊ líssa ţáfya 3alē*[3].

○ *ţáyyib, ħúţţi*[4] *da fi -ttalāga báʔa.*

◇ *ya nhār ábyaḑ! lē ya bínti -lhábal da?*[5]

○ *hábal ʔē bassᵊ ya bínti?*[6] *di ħāga basīţa niħálli bīha.*

◇ *mírsi ya ħabíbti, tíslam īdik.*

○ *tíslam īdik ínti. āgi asá3dik fi ħāga?*

◇ *laʔ, kullᵊ ħāga gáhza. yálla -dxúli iɣsíli īdik wi ta3āli 3a -ssúfra.*

(guest comes to the dining table)

○ *allāh allāh allāh... ʔē iššúɣl il3āli da bass?*[7]

◇ *di aʔállᵊ ħāga 3ándi ya bínti.*[8]

○ *miš kúnna 3amalnāha diš párti áħsan, bádal ma ta3ábti náfsik kída?*

◇ *ya šēxa rūħi kída. ínti biti3ráfi tiţbúxi asāsan. xálli -ţţābiʔ mastūr.*[9]

○ *māši! xallīki fákra ána 3aráḑtᵊ xadamāti w ínti -lli rafáḑti.*

◇ *ţab, yálla báʔa, míddi īdik wi kúli ʔablᵊ ma -lʔaklᵊ yíbrad. tiħíbbi aɣríflik ʔē?*

○ *laʔ, ma-tit3ibīš náfsik. ána hat3āmil.*

◇ *ţáyyib, ilbēt bētik báʔa, wi 3ēši ħayātik*[10]. *ána miš há3zim.*

(after finishing the meal)

○ *bi-gáddᵊ tíslam idēki wi 3inēki. ilʔáklᵊ túħfa.*

◇ *bi-lhána wi -ššífa ya ħabíbti. yálla ní3mil dōr šāy wi nākul ilħílwᵊ ma3ā báʔa.*

○ *lā, da -na yadōb álɦaʔ maȝād idduktōr.*
◇ *ínti gáyya tákli wi tímši? ma balāš ɣalāsa!*[11] *háȝmil iššāy bi-súrȝa.*
○ *ţáyyib, māši. háʔȝud šuwáyya kamān, bassᵊ miš háʔdar atʔáxxar gāmid.*
◇ *ma-tiʔlaʔīš*[12]. *yadōb haȝállaʔ ȝa -ššāy ȝála bāl ma tiɣsíli īdik.*

[1] = على طول *ȝála ţūl*

[2] = رايِق *rāyiʔ* = فاضي *fāḑi*

[3] = لِسّه شايْلاه مِن عالنّار. *líssa šaylā min ȝa-nnār.*

[4] = شيلي *šīli*

[5] This line is very informal and should only be used with a close friend.

[6] = وَلا هبل وَلا حاجة *wála hábal wála ɦāga*

[7] أيْه الشُّغْل الجّامِد ده؟ *ʔē -ššúgl iggāmid daʔ;* (slang) لا شُغْل فنادِق فِعْلاً! *laʔ šuglᵊ fanādiʔ fíȝlan!* (lit. Now, that's "hotel" work indeed!)

[8] شُفْتي بقى مِش سهْلين إحْنا. *šufti báʔa miš sahlīn íɦna.* (humorous) **See? We're not easy** (i.e., we are like no other)**.**

[9] (lit. keep the floor hidden) an Arabic proverb which people use to tell someone not to discuss an issue or to stop talking about something.

[10] = خُدي راحْتِك *xúdi ráɦtik*

[11] = متِبْقيش رِخْمة *ma-tibʔīš ríxma* (note: only use with close friends)

[12] = متْخافيش *ma-txafīš*

Vocabulary

meal invitation	*3uzūma*	عُزومة
breakfast	*fiţār*	فِطار
to have breakfast	*fíţir*	فِطِر
lunch	*ɣáda*	غدا
to have lunch	*itɣádda*	اِتْغدّى
dinner	*3áša*	عشا
to have dinner	*it3ášša*	اِتْعشّى
dessert	*ɧilw*	حِلْو
to have dessert	*ɧálla*	حلّى
water	*máyya*	مايّة
tea	*šāy*	شاي
a glass of tea	*kubbāyit šāy*	كُبّايِةْ شاي
coffee	*ʔáhwa*	قهْوَة
a cup of cofffee	*fingān ʔáhwa*	فِنْجان قهْوَة
dining table	*súfra*	سُفْرة
food	*akl*	أكْل
hot	*suxn*	سُخْن
cold, cool	*bārid*	بارِد
address	*3inwān*	عِنْوان
the way	*iţţarīʔ*	الطّريق
late	*mitʔáxxar*	مِتْأخّر

early	*bádri*	بدْري
to arrive	*wáṣal*	وَصل
to eat	*ákal*	أكل
to gather, collect	*lamm*	لمّ
tray	*ṣiníyya (ṣawāni)*	صينية (صَواني)
plate	*ṭábaʔ (aṭbāʔ)*	طبق (أطْباق)
fork	*šōka (šíwak)*	شوْكة (شِوَك)
spoon	*ma3láʔa (ma3āliʔ)*	معْلقة (معالِق)
pot	*ḫálla (ḫílal)*	حلّة (حِلل)
ladle	*maɣráfa (maɣārif)*	مغْرفة (مغارِف)
knife	*sikkīna (sakakīn)*	سِكّينة (سكاكين)
cup	*kubbāya (kubbayāt)*	كُبّايَة (كُبّايات)
bathroom	*ḫammām*	حمّام

Expressions

No, it's on me this time.	*laʔ, baʔúllak ʔē xallīha -lmarrādi 3aláyya.*	لا بقولّك أيْه خلّيها المرّة دي عليّا.
Everytime you do the same thing. There's no way this can happen. (to someone who insists on paying)	*ínta kullᵊ márra bití3mil kída 3ála fíkra, ma-yinfá3š.*	إنْتَ كُلّ مرّة بِتِعْمِل كِده على فِكْرة مَيِنْفعْش.
Who wants to finish off the food with tea?	*mīn 3āyiz yíḫbis bi-šāy?*	مين عايز يِحْبِس بِشاي؟

What's up with being right on time...? To the minute, wow!	*ʔē ilmawa3īd ilmaẓbūṭa di bass... gayyᵊ bi-ddiʔīʔa ya rábi.*	أيْه المواعيد المظْبوطة دي بسّ... جايّ بِالدّقيقة يا ربي.
(sarcastic, to someone who is late) Such punctuality! Why don't you just come tomorrow?	*ʔē ilmawa3īd iggamīla di bass... ma tīgi búkra áɧsan.*	أيْه المواعيد الجّميلة دي بسّ... ما تيجي بُكْرة أحْسن.
No greetings during eating. Come find yourself a chair and start eating (lit. stretch your hand).[1]	*la salām 3ála ṭa3ām. yálla šúflak kúrsi wi midd īdak.*	لا سلام على طعام. يَلّا شوفْلك كُرْسي و مِدّ إيدك.
You've brought us joy (lit. enlightened us). Today the prophet has visited us.[2]	*nawwartūna... da -ɧna zárna -nnábi -nnahárda.*	نوّرْتونا... ده إحْنا زارْنا النّبي النّهارْده.
(response) It's already enlightened by its inhabitants.	*mináwwir bi-ʔáhlu.*	مِنوّر بِاهْلُه.
I cannot get enough of your presence.	*ʔa3dítkum ma-yitšibi3š mínha wallāhi.*	قعْدِتْكُم مَيِتْشِبِعْش مِنْها والله.
Where are you going? It's still early.	*3ála fēn bass? líssa bádri.*	على فيْن بسّ؟ لِسّه بدري.
Compliments to the chef! (lit. Bless your hands!)	*tíslam īdak! tíslam idēk!*	تِسْلم إيدك! تِسْلم إيديْك!

An enduring dining table![3]	*súfra dáyma.*	سُفْرة دايْمة.
May [this house] always be filled with food and guests.	*dáyman 3āmir.*	دايْماً عامِر.
Thank God you are back / arrived safely / recovered.	*ɧamdílla 3a -ssalāma.*	حمْدِلْله عَ السّلامة.
(response) Thank you.	*allāh yisallímak.*	الله يِسلِّمك.
I hope you enjoyed the food.	*bi-lhána wi -ššífa.*	بِالهنا و الشِّفا.

[1] You say this when someone arrives when you and others are already eating, so you invite them to come straight to dining table to eat with them without needing to make the rounds greeting everyone.

[2] a folksy statement to show ultimate hopsitality and welcoming

[3] See dialogue 4 on p. 135.

Making Appointments ترْتيب مَواعيد

Egyptians have a laid-back attitude toward punctuality. If you make plans to meet friends somewhere at a certain time, you shouldn't be surprised if they arrive thirty minutes or even an hour late. You can either accept this cultural norm or grow increasingly frustrated by it. Horrendous traffic in Cairo doesn't help the situation, either. If you call or text your friend to ask where they are, you'll likely get an أنا جايّ في سِكّة. *ána gayyᵊ f síkka.* **I'm on my way.** (even if they haven't left the house yet). If you're told خمس دقايِق و هكُون هِناك. *xámas daʔāyiʔ wi hakūn hināk.* **I'll be there in five minutes.**[1], don't take it literally. It'll likely be longer than five minutes. Just reply ماشي، أنا مِسْتنّيك. *māši, ána mistannīk.* **Okay, I'm waiting for you.**[2] But when invited to someone's home, arriving late would be considered disrespectful. If you are running late, it's best to call the host and let them know.

[1] = أنا هَوْصل في خِلال خمس دقايِق. *ána háwṣal fi xlāl xámas daʔāyiʔ* = قُدّامي خمس دقايِق و اكون هِناك. *ʔuddāmi xámas daʔāyiʔ w akūn hināk.*

[2] طيِّب يَلّا متِتْأخّرْش *ṭáyyib, yálla ma-titʔaxxárš.* **Okay, don't be late.**; طيِّب، تِوْصَل بِالسّلامة. *ṭáyyib, tíwṣal bi-ssalāma.* **Okay, may God deliver you safely.**

Setting a Formal Appointment

○ كُنْت مِحْتاجة أتْكلِّم معَ حضْرِتك عن المشْروع.[1]

◇ معلِشّ أنا مشْغول[2] دِلْوَقْتي.

○ طيِّب، حضْرِتك فاضي[3] بعْد الضُهْر مثلاً؟

◇ آه مُمْكِن. على واحِد كِده يِبْقى تمام.

○ I wanted to talk to you about the project.

◇ Sorry, but I'm busy now.

○ All right, are you free this afternoon?

◇ Yes, around 1 p.m. should be fine.

○ *kuntᵊ miħtāga -tkállim má3a ħadrítak 3an ilmašrū3.*[1]

◇ *ma3alíšš. ána mašɣūl*[2] *dilwáʔti.*

○ *ṭáyyib, ħadrítak fāḍi*[3] *ba3d ilḍúhrᵊ másalan?*

◇ *āh, múmkin. 3ála wáħda kída yíbʔa tamām.*

[1] عايْزة أكلِّمك ضروري عن المشْروع. *áyza -kallímak ḍarūri 3an ilmašrū3.* **I urgently need to talk to you about the project.**

[2] مِش فاضي *miš fāḍi* **I'm not free**

[3] يِناسِب حضْرِتك؟ *yināsib ħadrítak?* **Does (that) suit you?**

In Arabic, there are no direct equivalents of "a.m." and "p.m." See the vocabulary section on p. 157.

Keep in mind that the weekend in Egypt is Friday and Saturday, when banks are closed. Sunday is the beginning of the work week. In the private sector, office hours are generally from 9 a.m. to 5 p.m., and in the public sector, only until 2 p.m. During the month of Ramadan, hours differ, and the eight-hour workday becomes seven. Barbers and hairdressers are typically closed on Mondays.

2

MAKING PLANS WITH A FRIEND

o بقولّك أيْه، ما تيجي نِروح السّينِما النّهارْده بعْد الشُّغْل.

◇ طب، ما تْخلّينا بِاللّيْل أحْسن.[1]

o خلاص نِدْخُل مِن سبْعة.

◇ ماشي نِتْقابِل[2] قُدّام[3] شِبّاك التّذاكِر على ٧ اِلّا رُبْع[4].

o Hey, how about we go to the movies after work today?

◇ Well, let's make it in the evening.

o Okay, let's see a 7-o'clock showing.

◇ All right. I'll meet you there at the ticket window at a quarter to seven.

o *baʔúllik ʔē, ma tīgi nrūħ issínima -nnahárda ba3d iššúɣl.*

◇ *ṭab, ma txallīna bi-llēl áħsan.*[1]

o *xalāṣ nídxul min sáb3a.*

◇ *māši nitʔābil ʔuddām šibbāk ittazākir 3ála sáb3a ílla rub3.*[2]

[1] خلّيها بِاللّيْل *xallīha bi-llēl*

[2] أشوفك *ašūfak* **I'll see you**

[3] عنْد *3and* **at, by**

[4] على سِتّة و نُصّ، سبْعة إلّا رُبْع كِده. *3ála sítta w nuṣṣ, sáb3a ílla rub3ᵊ kída.* **Around 6:30 or 6:45.**

Egyptians sometimes use the five daily prayer times as reference points for making appointments instead of numbered hours of the day. For example, بعْد العِشا *ba3d il3íša* **after the evening prayer** (one hour after sunset.

3

Agreeing on a Time (Formal)

○ طيِّب، حضْرِتك هتْكون فاضي يوْم الخميس السّاعة ١٢.

◇ لا الخميس صعْب خالِص[1] ١٢. مُمْكِن مِن السّاعة ١٠ أيْه رأْيَك؟

○ أنا لِلْأسف السّاعة ١٠ عنْدي اِجْتِماع. مُمْكِن بعْد الضُّهْر لَوْ حضْرِتك فاضي.

◇ لا أنا مشْغول خالِص النّهارْده و اِحْتِمال أمْشي بدْري كمان. خلّينا السّبْت أحْسن؟[2]

○ تمام يافنْدِم. السّبْت مُمْتاز. حضْرِتك شوف المعاد اللي يِناسِب حضْرِتك.

○ Okay, are you free at 12 p.m. on Thursday?

◇ No, Thursday will be too difficult around noon. Maybe around 10 a.m. What do you think?

○ Unfortunately, I have a meeting at 10. Maybe this afternoon if you are free?

◇ No, I'm extremely busy today, and I might leave early. How about Saturday?

○ Okay, sir. Saturday will be perfect. Just tell me what time suits you best.

○ *ṭáyyib, ḫaḍrítak hatkūn fāḍi yōm ilxamīs issā3a -tnāšar?*

◇ *laʔ, ilxamīs ṣa3b^{ə} xāliṣ*[1] *itnāšar. múmkin min issā3a 3ášara. ʔē ráʔyak?*

○ *ána li-lʔásaf issā3a 3ášara 3ándi -gtimā3. múmkin ba3d iḍḍúhr^{ə} law ḫaḍrítak fāḍi?*

◇ *laʔ, ána mašɣūl xāliṣ innahárda wi -ḫtimāl ámši bádri kamān. xallīna -ssabt áḫsan?*[2]

○ *tamām, yafándim. issábt^{ə} mumtāz. ḫaḍrítak šūf ilma3ād ílli yināsib ḫaḍrítak.*

[1] مُسْتحيل *mustaḫīl* **impossible**

[2] = أيْه رأْيَك يوْم السّبت؟ *ʔē ráʔyak yōm issábt?*

Agreeing on a Time (Informal)

○ أيْه يا مُعلِّم، هنِتْقابِل كام النّهارْده؟[1]
◇ عَ الغدا.[2] أيْه رأْيَك نِتْغدّى سَوا؟
○ لا يا عمّ، أنا أُمّي عامْلة أكْل جامِد[3] النّهارْده. خلّينا نِتْقابِل بِاللّيْل.
◇ ماشي بسّ بدْري على ٧ كِده عشان ألْحق محلّ الكُّمْبْيوتر قبْل ما أروّح[4].
○ لا متِقْلقْش، مِش بيِقْفِلوا قبْل ١١[5].

○ Hey, dude! When are we meeting up today?
◇ At lunchtime. How about we have lunch together?
○ No, man. My mom is making a killer meal today. Let's meet in the evening.
◇ Okay, but early, around 7 p.m. so I can get to the computer shop before I go back home.
○ Don't worry. They don't close until 11.

○ *ʔē ya mu3állim, hanitʔābil kām innahárda?*[1]
◇ *3a -lɣáda.*[2] *ʔē ráʔyak nitɣadda sáwa?*
○ *lā, ya 3amm, ána úmmi 3ámla aklᵊ gāmid*[3] *innahárda. xallīna nitʔābil bi-llēl.*
◇ *māši bassᵊ bádri 3ála sáb3a kída 3ašān álħaʔ maħáll ikkumbyūtir ʔablᵊ ma -ráwwaħ.*[4]
○ *laʔ, ma-tiʔláʔš, miš biyiʔfílu ʔablᵊ ħdāšar*[5].

[1] نِتْقابِل على كام؟ *nitʔābil 3ála kām?* **What time shall we meet?**

[2] عَ العصْر كِده. *3a -l3aṣrᵊ kída.* **Sometime in the afternoon.**; على ٣ و نُصّ *3ála talāta w nuṣṣ.* **Around three o'clock.**

[3] طابْخة حاجات جامْدة. *ṭábxa ħagāt gámda.* **She's cooked something great.**

[4] عايِز اعدّي على محلّ الكُّمْبْيوتر و أنا مِروّح *3āyiz a3áddi 3ála maħáll ikkumbyūtar wána mráwwaħ.* **I want to go by the computer shop on my way home.**

[5] فاتْحين لِحدّ ١١. *fatħīn li-ħádd iħdāšar.* **They're open until 11 p.m.**

5

Rescheduling

○ معلِشّ أنا كان عنْدي معاد معَ د.[1] هَيْثم الخميس[2] السّاعة ٥.

◇ آه مظْبوط يافنْدِم. كُنْت هتّصِل أكِّدْه على حضْرِتِك.

○ طيِّب، إحْنا يِنْفع نِبدّرْها في أيّ يوْم تاني؟[3] عشان لازِم اسافِر الخميس.

◇ لِلأسف. د. هيْثم مشْغول طول الأُسْبوع. لَوْ كِدِه مُمْكِن احْجِز لِحضْرِتك معاد الأُسْبوع الجّاي.[4]

○ طيِّب تمام ياريْت.[5]

○ Excuse me, I had an appointment with Dr. Haytham at 5 p.m. on Thursday.

◇ Ah, yes, miss. I was going to call to confirm with you.

○ Okay, can we make it earlier on any other day? Because I have to go out of town on Thursday.

◇ Unfortunately, Dr. Haytham is busy all week. In that case, we can set another appointment for next week.

○ Okay, yes, please!

○ *ma3alíšš, ána kān 3ándi ma3ād má3a duktōr háysam ilxamīs*[2] *issā3a xámsa.*

◇ *āh, maẓbūṭ yafándim. kuntᵊ hattáṣil aʔakkídu 3ála ḥaḍrítik.*

○ *ṭáyyib, íḥna yínfa3 nibaddárha fi ayyᵊ yōm tāni?*[3] *3ašān lāzim asāfir ilxamīs.*

◇ *li-lʔásaf. duktōr háysam mašɣūl ṭūl ilʔusbū3. law kída, múmkin áḥgiz li-ḥaḍrítak ma3ād ilʔusbū3 iggáyy.*[4]

○ *ṭáyyib tamām, yarēt.*[5]

[1] دُكْتوْر = د. *duktōr* **doctor** / [2] يوْم الخميس = *yōm ilxamīs* / [3] نِأجِّلْها لِلأُسْبوع الجّاي؟ *niʔaggílha li-lʔusbū3 iggāy?* **Can we postpone until next week?** / [4] آه مُمْكِن الأُسْبوع الجّاي يوْم التّلات نفْس المعاد. *āh, múmkin ilʔusbū3 iggáyy yōm ittalāt nafs ilma3ād.* **Yes, it can be next Thursday at the same time.** / [5] تمام مُناسِب جِدّاً. *tamām, munāsib gíddan.* **Okay, that's perfect.**

6

Canceling plans

- o بقولّك أيْه فاكِس[1] الحفْلة بِالنِّسْبالي النّهارْده[2]، اِنْطِلْقوا[3] إنْتو.
- ◇ ليْه يا عمّ بسّ أيْه اللي حصل؟
- o فيه ماسورة اِتْسدِّت في صرْف الحمّام و السّباك جايّ يِشْتغل[4] و مِش عارِف هَيْخلّص على كام.
- ◇ يا ساتِر! معلِشّ، إن شاء الله يِظبّطْها و لَوْ خلّص بِسُرْعة تعالى برْضُه.
- o هشوف كِده. ربِّنا يِسهِّل.

- o You know what, forget about me for the concert tonight. You guys go ahead.
- ◇ Why?! What happened?
- o A pipe is blocked in the bathroom sewage and a plumber is coming to fix it. I have no idea what time he will finish.
- ◇ Oh no! Don't worry. Hopefully, he'll fix it, and if he finishes early, go ahead and join us.
- o Okay, we'll see. Hopefully it'll go smoothly!

- o *baʔúllak ʔē, fākis[1] ilɧáfla bi-nnisbāli -nnahárda[2], inṭílʔu[3] íntu.*
- ◇ *lē ya 3ammᵊ bass ʔē ílli ɧáṣal?*
- o *fī masūra -tsáddit fi ṣarf ilɧammām wi -ssabāk gayyᵊ yištáɣal[4] wi miš 3ārif hayxállaṣ 3ála kām.*
- ◇ *ya sātir! ma3alíšš, in šāʔ allāh yiẓabbáṭha, wi law xállaṣ bi-súr3a ta3āla bárḍu.*
- o *hašūf kída. rabbína yisáhhil.*

[1] فاكِس *fākis* is slang used mostly by teenagers; older people may not understand this word. / [2] = فُكّك مِنّي في حفْلة النّهارْده. *fúkkak mínni fi ɧáfla -nnahárda.*; أنا مِش رايِح حفْلة النّهارْده. *ána miš rāyiɧ ɧáfla -nnahárda.* **I'm not going to the party tonight.** / [3] = روحوا *rūɧu* / [4] = يِصلّحْها *yiṣalláɧha*

- o بقولّك أيْه، مِش هنُخْرُج بقى في سنتْنا دي؟[1]
- ◇ يا ريْت واللهِ[2] يا بِنْتي، إنْتي واحْشاني جِدّاً[3].
- o طب، أيْه نِظامِك[4] الويك إنْد الجّاي؟
- ◇ أنا الجُّمْعة عنْدي رِحْلة بسّ السّبْت تمام معايا[5].
- o طيِّب، أيْه رأْيِك نِتْغدّى و نُدْخُل سينِما؟
- ◇ ما تْخلّيها فِطار طيِّب وَلّا أيْه رأْيِك؟ نِركب عجل و بعْديْن نِفْطر[6].
- o عجل أيْه؟ مِش الرّايْدات دي بِتِبْقى الجُّمْعة؟
- ◇ و بيِبْقى فيه السّبْت باين[7].
- o بقولّك أيْه، فُكِّك مِ العجل[8]. أنا أصْلاً مِش حِمْل فرْهدة[9].
- ◇ طيِّب، خلاص، خلّينا نِتْغدّى و نُدْخُل سينِما من ٤.
- o لا خلّينا نِتْغدّى على ٤ و بعْديْن نُدْخُل سينِما من ٧.
- ◇ مِش فارْقة كِتير[10]. ثانْيَة واحْدة[11] كِده... هُوَّ السّبْت ده مِوافِق أيْه[12]؟
- o ٢٣ مارِس.
- ◇ يا نْهار ابْيَض، ده أنا ناسْيَة خالِص إنيّ عنْدي معاد دُكْتوْر.
- o بِتْهزّري[13]... كام طيِّب؟
- ◇ السّاعة ٥.
- o يِبْقى خلّينا على فِطار بقى و نْشوف ساعِتْها لَوْ عِرِفْنا نِدْخُل سينِما.
- ◇ خلاص نأكِّد على بعْض الجُّمْعة بِاللّيْل.

- o Hey, aren't we ever going to go out?
- ◇ I really hope so, girl. I miss you so much.
- o Well, how about next weekend?
- ◇ Next Friday, I have a trip, but Saturday works for me.
- o Okay, how about we have lunch and go to the movies?

◇ Let's make it breakfast, or how about we go cycling and then have breakfast?

○ Cycling? Aren't those rides usually organized on Fridays?

◇ It seems some are on Saturdays, too.

○ You know what? Forget about cycling. I can't be bothered.

◇ Okay, let's have lunch and go to the cinema at 4 then.

○ No, let's have lunch at 4 and then go to the cinema at 7.

◇ Doesn't matter. Wait a minute! What date is this Saturday?

○ March 23.

◇ No way! I totally forgot that I have a doctor's appointment!

○ You must be kidding! What time is it at?

◇ At 5 p.m.

○ In that case, let's make it breakfast and then see if we can make it to the cinema.

◇ Okay, let's confirm with each other on Friday evening.

○ *baʔúllak ʔē, miš hanúxrug báʔa fi sanátna di?*[1]

◇ *ya rēt wallāhi*[2] *ya bínti, ínti waɧšāni gíddan*[3].

○ *ţab, ʔē nẓāmik*[4] *ilwīk ind iggáyy?*

◇ *ána -ggúm3a 3ándi ríɧla bass issábtᵊ tamām ma3āya*[5].

○ *ţáyyib, ʔē ráʔyik nitɣádda wi nídxul sínima?*

◇ *ma txallīha fţār ţáyyib, wálla ʔē ráʔyik? nírkab 3ágal wi ba3dēn nífţar*[6].

○ *3ágal ʔē? miš irraydāt di bitíbʔa -ggúm3a?*

◇ *wi biyíbʔa fī -ssábtᵊ bāyin*[7].

○ *baʔúllak ʔē, fúkkik mi -l3ágal*[8]. *ána áşlan miš ɧimlᵊ farháda*[9].

◇ *ţáyyib, xalāş, xallīna nitɣádda wi nídxul sínima min arbá3a.*

○ *laʔ, xallīna nitɣádda 3ála arbá3a wi ba3dēn nídxul sínima min sáb3a.*

◇ *miš fárʔa ktīr*[10]. *sánya wáɧda*[11] *kída... húwwa -ssábtᵊ da mwāfiʔ ʔē*[12]*?*

- ○ *talāta w 3išrīn māris.*
- ◇ *ya nhār ábyaḍ, da -na násya xāliṣ ínni 3ándi ma3ād duktōr.*
- ○ *bithazzári*[13]*... kām ṭáyyib?*
- ◇ *issā3a xámsa.*
- ○ *yíbʔa xallīna 3ála fṭār báʔa wi nšūf sa3ítha law 3irífna nídxul sínima.*
- ◇ *xalāṣ niʔákkid 3ála ba3ḍ iggúm3a bi-llēl.*

[1] ملْناش نصيب نِتْقابِل السّنة دي وَلّا أيْه؟ *ma-lnāš naṣīb nitʔābil issanā-di wálla ʔē?* (ironically) **Aren't we destined to meet this year or what?**

[2] نِفْسي جِدّاً *nífsi gíddan* **I really want to**

[3] = هموت و أشوفك *hamūt w ašūfak* **I'm dying to see you;** يَلّا بينا بِجدّ! *yálla bīna b-gadd!* **Let's do it!**

[4] وَراكي حاجة *warāki ḫāga* **you have something (to do)**

[5] مَوَراييش حاجة *ma-warayīš ḫāga* **I don't have anything (to do)**

[6] خلّينا نِفْطر. *xallīna níftar.* **Let's have breakfast!**

[7] تقْريباً *taʔrīban* **I guess**

[8] = بلاش عجل. = فاكِس عجل. *balāš 3ágal.* = *fākis 3ágal.*

[9] = مِش ناقْصة تعب *miš náʔṣa tá3ab*

[10] أيّ حاجة، مِش هتِفْرِق. *ayyᵊ ḫāga, miš hatífriʔ.* **Anything, it doesn't make any difference.**

[11] = ثَواني *sawāni* = لحْظة *láḫẓa;* اِسْتنّي *istánni* **Wait!**

[12] يوْم كام في الشّهر؟ *kām fi -ššahr?* **what day of the month?**

[13] = بِتِسْتهْبلي *bitistahbíli* (note: only use with close friends, never with strangers)

Vocabulary

appointment, meeting (time)	*ma3ād*	معاد
to meet	*it?ābil*	اِتْقابِل
meeting	*igtimā3*	اِجْتِماع
to book	*ɦágaz*	حجز
reservation	*ɦagz*	حجْز
to confirm	*?ákkid*	أكِّد
confirmation	*ta?kīd*	تأْكيد
to cancel	*láɣa* *kánsil*	لغى كنْسِل
phone	*tilifōn*	تِليفوْن
phone call	*mukálma*	مُكالْمة
to call	*ittáṣal bi-*	اِتّصل بِـ
hour	*sā3a*	ساعة
two hours	*sa3atēn*	ساعتيْن
three hours	*tálat sa3āt*	تلات ساعات
one minute	*di?ī?a wáɦda*	دِقيقة واحْدة
five minutes	*xámas da?āyi?*	خمس دقايِق
ten minutes	*3ášar da?āyi?*	عشر دقايِق
15 minutes, a quarter hour	*rub3ᵃ sā3a*	رُبْع ساعة
20 minutes	*tiltᵊ sā3a*	تِلْت ساعة

half an hour	*nuṣṣᵊ sā3a*	نُصّ ساعة
a quarter to	*sā3a ílla rub3*	ساعة إلّا رُبْع
one moment	*sánya wáḫda*	ثانْيَة واحْدة
Saturday	*issábt*	السّبْت
Sunday	*ilḫadd*	الحدّ
Monday	*ilʔitnēn*	الاِتْنينْ
Tuesday	*ittalāt*	التّلات
Wednesday	*ilʔárba3*	الأرْبع
Thursday	*ilxamīs*	الخميس
Friday	*iggúm3a*	الجُّمْعة
weekend	*āxir ilʔusbū3* *wīk ind*	آخِر الأُسْبوع ويك إنْد
during the week (not the weekend)	*nuṣṣ ilʔusbū3*	نُصّ الأُسْبوع
in the morning	*iṣṣúbḫ*	الصُّبْح
at noon	*iḍḍúhr*	الضُّهْر
in the (early) afternoon	*ba3d iḍḍúhr*	بعْد الضُّهْر
in the late afternoon	*il3áṣr*	العصْر
at sunset	*ilmáɣrib*	المغْرِب
in the evening	*il3íša*	العِشا
in the late evening, at night	*bi-llēl*	بِاللّيْل
early	*bádri*	بدْري

late	*mitʔáxxar*	مِتْأخّر
1:05	*wáɧda wi xámsa*	واحْدة و خمْسة
2:10	*itnēn wi 3ášara*	اِتْنين و عشرة
3:15	*talāta wi rub3*	تلاتة و رُبْع
3:20	*talāta wi tilt*	تلاتة و تِلْت
4:25	*arbá3a wi nuṣṣ ílla xámsa*	أرْبعة و نُصّ إلّا خمْسة
5:30	*xámsa wi nuṣṣ*	خمْسة و نُصّ
6:35	*sítta w nuṣṣ^{ə} w xámsa*	سِتّة و نُصّ و خمْسة
7:40	*tamánya ílla tilt*	تمانْيَة إلّا تِلْت
9:45	*3ášara ílla rub3*	عشرة إلّا رُبْع
10:50	*ɧidāšar ílla 3ášara*	حِداشر إلّا عشرة
11:55	*itnāšar ílla xámsa*	اِتْناشر إلّا خمْسة
12:00 a.m.	*itnāšar bi-llēl*	اِتْناشر بِاللّيْل
12:00 p.m.	*itnāšar iḍḍúhr*	اِتْناشر الضُّهْر
2:00 a.m.	*itnēn bi-llēl*	اِتْنين بِاللّيْل
2:00 p.m.	*itnēn iḍḍúhr*	اِتْنين الضُّهْر
1:00 a.m.	*wáɧda bi-llēl*	واحْدة بِاللّيْل
1:00 p.m.	*wáɧda iḍḍúhr*	واحْدة الضُّهْر
4:00 p.m.	*arbá3a -lfágr*	أرْبعة الفجْر
4:00 p.m.	*arbá3a -l3áṣr*	أرْبعة العصْر

(on the phone) Who's speaking?	*mīn ma3āya*	مين معايا؟
Meet me at the station in 10 minutes.	*ʔabílni kamān xámas daʔāyiʔ 3and ilmaħáṭṭa.*	قابِلْني كمان خمس دقايِق عنْد المحطّة.
Can we move our appointment to Monday?	*yínfa3 niɣáyyar ma3ádna li-yōm ilʔitnēn?*	يِنْفع نِغيرّ معادْنا لِيوْم الاِتْنينْ؟
Can we have the meeting an hour earlier?	*yínfa3 nibáddar ilʔigtimā3 sā3a?*	يِنْفع نِبدّر الاِجْتِماع ساعة؟
Can we make the meeting one hour later?	*yínfa3 niʔáxxar ilma3ād sā3a?*	يِنْفع نِأخّر المعاد ساعة؟
Cancel with them today.	*kánsil ma3āhum ma3ād innahárda*	كنْسِل معاهُم معاد النّهارْده
The appointment was canceled.	*ilma3ād itláɣa.*	المعاد اِتْلغى.
The outing was postponed until next week.	*ilxurūga itʔaggílit li-lʔusbū3 iggáyy.*	الخُروجة اِتْأجِّلِت لِلأُسْبوع الجّاي.
At what time?	*issā3a kām?*	السّاعة كام؟
How many hours?	*kām sā3a?*	كام ساعة؟
On which day?	*yōm ʔē?* *ánhi yōm?*	يوْم أيْه؟ أنْهي يوْم؟

At the Doctor's عِنْد الدُّكْتوْر

You can make an appointment with a doctor in a مُسْتَشْفى *mustášfa* **hospital** or a عِيادة *3iyāda* **private clinic**. Office hours vary from clinic to clinic, as do the systems for making appointments. Some clinic use apps to make the scheduling process easier. Double-check the time when making an appointment and call the day before your appointment to confirm. And always ask about the examination fees before scheduling an appointment. Before seeing a doctor for the first time, it's a good idea to check their patients' reviews and ratings online. It can take weeks to find an open slot with a doctor who has an excellent reputation and is in high demand. Most doctors offer a quick اِسْتِشارة *istišāra* **consultation** appointment at no charge (or a nominal fee) within two weeks of your first examination.

CHECKING IN WITH THE RECEPTIONIST

o مِن فضْلِك، كُنْت حاجْزة[1] معاد بِإسْم هِبة صلاح.

◇ آه حضْرِتِك رقم ٥. قُدّامِك حالْتينْ[2].

o تمام أقْدر[3] أدْخُل التُّواليْت؟

◇ آه اِتْفضّلي مِن هِنا.

o Excuse me, I've made an appointment under the name Heba Salah.

◇ Yes, your appointment number is 5. You have two cases ahead of you.

o Okay, may I use the restroom?

◇ Sure, it's this way.

o *min fáḍlik, kuntᵊ ḫágza[1] ma3ād bi-ʔísmᵊ híba ṣalāḫ.*

◇ *āh, ḫaḍrítik ráqam xámsa. ʔuddāmik ḫaltēn[2].*

o *tamām, áʔdar[3] ádxul ittuwalēt?*

◇ *āh, itfaḍḍáli, min hína.*

[1] = كان فيه حجْز *kān fī ḫagz*

[2] = لِسّه حالْتينْ قبْلِك *líssa ḫaltēn ʔáblik*

[3] = مُمْكِن *múmkin*

A useful website is www.vezeeta.com/en, where you can search for doctors near you, see their examination fees, and read patients' reviews.

In some clinics, there are two kinds of appointments (regular and urgent), especially in the clinics of renowned doctors. If you need to see the doctor within days or the coming couple weeks, you can make an urgent appointment, which is more expensive than a regular appointment, of course.

2

ASKING ABOUT A DOCTOR

o قوليلي مِن فضْلِك هُوَّ الدُّكْتوْر هِنا بِيِعْمِل زِراعِةْ أسْنان؟

◇ لا دُكْتوْر مُحمّد تخصُّصُه أعْصاب بسّ فيه دُكْتوْر مُراد بِييجي اِتْنينْ و خميس تخصّصُه جِراحة.

o و يِقْدر يِعْمِلّي زِراعِةْ اسْنان؟

◇ حضْرِتك بِتِحْجِز كشْف معاه و هُوَّ هَيْقولّك لَوْ الزِّراعة تِنْفع معَ[1] حضْرِتك.

o Can you tell me, please, if the dentist here does dental implants?

◇ No, Dr. Muhamed's specialty is nerve treatment, but there is Dr. Mourad who comes on Mondays and Thursdays, and his specialty is surgery.

o And can he do a dental implant for me?

◇ You can book an appointment with him, and he'll tell you if an implant is right for you.

o *ʔulīli min fáḍlik, húwwa -dduktōr hína biyí3mil zirā3it asnān?*

◇ *laʔ, duktōr muḫámmad taxaṣṣúṣu a3ṣāb, bassᵊ fī duktōr murād, biyīgi itnēn wi xamīs,taxaṣṣáṣu grāḫa.*

o *wi yíʔdar yi3mílli zirā3it asnān?*

◇ *ḫaḍrítak bitíḫgiz kašfᵊ ma3ā, wi húwwa hayʔúllak law izzirā3a tínfa3 má3a[1] ḫaḍrítak.*

1 = تِناسِب *tināsib*

3

BRINGING X-RAYS BACK TO THE DOCTOR

○ اِتْفضّلي يا دُكْتوْر الأشِعّة و التّحاليل اللي طلبْتيها مِنّي.

◇ الأشِعّة كُوَيِّسة. مفيش فيها أيّ حاجة[1] بسّ التّحاليل مِش عاجْباني.

○ ليْه بسّ كِده؟[2]

◇ معلِشّ هكْتِبْلك على كورْس حديد نِمْشي عليْه[3] ٣ شُهور و بعْديْن نِشوف.

○ Here you are, doctor: the x-rays and tests [analyses] you requested.

◇ The X-ray is clear. Nothing wrong there, but I don't like the results of the tests.

○ Why's that?

◇ I'll prescribe an iron course for you for three months and then we'll see.

○ *itfaḍḍáli ya duktōr ilʔaší33a wi -ttaɦalīl ílli ṭalabtīha mínni.*

◇ *ilʔaší33a kuwayyísa. ma-fīš fīha ayyᵊ ɦāga*[1]*, bass ittaɦalīl miš 3agbāni.*

○ *lē bassᵊ kída?*[2]

◇ *ma3alíšš, haktíblak 3ála kursᵊ ɦadīd, nímši 3alē*[3] *tálat šuhūr wi ba3dēn nišūf.*

[1] = أيّ مشاكِل *ayyᵊ mašākil*

[2] = ليْه خيْر مالْها؟ *lē xēr málha?*

[3] = نِسْتمِرّ عليْه *nistamírrᵊ 3alē*

Most doctors speak excellent English. Unless your Arabic is better than their English, it may be best to discuss serious matters with your doctor in English to ensure clear communication and avoid any misunderstandings.

o كُنْت واكِل سمك و حلّيْت بِشوكولاتة بسّ بعْمِلْها كِتير[1] و أوِّل مرّة يِحْصلّ الكّلام ده.

◇ الحسّاسية مُمْكِن أسْبابْها تِبْقى كِتير[2]، مِش بسّ عُضْوي وَلّا بسّ أكْل[3].

o طيِّب و العمل أيْه؟[4]

◇ هكْتِبْلك على ادْوية و أصْناف أكْل محْدودة[5] هِيَّ بسّ المسْموحة[6] لِمُدّة شهْر.

o I had fish and a chocolate dessert, but I do this a lot, and this is the first time this has happened.

◇ Allergies can have many causes, not just physical or just food.

o What should be done then?

◇ I'll prescribe some medications. And only limited kinds of food will be allowed for one month.

o *kuntᵊ wākil sámak wi ḫallēt bi-šukulāta bassᵊ ba3mílha kitīr*[1] *w áwwil márra yiḫṣálli -kkalām da.*

◇ *ilḫassasíyya múmkin asbábha tíbʔa kitīr*[2]*, miš bassᵊ 3úḍwi wálla bass akl*[3]*.*

o *ṭáyyib, wi -l3ámal ʔē?*[4]

◇ *haktíblak 3ála adwíyya w aṣnāf aklᵊ maḫdūda*[5] *híyya bass ilmasmūḫa*[6] *li-múddit šahr.*

[1] = متْعوِّد على كِده *mit3áwwid 3ála kída*

[2] = ليها أسْباب كِتير *līha asbāb kitīr*

[3] = مِش شرْط عُضْوي وَلّا شرْط أكْل *miš šarṭᵊ 3úḍwi wálla šarṭ akl*

[4] أيْه العِلاج؟ *ʔē -l3ilāg?* **What's the treatment?**

[5] = مُعيّنة *mu3ayyána*

[6] = المسْموح لك تاكْلْها *ilmasmūḫ lak takúlha*

DISCUSSING TEST RESULTS AND TREATMENTS

◇ أنا شايِف النّبْض كُوَيِّس و رسْم القلْب كمان مفيهوش حاجة.

○ أُمّال الألم اللي بحِسّ بية ده سببُه أيْه؟ و ليْه مِش بقْدر آخُد نفسي؟[1]

◇ غالبِاً اِلْتِهاب في عضلات الصّدْر. هُوَّ اللي بيِْخلّيك مِش قادِر تاخُد نفسك لِلْآخِر فا بيِْسبِّبْلك كُلّ ده.

○ طب، و عِلاجة أيْه يا دُكْتوْر؟

◇ أنا هكْتِبْلك على مرْهم تِدْهِنْه معَ أدْوية تمِْشي عليْها لِمُدِّةْ أُسْبوعيْن و لَوْ اِتْكرّر الألم تاني اِرْجعْلي.

◇ I can see your heartbeat is fine, and the EKG is also clear.

○ Then why do I feel this pain? And why can't I breathe normally?

◇ Most probably it's an inflammation in the chest muscles. That's why you cannot breathe properly and is causing all of this.

○ And how can this be treated, doctor?

◇ I'll prescribe an ointment for you to use alongside with some medications for two weeks. And if the pain comes back, let me check you again.

◇ *ána šāyif innábḍᵊ kuwáyyis, wi rasm ilʔálbᵊ kamān ma-fihūš ḫāga.*

○ *ummāl ilʔálam ílli baḫissᵊ bī da, sábabu ʔē? wi lē miš báʔdar āxud náfasi?*[1]

◇ *ɣālíban iltihāb fi 3aḍalāt iṣṣádr. húwwa -lli biyxallīk miš ʔādir tāxud náfasak li-lʔāxir, fa biysabbíblak kullᵊ da.*

○ *ṭab, wi 3ilāga ʔē ya duktōr?*

◇ *ána haktíblak 3ála márham tidhínu máa3a adwíyya tímši 3alēha li-múddit usbu3ēn, wi law itkárrar ilʔálam tāni irgá3li.*

[1] بحِسّ بِصُعوبة في التّنفُّس. *baḫissᵊ b-ṣu3ūba fi -ttanáffus.* **I'm having difficulty breathing.**

6

A BROKEN BONE

o أنا وِقِعْت على دِراعي و غالباً اِتْكسر و الألم فظيع[1].

◇ طيِّب، خلّينا نِعْمِل أشِعّة عليْها الأوّل قبْل أيّ حاجة و قوليلي وِقِعْتي عليْها إزّاي.

o كُنْت قايْمة مِن عَ السّرير في الضّلْمة[2] و وِقِعْت بِكُلّ جِسْمي على إيدي.

(after the x-rays come back)

◇ طيِّب، إحْنا هنِعْمِل جِبْس مُؤقّت لِحدّ الصُّبْح و الأحْسن تِتابْعي معَ اِسْتِشاري عِظام لإنّ اِحْتِمال يِحْتاج جِراحة.

o جِراحة ليْه؟

◇ الأشِعّة مْبيِّنة كسْر مُضاعف في كذا عضْمة، فا عشان كِده الدُّكْتوْر هُوَّ اللي هَيْحدِّد أيْه اللي هَيِتْعِمِل بِالظّبْط.

o I fell on my arm and it's probably broken. The pain is horrible.

◇ Okay, let's take an x-ray first before anything else. And tell me how you fell on it.

o I was getting up from bed in the dark and I fell with my whole body on top of my hand.

(after the x-rays come back)

◇ Okay, we'll make a temporary splint until tomorrow morning. And you'd better follow up with an orthopedic consultant because it might require surgery.

o Why surgery?

◇ The x-ray shows a compound fracture, and this is why the [orthopedic] doctor is the one who will determine what needs to be done exactly.

- ○ *ána wiʔíʒtᵊ 3ála dirā3i wi ɣālíban itkásar wi -lʔálam fazī3*[1].
- ◇ *ṭáyyib, xallīna ní3mil aší33a 3alēha -lʔáwwil ʔablᵊ ayyᵊ ħāga wi ʔulīli wiʔí3ti 3alēha izzāy.*
- ○ *kuntᵊ ʔáyma min 3a -ssarīr fi -ḍḍálma*[2] *wi wiʔí3tᵊ bi-kúllᵊ gísmi 3ála īdi.*

(after the x-rays come back)

- ◇ *ṭáyyib, íħna haní3mil gibsᵊ muʔáqqat li-ħádd iṣṣúbħᵊ wi -lʔáħsan titáb3i má3a istišāri 3iẓām li-ínn iħtimāl yiħtāg girāħa.*
- ○ *girāħa lē?*
- ◇ *ilʔaší33a mbayyína kasrᵊ muḍā3af fi káza 3áḍma, fa 3ašān kída idduktōr húwwa ílli hayħáddid ʔē ílli hayit3ímil bi-ẓẓábṭ.*

1 = بِشِع *bíši3* = رهيب *rahīb*

2 اِتْكَعْبِلْت في السِّجّادة. *ikka3bíltᵊ fi -ssiggāda.* **I tripped over the carpet.**

◇ بِتِشْتِكي مِن أيْه يا أُسْتاذة سارة؟

○ أنا بقالي شهْريْن في مصْر و مِن ساعِة ما جيْت و أنا مِعْدِتي بايْظة خالِص.

◇ إنْتي مِش مصْرية و نقلْتي هِنا يَعْني؟

○ آه بِالظّبْط يا دُكْتوْر. كان عنْدي قَوْلوْن عصبي زمان بسّ رِجِعْلي أوِّل ما جيْت هِنا.

◇ طيِّب، هل اِخْتِلاف الأكْل هُوَّ اللي مِسبِّبْلِك ده مثلاً؟

○ مِش عارْفة. مُمْكِن آه و مُمْكِن يِكون التّوَتُّر مِن التّغيُّرات دي كُلّها.

◇ طيِّب، أيْه اللي بِتِشْتِكي مِنُّه بِالظّبْط؟

○ دايْماً إحْساس بِالاِنْتِفاخ و مِعْدِتي على طول بِتِقْلِب.

◇ طيِّب، فيه عُسْر هضْم؟

○ آه بِيِحْصل كتير. بقْى باكُل عادي ساعِتْها و مِش بِيِتْعِبْني بسّ بعْدها بِيوْم ألاقي بطْني واجْعاني جِدّاً.

◇ طيِّب، فيه أيّ إحْساس بِحرقان أَوْ حموضة؟

○ لا مفيش بسّ برجّع كِتير.

◇ طيِّب، هُوَّ أنا شايِف مِن السّونار إنّ القَوْلوْن مُتضخّم. طبْعاً فا فيه اِلْتِهاب جامِد فيه.

○ ده حقيقي و ده اللي بِيْسبِّبْلي الإحْساس بِالاِنْتِفاخ على طول.

◇ طيِّب، الاِنْتِفاخ ده بِييجي مِن أكْل مُعيّن؟ وَلّا مِش مُرْتبِط[1] بِحاجة مُعيّنة؟

○ ساعات بعْد اكلات مُعيّنة و ساعات مِن التّوَتُّر.

◇ طيِّب، خلّيني اكْتِبْلك على شُوَيّة تحاليل تِعْمِليها و تِجيبيهالي.

○ تمام طيِّب هل هاخُد دَوا مثلاً أَوْ حاجة؟[2]

◇ خلّينا نْشوف الأوِّل نتيجةْ التّحاليل و على أساسْها اكْتِبْلِك العِلاج المُناسِب.
o تمام هعْمِلْهُم و أرجّع لِحضْرِتك في اقْرب فُرْصة.

◇ What seems to be the problem, Ms. Sara?
o I've been in Egypt for two months, and ever since I arrived, my stomach has been having problems.
◇ You're not Egyptian and [recently] moved here, huh?
o Yes, exactly, doctor. I used to have irritable bowel syndrome long ago, but it came back once I came here.
◇ Okay. Is the difference in food what is causing all of this?
o I'm not sure. Maybe, yes. And maybe it's the stress from all these changes.
◇ What are the symptoms you're suffering from then?
o A constant feeling of bloating and my stomach is always upset.
◇ Do you have indigestion?
o Yes, it happens a lot. I eat normally and it doesn't make me sick at the time, but the next day, I find my stomach hurting so much.
◇ Okay, is there any burning feeling?
o No, there isn't, but I throw up a lot.
◇ All right, I can see from the sonar that the colon is extremely large, and it's definitely severely inflamed.
o That's right. And that's what's causing the constant bloating.
◇ Okay, does this bloating come from a specific type of food? Or is it not connected to anything in particular?
o Sometimes after certain types of food, and sometimes just from stress.
◇ Okay, let me write down some tests [analyses] for you to get, and bring the results to me.
o All right. Will I take any medicine or anything?

◇ Let's wait for the results first, and based on them, I'll prescribe the appropriate treatment.

○ Okay, I'll get them done and bring them to you as soon as possible.

◇ *bitištíki min ʔē ya ustāza sāra?*

○ *ána baʔāli šahrēn fi maṣr, wi min sā3it ma gēt w ána mi3díti báyẓa xāliṣ.*

◇ *ínti miš maṣríyya wi naʔálti hína yá3ni?*

○ *āh, bi-ẓẓábṭᵊ ya duktōr. kān 3ándi qawlōn 3áṣabi zamān bassᵊ rigí3li áwwil ma gēt hína.*

◇ *ṭáyyib, hal ixtilāf ilʔáklᵊ húwwa ílli misabbíblik da másalan?*

○ *miš 3árfa. múmkin āh, wi múmkin yikūn ittawáttur min ittaɣayyurāt di kulláha.*

◇ *ṭáyyib, ʔē ílli btištíki mínnu bi-ẓẓábṭ?*

○ *dáyman iḫsās bi-lʔintifāx wi mi3díti 3ála ṭūl bitíʔlib.*

◇ *ṭáyyib, fī 3usrᵊ haḍm?*

○ *āh, biyíḫṣal kitīr. bábʔa bākul 3ādi sa3ítha wi miš biyit3íbni, bassᵊ ba3dáha bi-yōm alāʔi báṭni w ag3āni gíddan.*

◇ *ṭáyyib, fī ayyᵊ iḫsās bi-ḫaraʔān aw ḫamūḍa?*

○ *laʔ, ma-fīš bassᵊ barágga3 kitīr.*

◇ *ṭáyyib, húww- ána šāyif min issunār inn ilqawlōn mutaḍáxxam. ṭáb3an fa fī -ltihāb gāmid fī.*

○ *da ḫaʔīʔi wi da -lli biysabbíbli -lʔiḫsās bi-lʔintifāx 3ála ṭūl.*

◇ *ṭáyyib, ilʔintifāx da byīgi min aklᵊ mu3áyyan? wálla miš murtábiṭ*[1] *bi-ḫāga mu3ayyána?*

○ *sa3āt ba3d akalāt mu3ayyána wi sa3āt min ittawáttur.*

◇ *ṭáyyib, xallīni aktíblak 3ála šuwáyyit taḫalīl ti3milīha wi tigibihāli.*

○ *tamām ṭáyyib, hal hāxud dáwa másalan aw ḫāga?*[2]

◇ *xallīna nšūf ilʔáwwil natīgit ittaḫalīl wi 3ála asásha aktíblik il3ilāg ilmunāsib.*

○ *tamām, ha3mílhum w arágga3 li-ḫaḍrítak fi áʔrab fúrṣa.*

[1] وَلّا ملوش عِلاقة؟ *wálla ma-lūš 3ilāqa?* **Or is there no connection/ relationship?**

[2] هل فيه عِلاج همْشي عليْه؟ *hal fī 3ilāg hámši 3alē?* **Is there any medicine I'll be on?**

Vocabulary

hospital	*mustášfa*	مُسْتشْفى
clinic	*3iyāda*	عِيادة
private clinic	*3iyāda xáşşa*	عِيادة خاصّة
dispensary	*mustáwşaf*	مُسْتَوْصف
examination	*kašf*	كشْف
consultation	*istišāra*	اِسْتِشارة
emergency	*ţawāri?*	طَوارِئ
ambulance	*is3āf*	إسْعاف
insurance	*ta?mīn*	تأْمين
reservation, appointment	*ђagz*	حجْز
doctor	*duktōr*	دُكْتوْر
general practitioner	*mumāris 3amm*	مُمارِس عامّ
consultant (holding a Ph.D.)	*istišāri*	اِسْتِشاري
specialist (holding a master's degree)	*axişşā?i*	أخِصّائي
surgeon	*duktōr girāђa*	دُكْتوْر جِراحة
internist	*duktōr báţna*	دُكْتوْر باطْنة
osteopath, orthopedist	*duktōr 3azām*	دُكْتوْر عظام
obstetrician	*duktōr nísa wi wilāda*	دُكْتوْر نِسا و وِلادة
pediatrician	*duktōr aţfāl*	دُكْتوْر أطْفال
oncologist	*duktōr awrām*	دُكْتوْر أَوْرام

dentist	*duktōr sinān*	دُكْتوْر سِنان
nurse (female)	*mumarríḍa*	مُمرِّضة
illness, sickness, disease	*máraḍ (amrāḍ)*	مرض (أمْراض)
ulcer	*ʔúrɧa*	قُرْحة
heartburn	*ɧumūḍa*	حُموضة
indigestion	*3usrᵊ haḍm*	عُسْر هضْم
irritable bowel syndrome	*qawlōn 3áṣabi*	قَوْلوْن عصبي
tooth decay, cavities	*tasáwwus*	تسوُّس
extracting a tooth	*xal3ᵊ ḍirs*	خلْع ضِرْس
compound fracture	*kasrᵊ muḍā3af*	كسْر مُضاعف
inflammation	*iltihāb*	اِلْتِهاب
injury, wound	*garɧ*	جرْح
chronic disease	*máraḍ múzmin*	مرض مُزْمِن
high blood pressure	*ḍaɣṭ*	ضغْط
diabetes	*issúkar*	السُّكر
surgery	*girāɧa*	جِراحة
medicine	*dáwa (adwíyya)*	دَوا (أدْوية)
pill	*ɧabbāya*	حبّايَة
treatment; medication	*3ilāg*	عِلاج
tests, analyses	*taɧalīl*	تحاليل
x-ray	*aší33a*	أشِعّة

intensive care	*3ināya murakkáza*	عِنايَة مُركّزة

Expressions

○

Excuse me, doctor, this medicine makes me feel ill.	*min fáḍlak, ya duktōr, iddáwa da ta3ábni gíddan.*	مِن فضْلك يا دُكْتوْر، الدَّوا ده تعبْني جِدّاً.
When will I be able to stop these injections?	*húwwa ímta háʔdar awáʔʔaf ilḫúʔan di?*	هُوَّ إمْتى هقْدر أَوَقّف الحُقن دي؟
Excuse me, I made an appointment in advance but haven't been seen yet.	*min fáḍlak, ána ḫāgiz min bádri wi líssa ma-daxáltiš.*	مِن فضْلك، أنا حاجِز مِن بدْري و لِسّه مدخلْتِش.

◇

What is troubling you?	*bitištíki min ʔē?*	بِتِشْتِكي مِن أيْه؟
There are no openings before March 3rd.	*ma-fīš ḫagzᵊ ʔablᵊ yōm talāta māris.*	مفيش حجْز قبْل يوْم ٣ مارِس.
The doctor regrets he has to reschedule your appointment for next week.	*idduktōr biy3tízir 3an ilma3ād wi biyballáɣak law yínfa3 yitʔággil li-lʔusbū3 iggáyy.*	الدُّكْتوْر بِيْعْتِذِر عن المعاد و بِيْبلّغك لَوْ يِنْفع يِتْأجِّل لِلأُسْبوع الجّاي.
The doctor had an emergency and apologizes that your appointment will be delayed for one hour.	*idduktōr gālu ẓarfᵊ ṭāriʔ wi biyistáʔzin law yínfa3 niʔáxxar ilma3ād sā3a.*	الدُّكْتوْر جالُه ظرْف طارِئ و بِيِسْتأْذِن لَوْ يِنْفع نِأخّر المعاد ساعة.

Unfortunately, the uric acid level is a bit height.	*li-lʔásaf, nísbit ilyūrik āsid 3ályašuwáyya.*	لِلأسف نِسْبِةْ اليوريك أسيد عالْيَة شُوَيّة.
We need to run a few tests before the operation.	*miħtagīn ní3mil šuwáyyit taħalīl ʔabl il3amalíyya.*	مِحْتاجين نِعْمِل شُوَيّةْ تحاليل قبْل العملية.

See **Egyptian Colloquial Arabic Vocabulary**, section 11: Health and Medicine for more vocabulary and expressions.

At the Pharmacy في الصَّيْدلية

In Egypt, pharmacies open late in the morning and close between 10:30 p.m. and midnight. However, big pharmacy chains offer 24/7 services, some even having call centers with extra services for the clients: home delivery, home injection, measuring blood pressure, cannula insertion, providing care, and so on. Some of these services are not performed by pharmacists but by specialists who have an agreement with the pharmacy chain. In Egyptian culture, it is polite to wish someone good health upon hearing that they are ill or injured, using one of a handful of formulaic expressions, such as ألْف سلامة (عليْك) *alf^{ə} salāma (3alēk)* **A thousand good healths (to you)!** or سلامْتك *salámtak* **Your well-being!** You will almost certainly receive one of these well-wishes from your pharmacist when you explain your symptoms and likely again at the end of the transaction. When you are being handed your medication, you may also get a بِالشِّفا (إن شاء الله) *bi-ššífa (in šā? allāh)* **With health, (God willing)!**

Describing symptoms

o دِلْوَقْتي يا دُكْتوْرة، أنا عنْدي سُخونية فظيعة[1] و إسْهال و بطْني مقْلوبة[2] مِ الصُّبْح.

◇ ألْف سلامة عليْك. بسّ فيه حاجة أكلْتها و تعبِتك مثلاً؟

o بِصراحة أكلْت سلطة تونة بقالْها يومينْ.

◇ غالِباً دي اللي سبِّبِت تسمُّم. بُصّ أنا هدّيك[3] مُطهِّر معَوي و خافِض حرارة و حاوِل تاكُل حاجات خفيفة[4].

o Doctor, I have a terrible fever, diarrhea, and my stomach has been upset since this morning.

◇ Speedy recovery! Did you eat something that made you sick?

o To be honest, I ate a salad that had been made two days ago.

◇ That's probably what caused the food poisoning. I'll give you an anti-diarrheal and a fever reducer. Try to eat light foods.

o *dilwáʔti ya duktōra, ána 3ándi suxuníyya fazī3a*[1] *wi ishāl wi báṭni maʔlūba*[2] *mi -ṣṣubḫ.*

◇ *alfᵊ salāma 3alēk. bassᵊ fī ḫāga akaltáha wi ta3abítak másalan?*

o *bi-ṣarāḫa akáltᵊ sálaṭa tūna baʔálha yumēn.*

◇ *ɣālíban di -lli sabbíbit tasámmum. buṣṣ, ána haddīk*[3] *muṭáhhir má3awi wi xāfiḍ ḫarāra wi ḫāwil tākul ḫagāt xafīfa*[4].

[1] حاسِس إنّي حرارْتي عالْيَة *ḫāsis ínni ḫarárti 3álya*

[2] بطني مِكرْكِبة *báṭani mikarkíba*

[3] هكْتِبْلك *haktíblak* **I'll write (for) you**

[4] متْتقّلْش في الأكْل *ma-ttaʔʔálšᵊ fi -lʔakl* **not to overeat**

Even though pharmacists do not typically have a Doctor of Medicine degree (MD), Egyptians respectfully address pharmacists (and other medical professionals) as دُكْتوْر *duktōr* **Doctor**.

2

DESCRIBING SYMPTOMS

○ سلامٌ عليْكُم.

◇ وَعليْكُم السّلام، اِتْفضّل.

○ لَوْ سمحْت كُنْت مِحْتاج أيّ دَوا لِلصُّداع.

◇ عنْدك فِكْرة أيْه سبب الصّداع؟

○ مِش عارِف. يِمْكِن داخِل عليّا دوْر برْد. و الجُيوب الأنْفية مِبهْدِلاني[1].

◇ ألْف سلامة. طيِّب، مُمْكِن تاخُد بنادوْل[2] العادي مُؤَقّتاً لِحدّ ما تِظْهر أعْراض البرْد، ساعِتْها تِقْدر تاخُد بنادوْل بِتاع البرْد.

○ Hello.

◇ Hello. How may I help you?

○ I need some medicine for a headache, please.

◇ Do you have any idea what's causing the headache?

○ I don't know. Maybe I'm coming down with the flu. And my sinuses are torturing me.

◇ Get well soon. All right, you can take regular Panadol[1] for now until symptoms of the flu appear. Then you can switch to Panadol Flu.

○ *salāmu 3alēkum.*

◇ *wi 3alēkum issalām, itfáḍḍal.*

○ *law samáḥtᵊ kuntᵊ miḥtāg ayyᵊ dáwa li-ṣṣudā3.*

◇ *3ándak fíkra ʔē sábab iṣṣadā3?*

○ *miš 3ārif. yímkin dāxil 3aláyya dōr bard. wi -lguyūb ilʔanfíyya mbahdilāni[1].*

◇ *alfᵊ salāma. ṭáyyib, múmkin tāxud banadōl[2] il3ādi muʔaqqátan li-ḥáddᵊ ma tíẓhar a3rāḍ ilbárd, sa3ítha tíʔdar tāxud banadōl bitā3 ilbárd.*

[1] = مِعذِّباني *mi3azzibāni* = مِجنِّناني *migannināni*

[2] Panadol is a popular brand of acetaminophen (a pain killer) in Egypt.

3

Getting medicine for a headache

◇ مِن فضْلك، أنا حاسّة بِصُداع رهيب و مِحْتاجة أيّ دَوا لِلصُّداع.
○ طيِّب، الصُّداع ده حاسّة بية بقالِك قدّ أيْه؟
◇ مِن ساعِةْ ما نْزِلْت الصُّبْح. غالِباً عشان مفْطِرْتِش[1].
○ طيِّب، حاوْلي تاكْلي أيّ حاجة و خُدي المُسكِّن ده بعْدها على طول.
◇ تمام، هاكُل و أخْدُه على طول. مُتْشكِّرة أَوي.

◇ Excuse me. I have a terrible headache. I need some headache medicine.
○ Okay, how long have you had this headache?
◇ Ever since I went out this morning. Probably because I didn't have breakfast.
○ All right, try to eat something now and take this painkiller right afterward.
◇ Okay, I'll eat then take it right away. Thanks a lot.

◇ *min fáḍlak, ána ḫássa b-ṣudā3 rahīb. miḫtāga ayyᵊ dáwa li-ṣṣudā3.*
○ *ṭáyyib, iṣṣudā3 da ḫássa bī baʔālik ʔaddᵊ ʔē?*
◇ *min sā3it ma nzilt iṣṣúbḫ. ɣālíban 3ašān ma-fṭírtiš*[1].
○ *ṭáyyib, ḫáwli tákli ayyᵊ ḫāga wi xúdi -lmusákkin da ba3dáha 3ála ṭūl.*
◇ *tamām, hākul w áxdu 3ála ṭūl. mutšakkíra áwi.*

[1] In the Alexandrian accent, many verbs which have kasra (*i*) in Cairo are pronounced with fatha (*a*):

Cairene	Alexandrian	
نِزِل *nízil*	نزل *názal*	**to go out/down**
فِطِر *fíṭir*	فطر *fáṭar*	**to have breakfast**

Filling a prescription

○ مِن فضْلك، كُنْت عايْزة الأدْوية اللي في الرّوشِتّة دي.
◇ ثَواني و هجهِّزْهُمْلِك.

(a few minutes later)

◇ أنا كتبْتِلِك على كُلّ دَوا الجُرْعات بِتاعْتُه.
○ تمام حِلْو جِدّاً. حِسابْهُم كام؟[1]
◇ كِده الحِساب ١٢٥ جِنيْه. اِتْفضّلي. بِالشِّفا إن شاء الله.
○ أنا لِسّه جايْبة الأدْوية دي مِن شهْر. كانِت أرْخص كِتير[2]... عُموماً اِتْفضّلي الحِساب. مُتْشكِّرة جِدّاً.

○ I'd like to get fill this prescription, please.
◇ Just a moment, and I'll prepare it for you.

(a few minutes later)

◇ I've written the dosage on each medicine.
○ Okay, great! How much do I owe you?
◇ The total is 125 LE. Here you are. Feel better soon!
○ I just bought the same medications last month and it was much cheaper! Anyway, here's the money. Thank you!

○ *min fáḍlik, kuntᵊ 3áyza -lʔadwíyya ílli fi -rrušítta di.*
◇ *sawāni wi hagahhizhúmlik.*

(a few minutes later)

◇ *ána katabtílik 3ála kullᵊ dáwa -ggur3āt bitá3tu.*
○ *tamām! ḫilwᵊ gíddan. ḫisábhum kām?*[1]
◇ *kída -lḫisāb xámsa w 3išrīn ginēh. itfaḍḍáli. bi-ššífa in šāʔ allāh.*
○ *ána líssa gáyba -lʔadwíyya di min šahr. kānit árxaṣ kitīr*[2]*... 3umūman itfaḍḍáli -lḫisāb. mutšakkíra giddan.*

[1] = كِده الحِساب كام؟ *kída -lḫisāb kām?* = بِكام بقى؟ *bi-kām báʔa?*

[2] = سِعْرها كان أقلّ مِن كِده *si3ráha kān aʔáll min kída*

⑤

FILLING A PRESCRIPTION

o مِن فضْلِك، الدُّكْتوْر كان كتبْلي الدَّوا بسّ مِش لاقيه.

◇ هُوَّ ناقِص فِعْلاً، بسّ مُمْكِن تاخُد ده البديل بِتاعُه.

o طيِّب، ده آخْدُه كُلّ قدّ أيْه؟ و كام قُرْص و كِده؟

◇ ده بِيِتّاخِد قُرْصينْ قبْل الفِطار و العشا بِنُصّ ساعة.

o Excuse me. The doctor has prescribed this medicine for me but I haven't been able to find it.

◇ There's a shortage of it actually. But you can take this, its equivalent.

o All right. How often should I take it? And how many tablets, et cetera?

◇ Take two tablets a half an hour before breakfast and dinner.

o *min fáḍlik, idduktōr kān katábli -ddáwa bassᵊ miš laʔī.*

◇ *húwwa nāʔiṣ fíʒlan, bassᵊ múmkin tāxud da, ilbadīl bitā3u.*

o *ṭáyyib, da áxdu kullᵊ ʔaddᵊ ʔē? wi kām ʔurṣᵊ w kída?*

◇ *da biyittāxid ʔurṣēn ʔabl ilfiṭār wi -l3áša bi-núṣṣᵊ sā3a.*

Pharmacies sell a lot more than just medicine. You can also buy cosmetics, toiletries, contraceptives, items for babies, etc. Larger supermarkets also carry all of these, of course, but if you need of a toothbrush, for example, you'll have more luck trying your local pharmacy than a corner shop.

Pharmacists in Egypt are qualified to diagnose minor illnesses and recommend medication. In many cases, they know better than doctors when it comes to the nature of medicines and chemicals. Many medicines that would require a prescription from a doctor in the U.S. (antibiotics, for example) can be given over the counter by pharmacists in Egypt. However, a prescription *is* required by law for strong narcotics and antidepressants.

6

Refilling a prescription

○ لَوْ سمحْتي، الدُّكْتوْر كان كاتِبْلي الحُقن دي مرّة كُلّ تلات أيّام لِمُدِّة شهْر.

◇ مِحْتاج حدّ يِدّيهالك دِلْوَقْتي يَعْني؟

○ لا تمام. فيه حدّ هَيْدّيهالي في البيْت. كُنْت مِحْتاج بسّ الجُّرْعات اللي تِكفّي المدُّة دي.

◇ تمام، أنا حضّرْتِلك سِرِنْجات تلات سنْتي و أمْبولات الحُقن بِالعدد اللي هتِحْتاجُه.

○ مُتْشكِّر جِدّاً. و ياريْت لَوْ إزازِةْ كُحول و كيس قُطْن معاهُم.

○ Excuse me. My doctor has prescribed this injection for me once every three days for a month.

◇ So, you want someone to administer it to you now?

○ No, that' fine. Someone will give it to me at home. I just need doses that will be enough for this duration.

◇ All right, I have prepared for you 3-centimeter syringes and injection ampules in the quantity you will be needing.

○ Thank you very much. And a bottle of alcohol and a packet of cotton with that, please.

○ *law samáħti, idduktōr kān katíbli -lħúʔan di márra kullᵊ tálat ayyām li-múddit šahr.*

◇ *miħtāg ħaddᵊ yiddihālak dilwáʔti yá3ni?*

○ *laʔ, tamām. fī ħaddᵊ hayddihāli fi -lbēt. kuntᵊ miħtāg bass iggur3āt ílli tkáffi -lmúdda di.*

◇ *tamām, ána ħaḍḍartílak siringāt talāta sánti wi ambulāt ilħúʔan bi-l3ádad ílli hatiħtāgu.*

○ *mutšákkir gíddan. wi yarēt law izāzit kuħūl wi kīs ʔuṭnᵊ ma3āhum.*

7

Making a purchase

○ لَوْ سمحْتي، كُنْت عايِز أشْترِي فُرْشِةْ سِنان ناعْمة و معْجون لِلأسْنان الحسّاسة.

◇ تحْت امْرك يافنْدِم. مُمْكِن تِسْتخْدِم المعْجون ده كُوَيِّس جِدّاً معَ الأسْنان الحسّاسة.

○ طيِّب، لَوْ كِده هاتيلي الأنْبوبة الكِّبيرة بقى.

◇ اِتْفضّل يافنْدِم. كِده الحِساب ٢٥ جِنيْهْ.

○ Excuse me. I wanted to buy a soft toothbrush and toothpaste for sensitive teeth.

◇ My pleasure. You can use this toothpaste. It's really good for sensitive teeth.

○ Okay. In that case, give me the large tube.

◇ Here you are, sir. That will be 25 pounds.

○ *law samáђti, kuntᵊ 3āyiz aštíri fúršit sinān ná3ma wi ma3gūn li-lʔasnān ilђassāsa.*

◇ *taђtᵊ ámrak yafándim. múmkin tistáxdim ilma3gūn da kuwáyyis giddan má3a -lʔasnān ilђassāsa.*

○ *ţáyyib, law kída hatīli -lʔanbūba -kkibīra báʔa.*

◇ *itfáďďal yafándim. kída -lђisāb xámsa w 3išrīn ginēh.*

Besides just preparing prescriptions and selling over-the-counter medicine, pharmacies offer a variety of health-related services, such as giving injections, measuring blood pressure, blood sugar, weight, and height, and changing dressings on wounds. Many pharmacies provide home visit services and deliveries.

Handwritten prescriptions are hard to read, even for Egyptians. Yes, it seems doctors having horrible penmanship is a universal trait! Fortunately, pharmacists are experts at deciphering prescriptions.

○ لَوْ سمحْتي، أنا لِسّه واصِل مصْر مِن أُسْبوعيْن و بتْعب كِتير.

◇ حمْدِلْله عَ السّلامة.[1] بسّ أيْه سبب التّعب؟[2]

○ غالباً تغْيير الجّوّ. و لِسّه مِش واخِد عَ[3] الأكْل. فا كُنْت مِحْتاج كام حاجة[4] كِده لِلطَّوارِئ تِكون عنْدي.

◇ هِيَّ مسْألِةْ وَقْت. هتِتْعوِّد إن شاء الله. اِتْفضّل.

○ كُنْت مِحْتاج تِرْمومِتْر و بِلاسْتر و مُطهِّر و مُسكِّن مثلاً. أيْه تاني مُمْكِن يِكون عنْدي لِلطَّوارِئ؟

◇ مُمْكِن نِزوِّد... مرْهم ميبو لِلحُروق... هيموكْلار لِلكّدمات... فولْتارين مرْهم مُسكِّن لِلْعضلات... بنادوْل و كونْجِسْتال لِلْبرْد... برِيزوْلين قطْرة لالْتِهاب العينيْن.

○ كُوَيِّس جِدّاً! أنا كِده معايا صَيْدلية في البيْت لِاى طَوارِئ.

◇ بِالظّبْط كِده! عُموماً ألْف سلامة على حضْرِتك. و لَوْ اِحْتجْت[5] أيّ حاجة برْضُه ده رقم الصَّيْدلية. مُمْكِن تِتّصِل بينا في أيّ وَقْت، و نِبْعتْلك أيّ حاجة مِحْتاجْها لِلْبيْت.

○ أيْه ده... إنْتو عنْدُكو خِدْمِةْ تَوْصيل لِلْمنْزِل؟

◇ أَيْوَه يافنْدِم، و عنْدِنا خِدْمِةْ واتْساب كمان تِقْدر تِبْعتْلِنا صُوَر أيّ دَوا أَوْ روشِتّة مِش قادِر[6] تِقْراها و إحْنا نِبْعتْلك المطْلوب بِالظّبْط.

○ دي خِدْمة مُمْتازه! أنا سمعْت إنّ كْتير مِن الدّكاتْرة هِنا فِعْلاً خطُّهُم صعْب يِتْقِري[7]. مُتْشكِّر جِدّاً.

◇ العفْو يافنْدِم، تحْت أمْرك في أيّ وَقْت.

○ Excuse me, I just arrived in Egypt a week ago and I keep getting sick.

◇ Welcome! But what's causing the sickness?

○ Probably the change of climate, and I'm still not used to the food. That's why I need some stuff on hand for any emergency.

◇ It's a matter of time. You'll get used to it, God willing. Go on then.

○ I needed a thermometer, bandages, antiseptic, and a pain killer, I guess. What else could I have for emergencies?

◇ We can add Mebo ointment for burns, Hemoclar for bruises, Voltaren gel (a muscle relaxant), Panadol and Congestal for colds and flus, and Prisoline drops for eye inflammation.

○ Excellent! Then I have a pharmacy with me at home for any emergency.

◇ Exactly! Anyways, get well soon. And if you need anything, this is the pharmacy's number. You can call us anytime, and we can deliver anything you need to your home.

○ Oh yeah? You have home delivery service?

◇ Yes, sir! And we have a Whatsapp service, too. You can send us pictures for any medicine or a prescription you cannot read and we will send you the exact medication.

○ That's a great service! I have heard lots of doctors' handwriting here is hard to read!

◇ You're most welcome, sir. Always at your service!

○ *law samáħti, ána líssa wāṣil maṣrᵊ min usbu3ēn wi bát3ab kitīr.*

◇ *ħamdílla 3a -ssalāma*[1]*. bassᵊ ʔē sábab ittá3ab?*[2]

○ *ɣālíban taɣyīr iggáww. wi líssa miš wāxid 3a*[3] *-lʔakl. fa kuntᵊ miħtāg kām ħāga*[4] *kída li-ṭṭawāriʔ tikūn 3ándi.*

◇ *híyya masʔálit waʔt. hatit3áwwid in šāʔ allāh. itfáḍḍal.*

○ *kuntᵊ miħtāg tirmumítrᵊ wi bilástar wi muṭáhhir wi musákkin másalan. ʔē tāni múmkin yikūn 3ándi li-ṭṭawāriʔ?*

◇ *múmkin nizáwwid... márham mību li-lħurūʔ... himuklār li-kkadamāt... vultarīn márham... musákkin li-l3aḍalāt... banadōl wi kunžistāl li-lbard... birizulīn ʔáṭra li-ltihāb il3inēn.*

○ *kuwáyyis gíddan! ána kída ma3āya ṣaydalíyya fi -lbēt li-ayyᵊ ṭawāriʔ.*

◇ *bi-ẓẓábṭᵊ kída! 3umūman alfᵊ salāma 3ála ḫaḍrítak. wi law iḫṭágt*[5] *ayyᵊ ḫāga bárḍu da ráqam iṣṣaydalíyya. múmkin tittíṣil bīna fi ayyᵊ waʔt, wi nib3átlak ayyᵊ ḫāga miḫtágha li-lbēt.*

○ *ʔē da... íntu 3andúku xídmit tawṣīl li-lmánzil?*

◇ *áywa, yafándim, wi 3andína xídmit watsāp kamān tíʔdar tib3atlína ṣúwar ayyᵊ dáwa aw rušítta miš ʔādir*[6] *tiʔrāha w íḫna nib3átlak ilmaṭlūb bi-ẓẓábṭ.*

○ *di xídma mumtāza! ána samá3t innᵊ ktīr min iddakátra hína fí3lan xaṭṭúhum ṣa3bᵊ yitʔíri*[7]*. mutšákkir gíddan.*

◇ *il3áfwᵊ yafándim, taḫtᵊ ámrak fi ayyᵊ waʔt.*

[1] حمْدِلْله عَ السّلامة *ḫamdílla 3a -ssalāma* and حمْدِلْله على سلامْتك *ḫamdílla 3ála salámtak* **Thank God you arrived safely!** is a formulaic greeting to someone who has arrived from a long trip.

[2] = أيْه اللي تاعْبك؟ *ʔē ílli tá3bak?*

[3] = مِش مِتْعوِّد عَ *miš mit3áwwid 3a*

[4] = شْوَيِّة حاجات *šuwáyyit ḫagāt*

[5] = عُزْت *3uzt*

[6] = عارِف *3ārif*

[7] = مَيِتْقِريش *ma-yitʔirīš*

Vocabulary

Symptoms		
a cold	*dōr bard*	دوْر برْد
constipation	*imsāk*	إمْساك
cough	*kúɧɧa*	كُحّة
diarrhea	*ishāl*	إسْهال
flu	*anfilwánza*	أنْفِلْوَنْزا
fever	*suxuníyya*	سُخونية
headache	*ṣudā3*	صُداع
pain	*álam*	ألم
poisoning	*tasámmum*	تسمُّم
upset stomach	*báṭnu maʔlūba*	بطْنُه مقْلوبة
vomiting	*qēʔ* *targī3*	قيْء ترْجيع

Medicine and Supplies		
antibiotic	*muḍádd^ə ɧáyawi*	مُضادّ حَيَوي
adhesive bandage, Band-Aid	*bilástar*	بِلاسْتر
anti-diarrheal medicine	*muṭáhhir má3awi*	مُطهِّر معَوي
cotton	*ʔuṭn*	قُطْن
eye-drops	*ʔáṭra*	قطْرة
gauze, dressing	*šāš*	شاش
fever reducer	*xāfiḍ li-lɧarāra*	خافِض لِلْحرارة

medicine	*dáwa (adwíya)*	دَوا (أدْوِيَة)
ointment	*márham (marāhim)*	مرْهم (مراهِم)
painkiller	*musákkin*	مُسكِّن
pill	*ђabbāya* *biršāma*	حبّايَة بِرْشامة
rubbing alcohol	*kuђūl*	كُحول
syringe	*siríŋga*	سِرِنْجة
tablet	*ʔurṣ (aʔrāṣ)*	قُرْص (أقْراص)
thermometer	*tirmumítr*	تِرْمومِتْر

Other Things You Can Buy at a Pharmacy

baby bottle	*bibrūna*	بِبْرونة
baby pacifier	*titīna*	تيتينة
shampoo for dry hair	*šámbu li-ššaʒr iggáff*	شامْبو لِلشّعْر الجّافّ
shampoo for normal hair	*šámbu li-ššaʒr ilʒādi*	شامْبو لِلشّعْر العادي
shampoo for oily hair	*šámbu li-ššaʒr iddúhni*	شامْبو لِلشّعْر الدُّهْني
anti-dandruff shampoo	*šámbu ḍidd ilʔíšra*	شامْبو ضِدّ القِشْرة
shaving blades	*šafarāt ђilāʔa*	شفرات حِلاقة
toothbrush	*fúršit sinān*	فُرْشِةْ سِنان
toothpaste	*maʒgūn*	معْجون
tube	*anbūba*	أنْبوبة

Misc.		
dose	*gúr3a*	جُرْعة
manufacture date	*tarīx ilʔintāg*	تاريخ الاِنْتاج
expiration date	*(tarīx) intihāʔ ṣalaɦíyya*	(تاريخ) اِنْتِهاء صلاحية
to measure	*ʔās (yiʔīs)*	قاس (يِقيس)
measuring blood pressure	*ʔiyās iḍḍáɣṭ*	قِياس الضّغْط
prescription	*rušítta*	روشِتّة
sick, ill	*3ayyān*	عيّان
to get sick	*tí3ib*	تِعِب
to make sick	*tá3ab*	تعب
sinuses	*guyūb anfíyya*	جُيوب أنْفية
stitches	*xiyāṭa*	خِياطة
stomach	*báṭn*	بطْن
temperature	*ɦarāra*	حرارة
wound	*garɦ*	جرْح

Expressions

○		
Can you read what medicine is written in this prescription?	*múmkin tiʔrāli -ddáwa -lli fi -rrušítta di?*	مُمْكِن تِقْرالي الدَّوا اللي في الرّوشِتّة دي؟

I need to measure my blood pressure.	*kuntᵊ miħtāg aʔīs ḍáɣṭi.*	كُنْت مِحْتاج أقيس ضغْطي.
Can I get my weight and height measured?	*múmkin aʔīs wázni wi ṭūli?*	مُمْكِن أقيس وَزْني و طولي؟
I need to change this bandage on this wound.	*miħtāg aɣáyyar 3ála -lgárħᵊ da.*	مِحْتاج أغيرّ على الجّرْح ده.
My stomach is upset.	*báṭni maʔlūba.*	بطْني مقْلوبة.
My head is going to explode.	*dimāɣi hatitfártik.*	دِماغي هتِتْفرْتِك.

◇

Speedy recovery!	*alfᵊ salāma!*	ألْف سلامة!
Get well soon!	*bi-ššífa!*	بِالشِّفا!
But this [medicine] requires a stamped prescription.	*bassᵊ da lāzim yitṣírif bi-rušítta maxtūma.*	بسّ ده لازِم يِتْصِرِف بِروشِتّة مخْتومة.
You need to change the dressing on those stitches.	*lāzim tiɣáyyar 3ála -lxiyāṭa di.*	لازِم تِغيرّ على الخِياطة دي.
Try to get to your doctor to prescribe another medicine	*ħāwil tírga3 li-dduktōr yiktíblak dáwa tāni.*	حاوِل ترْجع لِلدُّكْتوْر يِكْتِبْلك دَوا تاني.
There is a shortage of this medicine on the market.	*iddáwa da nāʔiṣ fi -ssūʔ.*	الدَّوا ده ناقِص في السّوق.

At the Gym

جُوّه الجّيم

Gyms are abundant in Egypt. You'll likely be able to find a decent one in your neighborhood, within walking distance or a short taxi ride away. They do vary in services offered, quality, and fees. Some are quite fancy with state-of-the-art equipment, hot tubs or spas, offer fitness classes and personal training, and even massage. Some gyms have separate areas for men and women, while others have specific hours of the day for women only. There are also women-only gyms, which many Egyptian women prefer, for privacy and religious piety. In the first dialogue, you learn useful phrases and vocabulary so that you can go by and check out your potential new gym.

1

Asking about Gym Membership

○ كُنْت عايْزة أشْترِك في الجّيمّ. و حابّة أعْرف العُضْوية أَوْ الاِشْترِاك بِكام؟

◇ أهْلاً بيكي يافنْدِم. بُصّي حضْرِتك هُوَّ فيه ٢٠٠ جِنيْه لِلْعُضْوية و

بعْديْن ٥٠٠ في الشّهْر. و فيه خصْم لَوْ حضْرِتك عملْتي اِشْتِراك سنَوي أَوْ نِصْف سنَوي.

- ○ آه... طيِّب أيْه هِيَّ السّاعات اللي الجِّيم فاتِح فيها؟[1]
- ◇ فاتِح كُلّ يوْم مِن السّاعة ٦ الصُّبْح لِحدّ ١٢ بِاللّيْل.
- ○ عظيم أَوي. طيِّب مُمْكِن آخُد لفّة[2] أشوف الأجْهِزة؟[3]
- ◇ أكيد طبْعاً. اِتْفضّلي و أنا هَوَرّي حضْرِتك.

- ○ I wanted to join the gym and was wondering about the membership fees.
- ◇ Welcome, miss. It's 200 LE for membership and then 500 LE per month. There's a discount if you get a quarterly or half-year membership.
- ○ I see. What are the gym's hours?
- ◇ It's open every day from 6 a.m. to midnight.
- ○ That's great! Can I take a look around to see the machines?
- ◇ For sure. Follow me. I'll show you around.

- ○ *kuntᵊ 3áyza -štírik fi -žžīmm. wi ɧábba á3raf il3uɖwíyya aw ilʔištirāk bi-kām?*
- ◇ *áhlan bīki yafándim. búʂʂi ɧaɖrítik húwwa fī mitēn ginēh li-l3uɖwíyya wi ba3dēn xumsumíyya fi -ššáhr. wi fī xaʂmᵊ law ɧaɖrítik 3amálti -štirāk sánawi aw niʂfᵊ sánawi.*
- ○ *āh... ʈáyyib ʔē híyya -ssa3āt ílli -žžīm fātiɧ fīha?*[1]
- ◇ *fātiɧ kullᵊ yōm min issā3a sítta -ʂʂúbɧᵊ li-ɧádd itnāšar bi-llēl.*
- ○ *3aʐīm áwi. ʈáyyib múmkin āxud láffa*[2] *ašūf ilʔaghíza?*[3]
- ◇ *akīd ʈáb3an. itfaɖɖáli w ána hawárri ɧaɖrítik.*

[1] = مَواعيد الجِّيمّ مِن كام لِكام؟ *mawa3īd ižžīmmᵊ min kām li-kām?* = أيْه مَواعيد الجِّيمّ؟ *ʔē mawa3īd ižžīmm?* / [2] = جَوْلة *gáwla* **tour** / [3] مُمْكِن تِوَرّيني الجِّيمّ و أشوف الأجْهِزة؟ *múmkin tiwarrīni -žžīmm w ašūf ilʔaghíza?* **Can you show me the gym so I can see the equipment?;** مُمْكِن أبُصّ بصّة كِده على الأجْهِزة؟ *múmkin abúʂʂᵊ báʂʂa kída 3ála -lʔaghíza?* **Can I take a look at the equipment?**

2

MAKING A FITNESS PLAN WITH A TRAINER

◇ طيِّب، إنْتَ أيْه اللي عايز تِوْصلُّه بِالظّبْط؟
○ أنا بسّ عايِز[1] أظْبُط شكْلي عامّةً[2].
◇ طيِّب، و حابِب تِتْمرّن[3] كام يوْم في الأُسْبوع؟
○ مبْدأيّاً مُمْكِن تلات أيّام. مُمْكِن آجي مثلاً حدّ و تلات و خميس.
◇ حِلْو جِدّاً. طيِّب أنا هعْمِلّك بِرْنامِج لِلتّلات أيّام عشان نِحْرق الدُّهون و نِبْني شُوَيِّةْ عضلات.

◇ What are your goals exactly?
○ I just want to get in better shape in general.
◇ How many days a week do you want to work out?
○ Maybe three to start with. I can come to the gym on Sundays, Tuesdays, and Thursdays.
◇ Perfect. I'll create a 3-day workout plan to burn fat and build muscle.

◇ *ṭáyyib, ínta ʔē ílli 3āyiz tiwṣállu bi-ẓẓábṭ?*
○ *ána bassᵊ 3āyiz[1] áẓbuṭ šákli 3ammátan[2].*
◇ *ṭáyyib, wi ḩābib titmárran[3] kām yōm fi -lʔusbū3?*
○ *mabdaʔíyyan múmkin tálat ayyām. múmkin āgi másalan ḩaddᵊ wi talāt wi xamīs.*
◇ *ḩilwᵊ gíddan. ṭáyyib ána ha3míllak birnāmig li-ttálat ayyām 3ašān níḩraʔ idduhūn wi níbni šwáyyit 3aḍalāt.*

[1] مِحْتاج *miḩtāg* **need**

[2] أخِسّ ١٠ كيلو *axíss 3ášara kīlu* **(I) lose ten kilograms;** أعْمِل فورْمة *á3mil fúrma* **(I) get in shape;** أزوِّد حجْم العضلات *azáwwid ḩagm il3aḍalāt* **(I) increase muscle mass**

[3] = تِتْدرّب *titdárrab*

3

Waiting to use equipment

○ حضْرتك بِتِسْتخْدِم الجِّهاز ده؟[1]

◇ آه باقي راوْنْد واحْدة و أخلّص[2].

○ آه تمام.

(waits a bit)

◇ تمام أنا خلّصْت. تِقْدر تِتْفضّل.

○ شُكْراً جِدّاً.

○ Are you using this machine?

◇ Ah yes, I just have one more set left.

○ Ah okay...

(waits a bit)

◇ Okay, I'm done. It's all yours.

○ Thank you.

○ *ḫadrítak bitistáxdim iggihāz da?*[1]

◇ *āh, bāʔi rawndᵊ wáḫda w axállaṣ*[2].

○ *āh, tamām.*

(waits a bit)

◇ *tamām, ána xallášt. tíʔdar titfáḍḍal.*

○ *šúkran gíddan.*

[1] قُدّامك كِتير؟ *ʔuddāmak kitīr?* **Do you still have much to go [on this machine]?**

[2] قرّبْت اخلّص *ʔarrábt axállaṣ* **I'm almost done**

Asking for Help with Equipment

o مِن فضْلِك، تِعْرفي إزّاي[1] أقْدر اظْبُط القعْدة عَ الجِّهاز ده؟

◇ آه طبْعاً. اِسْتنّي كِده أوَرّيكي. بُصّي بِتْشِدّي المُسْمار ده لْبرّه و تِحرّكي القعْدة بِراحْتِك[2].

o آه تمام. أنا مكُنْتِش شايْفة المُسْمار.[3] تِسْلمي.

◇ وَلا يِهِمِّك.[1]

o Excuse me, do you know how to adjust the seat on this machine?

◇ Sure! Wait and I'll show you. Look, You just have to pull out the pin underneath and slide the seat as you'd like it.

o Ah, I see! I didn't see the pin. Thank you!

◇ No problem!

o *min fáḍlik, ti3ráfi -zzāy*[1] *áʔdar áẓbuṭ ilʔá3da 3a -ggihāz da?*

◇ *āh, ṭáb3an. istánni kída awarrīki. búṣṣi, bitšíddi -lmusmār da lbárra wi tiḫarráki -lʔá3da bi-ráḫtik*[2].

o *āh, tamām. ána ma-kúntiš šáyfa -lmusmār.*[3] *tislámi.*

◇ *wála yhímmik.*[4]

[1] مُمْكِن تِوَرّيني إزّاي...؟ *múmkin tiwarrīni -zzāy...?* **Can you show me how to...?**

[2] = زيّ ما إنْتي عايْزة *zayyᵊ má-nti 3áyza*

[3] = المُسْمار مكانْش بايِن خالِص *ilmusmār ma-kánšᵊ bāyin xāliṣ*

[4] العفْو على أيْه؟ *il3áfwᵊ 3ála ʔē?* **You're welcome.**

WORKING WITH A TRAINER

◇ طيِّب، إحْنا كِده هنِعْمِل تلات مجْموعات مِن عشر رفعات. جاهِز؟

○ جاهِز!

◇ واحِد... اِتْنينْ... تلاتة...

○ لا بسّ دي تِقيلة شُوَيّة عليّا.[1]

◇ طيِّب، خلّينا نِجرّب الخمسْتاشر كيلو بدالْها... أيْه الأخْبار؟[2]

○ مْمْم... أَيْوَه... ده أحْسن شُوَيّة.

◇ Okay, we'll do three sets of ten reps. Ready?
○ Ready!
◇ One... two... three...
○ Oh, this is a bit heavy for me!
◇ Okay, let's try 15 kg instead. How is that weight?
○ Um, yes. That's a bit better.

◇ *ṭáyyib, íḫna kída haní3mil tálat magmu3āt min 3ášar rafa3āt. gāhiz?*
○ *gāhiz!*
◇ *wāḫid... itnēn... talāta...*
○ *laʔ, bassᵊ di tʔīla šwáyya 3aláyya.*[1]
◇ *ṭáyyib, xallīna ngárrab ilxamastāšar kīlu badálha... ʔē -lʔaxbār?*[2]
○ *mmm... áywa... da áḫsan šuwáyya.*

[1] خفيفة عليّا *xafīfa 3aláyya* **too light for me**

[2] تمام كِده؟ *tamām kída?* **Is that okay?**

6

TAKING AN AEROBICS CLASS

◇ يَلّا نِبْدأ التّمْرين ده. جاهْزة؟

o آه... معاكي.

◇ واحِد اِتْنينْ تلاتة فوْق ... واحِد اِتْنينْ تلاتة تحْت...

o لا معلِشّ[1]. مُمْكِن تِعْمِلي[2] الحركة دي تاني بِالرّاحة[3]؟

◇ Let's start this exercise. Ready?
o Yes, I'm following you.
◇ One, two, three up... one two three down.
o Sorry! Can you repeat that movement again slowly?

◇ *yálla níbdaʔ ittamrīn da. gáhza?*
o *āh... ma3āki.*
◇ *wāḥid itnēn talāta fōʔ... wāḥid itnēn talāta taḥt...*
o *laʔ, ma3alíšš[1]. múmkin ti3míli[2] -lḥáraka di tāni bi-rrāḥa[3]?*

[1] اِسْتنّي *istánni* **wait!**

[2] = تِعيدي *ti3īdi*

[3] = بِشْويْش *bi-šwēš*; واحْدة واحْدة *wáḥda wáḥda* **step by step**

Egyptians are modest when it comes to nudity, even in the locker room. Showers are always individual stalls, never open showers. Full nudity (outside of your private shower stall) is not acceptable. Be sure to stay covered at least below the waist with your towel and slip your underwear on and off from under the towel so as not to expose yourself.

Most gyms in Egypt offer programs to attract women, such as Zumba fitness classes, belly dancing classes, yoga, and meditation classes.

Some gyms have playrooms where you can leave your children while you work out. Make sure the playroom is closed-in and secure.

Extended Dialogue

○ مِن فضْلك، كُنْت عايْزة اشْترِك معاكُم[1] في الجّيم.
◇ أهْلاً بيكي يافنْدِم. تِحِبّي اِشْتراك سنَوي وَلّا نُصّ سنَوي وَلّا رُبْع سنَوي وَلّا شهْري؟
○ أنا حابّة أجرّب شهْر واحِد بسّ. هتِفْرِق في حاجة؟[2]
◇ هُوَّ لَوْ شهْري هَيِبْقى ٦٠٠ جِنيْه.
○ طب، و لَوْ تلات شُهور على بعْض؟
◇ هَيِبْقى بـ ١٥٠٠.
○ مْمْم... طيِّب خلّيني اعْرف[3] الأوِّل أيْه الأيّام و المَواعيد.
◇ لَوْ حابّة تيجي في الصّالة المفْتوحة ليكي كُلّ الأيّام مِن السّاعة ٧ الصُّبْح لِحدّ ١ بِاللّيْل.
○ دي ميكْس[4] يَعْني؟
◇ آه بِالظّبْط و فيه مَواعيد بِتِبْقى لِلْسّيِّدات فقط بِتِبْقى سبْت اِتْنيْن ارْبع مِن ٢ الضُّهْر لِحدّ ٧ بِاللّيْل.
○ طيِّب، و فيه أيْه تاني الجّيم بِيْقدِّمُه؟[5]
◇ مُمْكِن يِبْقى ليكي مُدرِّب خاصّ بِإضافةْ ٥٠٠ جِنيْه في الشّهْر، يِتابِع معاكي بِرْنامِج التّمْرين.
○ أنا سِمِعْت[6] إنّ عنْدُكُم مساج و حاجات تانْيَة.
◇ فيه فِعْلاً يافنْدِم جلسات مساج بسّ بِتِبْقى بِالحجْز و فيه جاكوزي كمان.
○ طيِّب، و جلْسِةْ المساج سِعْرها كام؟[7]
◇ الكِتْف و الضّهْر بـ ٢٠٠ نُصّ ساعة و الجِّسْم كُلُّه ٥٠٠ في السّاعة.
○ طيِّب، خلّيني ابْدأ معاكُم شهْر واحِد بسّ و بعْد كِده هشوف[8].
◇ تحْت أمْرك يافنْدِم.

○ Excuse me, I wanted to join your gym.

◇ Welcome, miss! Would you prefer an annual, half-year, quarterly or monthly membership?

○ I want to try just one month, but is there even a difference?

◇ If it's monthly, it will be 600 LE.

○ What if it's 3 months altogether?

◇ Then it will be 1500 LE.

○ Hmmm... okay, let me know the days and hours [of operation] first.

◇ If you want to come during to the "open" gym, it's available to you all days from 7 a.m. until 1 a.m.

○ It's mixed [for men and women], you mean?

◇ Yes, exactly, And there are certain sessions for ladies only: Saturdays, Mondays, and Wednesdays from 2 p.m. until 7 p.m.

○ Okay. What else do you offer at the gym?

◇ You can get a personal trainer for an extra 500 LE per month, and they'll follow a monthly exercise program with you.

○ I heard you also have massage and other things.

◇ Yes, indeed, miss. There are massage sessions, but they need to be booked in advance, and there is also a hot tub.

○ And how much is a massage session?

◇ Upper back and shoulders is 200 LE per hour and "whole body" is 500 per hour.

○ Okay, let me start with just one month with you guys, and then I'll see later.

◇ Sure, whatever you wish, miss.

○ *min fáḑlak, kuntᵊ 3áyza aštírik ma3ākum[1] fi -žžīmm.*

◇ *áhlan bīki yafándim. tiɧíbbi -štirāk sánawi wálla nuşşᵊ sánawi wálla rub3ᵊ sánawi wálla šáhri?*

○ *ána ɧábba -gárrab šahrᵊ wāɧid bass. hatífri? fi ɧāga?[2]*

◇ *húwwa law šáhri hayíb?a sittumīt ginēh.*

○ *ţab, wi law tálat šuhūr 3ála ba3ḑ?*

◇ *hayíbʔa bi-álfᵊ w xumsumíyya.*
○ *mmm... ṭáyyib xallīni á3raf*[3] *ilʔáwwil ʔē ilʔayyām wi -lmawa3īd.*
◇ *law ḫábba tīgi fi -ṣṣāla -lmaftūḫa līki kull ilʔayyām min issā3a sáb3a -ṣṣúbḫᵊ li-ḫáddᵊ wáḫda bi-llēl.*
○ *di miksᵊ*[4] *yá3ni?*
◇ *āh, bi-ẓẓábṭ, wi fī mawa3īd bitíbʔa li-ssayyidāt fáqaṭ, bitíbʔa sabt itnēn árba3 min itnēn iḍḍúhrᵊ li-ḫádd sáb3a bi-llēl.*
○ *ṭáyyib, wi fī ʔē tāni -žžīm biyʔaddímu?*[5]
◇ *múmkin yíbʔa līki mudárrib xaṣṣ, bi-ʔiḍāfit xumsumīt ginēh fi -ššahr, yitābi3 ma3āki birnāmig ittamrīn.*
○ *ána smí3t*[6] *innᵊ 3andúkum masāž wi ḫagāt tánya.*
◇ *fī fí3lan yafándim galasāt masāž bassᵊ btíbʔa bi-lḫágz, wi fī žakūzi kamān.*
○ *ṭáyyib, wi gálsit ilmasāž si3ráha kām?*[7]
◇ *ikkítfᵊ wi -ḍḍáhrᵊ b-mitēn nuṣṣᵊ sā3a wi -ggísmᵊ kúllu xumsumīyya fi -ssā3a.*
○ *ṭáyyib, xallīni ábdaʔ ma3ākum šahrᵊ wāḫid bassᵊ wi ba3dᵊ kída hašūf*[8].
◇ *taḫtᵊ ámrak yafándim.*

[1] = عنْدُكُم *3andúkum*

[2] = أيْه الفرْق يَعْني؟ *ʔē ilfárʔᵊ yá3ni*

[3] قولّي... *ʔúlli...* **tell me...**

[4] = مُشْترَكة *muštáraka*

[5] = أيْه كمان الخدمات اللي بِتْقدِّموها؟ *ʔē kamān ilxadamāt ílli bitʔaddimūha?*

[6] بِيْقولوا... *biyʔūlu...* **they say...**

[7] = بِكام؟ *bi-kām?*

[8] أفكّر *affákkar* **I'll think about it;** أقرّر *aqárrar* **I'll decide**

Vocabulary

gym, health club	*žīmm*	جيمّ
fitness	*liyāʔa* *fítnis*	لِياقة فيتْنِس
member	*3uḍw (a3ḍāʔ)* *muštárik*	عُضْو (أعْضاء) مُشْترِك
membership	*3uḍwíyya*	عُضْوية
to join a gym	*ištárak fi žīmm*	اِشْترك في جيمّ
monthly (membership) fee	*ištirāk šáhri*	اِشْتِراك شهْري
personal trainer	*mudárrib šáxṣi*	مُدرِّب شخْصي
training session	*ḥíṣṣit tadrīb*	حِصّةْ تدْريب
workout	*tamrīna*	تمْرينة
exercise	*tamrīn (tamarīn)* *tadrīb*	تمْرين (تمارين) تدْريب
to exercise, work out	*itdárrab* *itmárran*	اِتْدرّب اِتْمرّن
to get in shape	*ẓábaṭ šáklu*	ظبط شكْلُه
to be tired	*tí3ib*	تِعِب
calisthenics	*tamarīn riyaḍíyya*	تمارين رِياضية
gymnastics	*gumbāz*	جُمْباز
to do pull-ups	*lí3ib 3úʔla*	لِعِب عُقْلة
to do push-ups	*lí3ib ḍaɣṭ*	لِعِب ضغْط

to do sit-ups, work one's abs	*lí3ib baṭn*	لِعِب بطْن
to jump rope	*naṭṭ ilḥábl*	نطّ الحبْل
to do yoga	*lí3ib yōga*	لِعِب يوْجا
to do aerobics	*lí3ib ayrōbiks*	لِعِب أَيْروْبِكْس
to sweat	*3íriʔ*	عِرِق
equipment, machines	*adawāt*	أدَوات
to do cardio exercise	*lí3ib tamarīn kárdiyu*	لِعِب تمارين كارْدِيو
to burn calories	*ḥáraʔ issu3rāt ilḥararíyya*	حرق السُّعْرات الحرارية
cardio machine	*aghízit kárdiyu (taxsīs)*	أجْهِزةْ كارْدِيو (تخْسيس)
treadmill, running machine	*tridmīl* *maššāya*	تْريدْميل مشّايَة
to run	*gíri*	جِري
elliptical machine	*gihāz ilibtikāl*	جِهاز إيليبْتيكال
(stationary) bicycle	*3ágala*	عجلة
weight lifting	*raf3 asqāl*	رفْع أثْقال
weight machine	*gihāz ḥadīd*	جِهاز حديد
free weights	*awzān ḥúrra*	أَوْزان حُرّة
dumbbell(s)	*dámbal*	دامْبل
barbell	*bār ḥadīd*	بار حديد
bench	*3áḍalit ṣidr*	عضلِةْ صِدْر

a rep	*3ádda*	عدّة
a set	*magmū3a (magamī3)*	مجْموعة (مجاميع)
to bulk up, put on muscle mass	*bána 3aḑalāt*	بنى عضلات
to adjust the weight	*ẓábaṭ ilwázn*	ظبط الوَزْن
to lift weights	*šāl ђadīd/awzān*	شال حديد/أَوْزان
to spot (lit. help in lifting a weight)	*sā3id fi raf3 ilwázn*	ساعِد في رفْع الوَزْن
to lower	*názzil*	نزِّل
to pull	*šadd*	شدّ
to push	*zaʔʔ*	زقّ
thin	*rufáyya3*	رُفيّع
fat (adjective)	*tixīn*	تِخين
to gain weight, get fat	*tíxin*	تِخِن
muscular	*mi3áḑḑal*	مِعضّل
in shape	*šáklu maẓbūṭ* *gísmu mutanāsiʔ*	شكْلُه مظْبوط جِسْمُه مُتناسِق
out of shape	*šáklu miš mitẓábbaṭ* *gísmu miš mitnāsiʔ*	شكْلُه مِش مِتْظبّط جِسْمُه مِش مِتْناسِق
fat (noun)	*duhūn*	دُهون
muscle	*3áḑala*	عضلة
abs; belly	*baṭn*	بطْن
arm	*dirā3*	دِراع

back	*ḍahr*	ضهْر
chest	*ṣidr*	صِدْر
knee	*rúkba (rúkab)*	رُكْبة (رُكب)
leg	*rígl (riglēn)*	رِجْل (رِجْلينْ)
shoulder	*kitf (kitāf)*	كِتْف (كِتاف)
wrists	*rusɣ (arsāɣ)*	رُسْغ (أرْساغ)
locker	*lōkar*	لوْكر
locker room	*ɣúrfit taɣyīr ilmalābis* *vastayīr*	غُرْفِة تغْيير الملابِس فسْتيير
gym clothes, workout clothes	*hidūm žīmm*	هِدوم جيمّ
to change one's clothes	*ɣáyyar hidūmu*	غيرّ هِدومُه
sweat towel, hand towel (to wipe sweat with)	*fūṭa* *3arrāʔa*	فوطة عرّاقة
shower	*dušš*	دُشّ
towel (for showering)	*baškīr (bašakīr)*	بشْكير (بشاكير)
hair dryer	*sišwār*	سِشْوار
(bathroom) scale	*mizān (mawazīn)*	ميزان (مَوازين)
to weigh oneself	*wázan náfsu*	وَزن نفْسُه
to go on a diet	*3ámal rižīm* *míši 3ála rižīm*	عمل رِجيم مِشي على رِجيم
to lose weight	*xass*	خسّ
to gain weight	*záwwid wazn*	زوِّد وَزْن

to breathe in	*áxad náfas*	أخد نفس
to breathe out	*ţálla3 náfas*	طلّع نفس
up	*fōʔ*	فوْق
down	*taḩt*	تحْت
right	*yimīn*	يمِين
left	*šimāl*	شِمال
to jump	*naţţ*	نطّ
to sit	*ʔá3ad*	قعد
to stand	*wíʔif*	وِقِف
to squat	*skwāt*	سْكْوات

Expressions

Where is the locker room?	*fēn uḑt illōkar?*	فينْ أوضْة اللّوْكر؟
Where is the toilet?	*fēn ilḩammām?*	فينْ الحمّام؟
My goal is to gain muscle.	*3āyiz azáwwid 3áḑal.*	عايِز أزوِّد عضل.
Is there a contract?	*fī 3aʔd?*	فيه عقْد؟
How much does it cost per training session?	*ḩişşit ittadrīb fi -lmárra bi-kām?*	حِصّةْ التّدْريب في المرّة بِكام؟
How much is a monthly membership at this gym?	*ištirāk ižžīmm[ə] da bikām fi -ššahr?*	اِشْترِاك الجّيمّ ده بِكام في الشّهْر؟

I feel like I've gained a bit of weight.	*ana ɧāsis ínni zidt*^{ə} *šuwáyya.*	أنا حاسِس إنّي زِدْت شُوَيّة.
I need to lose five kilos.	*3āyiz axíss*^{ə} *xámsa kīlu.*	عايِز أخِسّ خَمْسة كيلو.
I try to exercise at least twice a week.	*baɧāwil atdárrab 3ála -lʔaʔáll*^{ə} *marritēn fi -lʔusbū3.*	بحاوِل أتْدرّب على الأقلّ مرّتيْن في الأُسْبوع.
I want to lose weight.	*3āyiz axíss.*	عايِز أخِسّ.
I'd like to hire a personal trainer.	*3āyiz mudárrib šáxṣi.*	عايِز مُدرِّب شخْصي.
I'm on a diet.	*ána 3āmil rižīm.* *ána māši 3ála rižīm.*	أنا عامِل رِجيم. أنا ماشي على رِجيم.
Excuse me, how do you use this machine?	*ba3d íznak, izzāi astá3mil iggihāz da?*	بعْد إذْنك، إزّاي أسْتعْمِل الجِّهاز ده؟
Could you spot me?	*múmkin tisa3ídni fi raf3 ilwázn?*	مُمْكِن تِساعِدْني في رفْع الوَزْن؟

◇

Adjust the weight before you get on the machine.	*úẓbuṭ ilwázn*^{ə} *ʔabl*^{ə} *ma tištáɣal 3ála -ggihāz.*	اُظْبُط الوَزْن قبْل ما تِشْتغل على الجِّهاز.
Do three sets of ten reps each.	*íl3ab 3ášar 3addāt fi tálat magmu3āt.*	اِلْعب عشر عدّات في تلات مجْموعات.
Rest for one minute between sets.	*ráyyiɧ diʔīʔa bēn kull*^{ə} *magmū3a.*	ريِّح دِقيقة بيْن كُلّ مجْموعة.

Lift the barbell over your head, then slowly lower it back down.	*írfa3 ilbār fōʔ rāsak wi nazzílu bi-búṭʔ.*	اِرْفع البار فوْق راسك و نزِّلُه بِبُطْء.
Don't forget to breathe!	*ma-tinsāš titnáffis!*	متِنْساش تِتْنفِّس!
Come on! You're doing great!	*3ās ya waђš!*	عاش يا وَحْش!
Excuse me. Your outfit does not meet our dress code.	*min fáḍlak, illíbsᵊ da ma-yinfá3šᵊ má3a -ddrīs kōd bitā3 ilmakān.*	مِن فضْلك، اللِّبْس ده مَيِنْفعْش معَ الدّْريس كوْد بِتاع المكان.
Could you please review our dress code at the front desk?	*múmkin ђaḍrítak tišūf ilʔiršadāt ilxáṣṣa bi-lmalābis bárra fi máktab ilʔistiʔbāl?*	مُمْكِن حضْرِتك تِشوف الاِرْشادات الخاصّة بِالملابِس برّه في مكْتب الاِسْتِقْبال؟

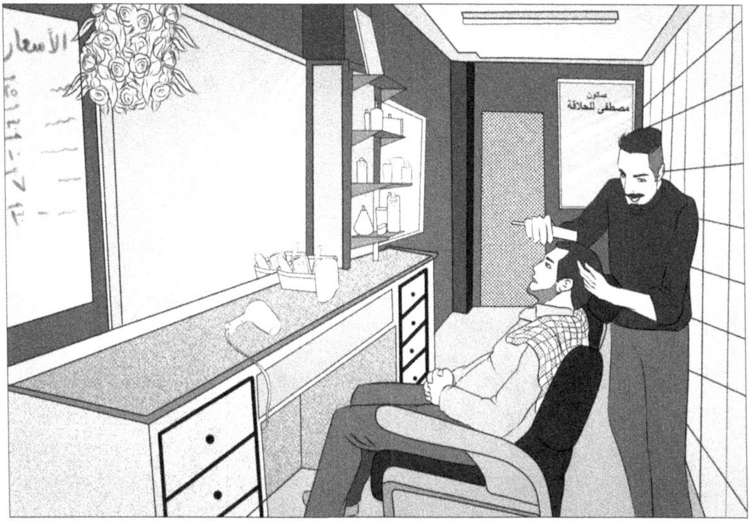

At a Barbershop عنْد الحلّاق

Barbers are usually quite chatty and like to entertain their customers. Because of this, they can be considered the center of information for a neighborhood, knowing things like who is selling their home, who is renting, who is looking for a new car, and so on. This also makes it an excellent opportunity to practice your Arabic. But not on Mondays. Barbershops are closed on Mondays in Egypt. Barbershops are strictly a man's domain. You would only see a woman in a barbershop if she's bringing in her young son for a haircut (but there are hairdressers who specialize in cutting children's hair, so even this is a rare scenario). In more affluent neighborhoods, unisex hair salons are common, but these tend to be more expensive, as well. After your barber has finished cutting your hair, he may say to you نعيماً *na3īman,* which doesn't translate well, but it is the standard formulaic greeting/wish to someone who has just had a haircut. If friends notice your new haircut, they may also say نعيماً *na3īman*. Your reply should be الله يِنْعِم عليْك *allāh yín3im 3alēk* to a man and الله يِنْعِم عليْكي *allāh yín3im 3alēki* to a woman.

ASKING ABOUT AVAILABILITY

o الدُّنْيا زحْمة كِده ليْه؟[1]

◇ معلِشّ بقى يوْم جُمْعة و كُلُّه عايِز يِحْلق بعْد الصّلاة.

o طب، أجيلك إمْتى تِحْلقْلي و تِكون فاضي[2]؟

◇ تعالالي بعْد العصْر أرْوَق[3].

o Why is it so crowded?

◇ Sorry about that, but it's Friday, and everyone is trying to get a haircut after the prayers.

o So, when should I come to you for a haircut and you're free?

◇ You'd better come later in the afternoon.

o *iddúnya záħma kída lē?*[1]

◇ *ma3alíšš^ə^ báʔa yōm gúm3a wi kúllu 3āyiz yíħlaʔ ba3d iṣṣála.*

o *ṭab, agīlak ímta tiħláʔli wi tkūn fāḍi*[2]*?*

◇ *ta3alāli ba3d il3áṣr árwaʔ*[3].

[1] = أيْه الزّحْمة دي كُلّها؟ *ʔē izzáħma di kulláha*

[2] = رايِق *rāyiʔ*

[3] أحْسن *áħsan* better; أفْضى *áfḍa* emptier, less crowded

Avoid getting a shave using the straight razor used by barbers as these are well known to cause infections.

2

SPECIFYING WHAT SERVICES YOU WOULD LIKE

◇ أُؤْمُر يا باشا.

o عايِز أحْلق شعْري و أظبّط وِشّي كِده.

◇ تِحِبّ أعْمِلّك وِشّك بِفتْلة؟

o لا أنا عايِز فوطة سُخْنة و ماسْك حِلْو كِده بعْد الحِلاقة.

◇ مِن عينيّا[1].

◇ How can I help you?

o I'd like to have a haircut [and shave] and get some facial care.

◇ Would you like me to apply some threading to your face?

o No, I just need a hot towel and a nice mask after the shave.

◇ My pleasure!

◇ *úʔmur ya bāša.*

o *3āyiz áḫlaʔ šá3ri w aẓábbaṭ wáši kída.*

◇ *tiḫíbb a3míllak wiššak bi-fátla?*

o *laʔ, ána 3āyiz fūṭa súxna wi mask ḫilwᵊ kída ba3d ilḫilāʔa.*

◇ *min 3ináyya*[1].

[1] = إنْتَ تُؤْمُر *ínta túʔmur* = تحْت أمْرك *taḫtᵊ ámrak* = حاضِر *ḫāḍir*

فتْلة *fátla* **threading** is a traditional technique removing cheek and eyebrow hairs, and sometimes hairs on your ears. Your barber will ask you if you want this option after getting your hair cut. He will hold one end of a thread in his teeth and the other in his hand against your face, moving his head back and forth to twist the thread which then pulls unwanted hairs out by the root.

3

SPECIFYING HOW YOU WANT YOUR HAIR CUT

◇ تِحِبّ اخِفِّلك[1] الجّناب وَلّا كُلُّه سِوا واحِد؟

o لا بقولّك أيْه الدُّنْيا حرّ[2] هاتْها زيرو[3].

◇ طب، و الدّقْن؟

o لا سيبْها[4] زيّ ما هِيَّ.

◇ Would you like the sides to be a bit shorter or all one length?

o You know what, it's so hot. Shave it all off.

◇ What about the beard?

o No, leave it as it is.

◇ *tiɦíbb axiffílak*[1] *igganāb wálla kúllu síwa wāɦid?*

o *laʔ, baʔúllak ʔē, iddúnya ɦarr*[2]*. hátha zīru*[3]*.*

◇ *ṭáb, wi -ddáʔn?*

o *laʔ, síbha*[4] *zayyᵊ ma híyya.*

[1] = أدرّجْلك *adarráglak*

[2] = الجّوّ حرّ *iggáwwᵊ ɦarr*

[3] = خلّيها زيرو *xallīha zīru*

[4] = خلّيها *xallīha*

A MOTHER BRINGS HER SMALL SON IN FOR A HAIRCUT.

◇ أيْه ده؟ أيْه اللي عمل فيك كِده؟[1]

o كان بِيِلْعب بِالمقصّ الأُسْتاذ[2]!

◇ ثَواني أجيب الخشبة يُقْعُد عليْها و أساويهولُه[3]. متِقْلقيش.

o بسّ متِعْمِلْهاش زيرو[4] الله يِخلّيك.

◇ What's this? What happened to you?

o This little guy was playing with scissors!

◇ Just a moment. I'll bring a wooden booster for him to sit on, and I'll fix it for him. Don't worry.

o But please don't make it a buzz cut.

◇ *ʔē da? ʔē ílli 3ámal fīk kída?*[1]

o *kān biyíl3ab bi-lmaʔáṣṣ ilʔustāz*[2]*!*

◇ *sawāni agīb ilxášaba yúʔ3ud 3alēha wi asawihūlu*[3]*. ma-tiʔlaʔīš.*

o *bassᵊ ma-ti3milhāš zīru*[4] *allāh yixallīk.*

[1] أيْه اللي حصل؟ *ʔē ílli ḫáṣal?* **What happened?;** أيْه اللي بوّظ شعْرك كِده؟ *ʔē ílli báwwaẓ šá3rak kída?* **What the heck happened to your hair?**

[2] الأُسْتاذ *ilʔustāz* **the mister,** الباشا *ilbāša* **the Pasha,** البيْه *ilbēh* **the sir** can be used sarcastically.

[3] = أظبّطْهولُه *aẓabbaṭhūlu*

[4] مِش عايْزاك تِحْلقْلُه زيرو. *miš 3ayzāk tiḫláʔlu zīru.* **I don't want you to make it a buzz cut.**

5

GETTING YOUR BEARD SHAVED

○ بقولّك أيْه، عايز أحْلق[1] دقْني بِالموس.
◇ و لَوْ إنّ شكْلك حِلْو[2] بسّ تحْت أمْرك[3].
○ طب، أقولّك[4]، اِعْمِلّي[5] سكْسوكة أحْسن.
◇ هتِبْقى حِلْوَة عليْك.[6]

○ Hey! I'd like to get my beard shaved off with a razor.
◇ You look nice [with it], but as you wish.
○ You know what? Let's make it a goatee. That would be better.
◇ That'll look nice.

○ *baʔúllak ʔē, 3āyiz áḥlaʔ*[1] *dáʔni bi-lmūs.*
◇ *wi law innᵊ šáklak ḥilwᵊ*[2] *bassᵊ taḥtᵊ ámrak*[3].
○ *ṭab, aʔúllak*[4] *i3míllī*[5] *saksūka áḥsan.*
◇ *hatíbʔa ḥílwa 3alēk.*[6]

[1] = أشيل *ašīl*

[2] = لَوْ إنّها حِلْوَة عليْك *law innáha ḥílwa 3alēk*

[3] = بسّ اللي إنْتَ عايْزُه *bass íll- ínta 3áyzu*

[4] = بقولّك *baʔúllak* = بُصّ *buṣṣ*

[5] = خلّيها *xallīha*

[6] هتْليق عليْك. *hatlīʔ 3alēk.* **That will suit you.**

6

PAYING FOR YOUR HAIRCUT

◇ نعيماً[1] يا باشا!
o الله يِنْعِم عليْك. حِسابْنا كام كِده؟
◇ كِده ٢٠ إن شاء الله.
o تمام اِتْفضّل. تِسْلم إيدك[2].
◇ الله يِسلِّمك. كُلّ مرّة و إنْتَ طيِّب.

◇ There you go, sir!
o Thank you! How much is the total?
◇ That's 20 LE, please.
o Okay, here you are. Bless your hands!
◇ Bless you, too, and be well always.

◇ *na3īman*[1] *ya bāša!*
o *allāh yín3im 3alēk. ḫisábna kām kída?*
◇ *kída 3išrīn in šāʔ allāh.*
o *tamām, itfáḍḍal. tíslam īdak*[2].
◇ *allāh yisállímak. kullᵊ márra w ínta ṭáyyib.*

[1] نعيماً *na3īman* is said to someone who you notice has a new haircut or has just showered. The response is الله يِنْعِم عليْك *allāh yín3im 3alēk.*

[2] تِسْلم إيدك *tíslam īdak* is the formulaic thank-you to someone who has skillfully done something for you, such as cut your hair or prepare a meal. The response is الله يِسلِّمك *allāh yisallímak.*

- ○ أهْلاً صباح الفُلّ[1] يا مُصْطفى.
- ◇ صباح النّور يا أُسْتاذ مجدي. ثَواني و اكون معَ حضْرتك.
- ○ خُد وَقْتك يا حبيبي[2].

(a few minutes later)

- ◇ أُؤْمُر[3] يا باشا.
- ○ بُصّ بقى يا سيدي[4]، أنا عنْدي مُناسْبة مُهِمّة فا عايْزك تِظبّطْني.
- ◇ مِن عينيّا. هنِحْلق وَلّا نِخِفّ بسّ؟
- ○ لا عايز أخِفّ شعْري شُوَيّة بسّ و ساويه.
- ◇ و الدقْن؟
- ○ بُصّ مُمْكِن تِساويهالي بِالمكنة مِن غيرْ ما تِخِفّها جامِد[5].
- ◇ تمام تِحِبّ أعْمِلّك فتْلة بعْدها؟
- ○ لا لا بلاش. بسّ مُمْكِن فوطة سُخْنة و ماسْك حِلْو كِده.
- ◇ مِن عينيّا. فيه ماسْك لِسّه جايْبُه جِديد مُمْتاز.
- ○ تمام، اِعْمِلْهولي بسّ خلّينا نِخلّص الحِلاقة الأوِّل.
- ◇ تحْت أمْرك.

(barber finishes cutting)

- ○ تِسْلم إيديْك و عينيْك يا دِرْش[6]!
- ◇ نعيماً يا باشا. أيْه رأْيَك؟
- ○ لا تمام جِدّاً[7]. الله يِنوّر بسّ بِالمرّة بقى ساويلي بِفتْلة. معلِشّ رَوَشْتك[8].
- ◇ لا يا باشا وَلا يِهِمّك. ثَواني.

(barber finishes threading)

- ○ تمام كِده الله يِنوّر!

◇ كُلّ مرّة و إنْتَ طيِّب يا باشا.

○ و إنْتَ طيِّب يا حبيبي. كِده حِسابْنا كام؟

◇ كِده كُلُّه ٧٥ جِنيْهْ.

○ ماشي اِتْفضّل يا جميل[9].

◇ خلّي[10] يا باشا!

○ Hello! Good morning, Mustafa!

◇ Good morning, Mr. Magdy. I'll be right with you.

○ Take your time, my friend.

(a few minutes later)

◇ What can I do for you, sir?

○ Listen, man, I have an important event, so I want you to pamper me.

◇ My pleasure! Are we going to cut it or just a trim?

○ I just want to get my hair trimmed a bit and make it all even.

◇ What about the beard?

○ You can just even it up with the clippers without taking off too much.

◇ All right. Would you like me to do some threading afterward?

○ No, no, don't! Just a hot towel and a nice mask.

◇ My pleasure. There is this new mask I just got, and it's excellent.

○ Okay, you can apply it, but let's get the haircut done first.

◇ You're the boss!

(barber finishes cutting)

○ Bless your hands and eyes, Darsh!

◇ There you are! What do you think?

○ It's great! Nice work! But let's make the beard even with some threading. Sorry for the hassle.

◇ No, sir, it's nothing. Just a second.

(barber finishes threading)

- ○ Perfect!
- ◇ Be well always, sir!
- ○ You too, my friend. How much do I owe you?
- ◇ Altogether, it's 75 LE.
- ○ Okay, handsome, here you are.
- ◇ Keep it, please!

- ○ *áhlan ṣabāḫ ilfúll*[1] *ya muṣṭáfa.*
- ◇ *ṣabāḫ innūr ya ustāz mágdi. sawāni w akūn má3a ḫaḍrítak.*
- ○ *xud wáʔtak ya ḫabībi*[2].

(a few minutes later)

- ◇ *úʔmur*[3] *ya bāša.*
- ○ *buṣṣᵊ báʔa ya sīdi*[4], *ána 3ándi munásba muhímma. fa 3áyzak taẓabbáṭni.*
- ◇ *min 3ináyya. haníḫlaʔ wálla nixíffᵊ bass?*
- ○ *lā, 3āyiz axíff šá3ri šwáyya bass, wi -sawī.*
- ◇ *wi -ddáʔn?*
- ○ *buṣṣ, múmkin tisawihāli bi-lmákana min ɣēr ma txíffaha gāmid*[5].
- ◇ *tamām, tiḫíbb a3míllak fátla ba3dáha?*
- ○ *lā lā, balāš. bassᵊ múmkin fūṭa súxna wi mask ḫilwᵊ kída.*
- ◇ *min 3ináyya. fī mask líssa gáybu gidīd mumtāz.*
- ○ *tamām, i3milhūli, bassᵊ xallīna nxállaṣ ilḫilāʔa ilʔáwwil.*
- ◇ *taḫtᵊ ámrak.*

(barber finishes cutting)

- ○ *tíslam idēk wi 3inēk ya darš*[6]!
- ◇ *na3īman ya bāša. ʔē ráʔyak?*
- ○ *lā, tamām gíddan*[7]. *allāh ynáwwar, bassᵊ bi-lmárra báʔa sawīli bi-fátla. ma3alíššᵊ rawáštak*[8].
- ◇ *lā, ya bāša, wála yihímmak. sawāni.*

(barber finishes threading)

- ○ *tamām kída, allāh yináwwar!*
- ◇ *kullᵊ márra w ínta ṭáyyib ya bāša.*
- ○ *w ínta ṭáyyib ya ḫabībi. kída ḫisábna kām?*
- ◇ *kída kúllu xámsa w sab3īn ginēh.*
- ○ *māši itfáḍḍal ya gamīl*[9].
- ◇ *xálli*[10] *ya bāša!*

[1] صباح الفُلّ *ṣabāḫ ilfúll* (lit. morning of jasmine) is an informal greeting used with people you know (and usually with the same gender so as not to be misunderstood). Similar gretings are صباح الوَرْد *ṣabāḫ ilwárd* (lit. morning of roses), صباح العسل *ṣabāḫ il3ásal* (lit. morning of honey), and صباح القِشْطة *ṣabāḫ ilʔíšṭa* (lit. morning of cream). If you are not on familiar terms with someone, it is better to use the standard صباح الخيْر *ṣabāḫ ilxēr*. The response to all is صباح النّور *ṣabāḫ innūr*.

[2] يا حبيبي *ya ḫabībi* (lit. my dear) is an affectionate form of address, better translated as **my friend** or **buddy**.

[3] (lit. Order...!) = أوامْرك *awámrak*

[4] = شوف بقى يا عمّ *šuf báʔa ya 3amm*

[5] = أَوي *áwi*

[6] درْش *darš* **Darsh** is the nickname for Mustafa.

[7] لا ده مية مية *lā, da míyya míyya*

[8] = عذّبْتك معايا *3azzíbtak ma3āya* = تعبْتك *ta3ábtak* (the response to which is وَلا تعب وَلا حاجة *wála tá3ab wála ḫāga* or تعبك راحة *tá3abak rāḫa*)

[9] = يا حبيبي *ya ḫabībi*

[10] خلّي *xálli* (lit. keep (it)) is not to be taken literally. See note 3 on p. 4.

Vocabulary

barbershop	*ṣalōn ɧilāʔa*	صالوْن حِلاقة
barber	*ɧallāʔ*	حلّاق
barber's assistant	*ṣábi ɧallāʔ*	صبي حلّاق
haircut; shave	*ɧilāʔa*	حِلاقة
to get a haircut; to cut (hair)	*ɧálaʔ*	حلق
to shave (one's head)	*ɧálaʔ zīru*	حلق زيرو
scissors	*maʔáṣṣ*	مقصّ
straight razor	*mūs*	موس
blade	*šáfra*	شفْرة
hair clippers	*mákanit ɧilāʔa*	مكنِةْ حِلاقة
comb	*mišṭ*	مِشْط
brush	*fúrša (fúraš)*	فُرْشة (فُرش)
mirror	*mirāya*	مِرايَة
towel	*fūṭa*	فوطة
thread(ing)	*fátla*	فتْلة
mask	*mask*	ماسْك
cream	*kirīm*	كِريم
gel	*žill*	جِلّ
dye	*ṣábɣa*	صبْغة
shampoo	*šámbu*	شامْبو

hair	*ša3r*	شعْر
face	*wišš*	وِشّ
beard	*daʔn*	دقْن
mustache	*šánab*	شنب
goatee, circle beard	*saksūka*	سكْسوكة
"zero" cut, very short buzz cut	*zīru*	زيرو
bangs	*ʔúṣṣa*	قُصّة
front	*ʔuddām*	قُدّام
top	*fōʔ*	فوْق
back	*wára*	وَرا
sides	*gināb*	جِناب
right side	*iggámb ilyimīn*	الجّنْب اليمين
left side	*iggámb iššimāl*	الجّنْب الشِّمال
sideburns	*sawālif*	سَوالِف

Expressions

○

I had my hair cut about a month ago.	*ána ḫaláʔt ilḫálʔa di min ḫawāli šahr.*	أنا حلقْت الحلْقة دي مِن حَوالي شهْر.
Give me a shave and haircut.	*iḫláʔli dáʔnᵊ wi ša3r.*	اِحْلقْلي دقْن و شعْر.
Please wash my hair before cutting it.	*iɣsílli šá3ri ʔablᵊ ma tíḫlaʔ.*	اِغْسِلّي شعْري قبْل ما تِحْلق.

Let's even up the hair.	*nisāwi -ššа3r.*	نِساوي الشّعْر.
Not too short.	*miš ʔuṣáyyar áwi.*	مِش قُصيرّ أَوي.
A little shorter, please.	*yínfa3 áʔṣar šuwáyya/sínna/sīka.*	يِنْفع أقْصر شُوّيَه/سِنّة/سيكا.
I just want you to take 2-3 centimeters off the top.	*xúdli daragtēn talāta min fōʔ.*	خُدْلي درجْتينْ تلاتة مِن فوْق.
I just want you to take 2-3 centimeters off the top.	*3áyzak bas tiʔúṣṣ yīgi -tnēn talāta sánti min fōʔ*	عايْزك بسّ تِقُصّ ييجي اِتْنينْ تلاتة سنْتي مِن فوْق.
Let's use setting 3 on the hair clippers.	*3āyiz áḫlaʔ 3ála talāta.*	عايِز أحْلق على ٣.
Show me the back of my hair with a mirror.	*warrīni šá3ri min wára bi-lmirāya.*	وَرّيني شعْري مِن وَرا بِالمِرايَة.
I want to have my beard shaved with a straight razor.	*3āyiz áḫlaʔ dáʔni bi-lmūs.*	عايِز أحْلق دقْني بِالموس.
Can you fix my beard with some threading?	*múmkin ti3mílli dáʔni bi-fátla?*	مُمْكِن تِعْمِلّي دقْني بِفتْلة؟
I want you to thin out the sides but leave one of them for (covering) the bald spot.	*3áyzak tixíff iggināb wi tsíbli náḫya 3ašān iṣṣál3a.*	عايْزك تِخِفّ الجِّناب و تِسيبْلي ناحْيَة عشان الصّلْعة.
Shave my beard but leave the mustache.	*íḫlaʔ iddáʔnᵊ wi sīb iššánab.*	اِحْلق الدّقْن و سيب الشّنب.

◇

[Are you here for] a shave, haircut, or both?	*dáʔnᵊ wálla šá3r wálla -lʔitnēn?*	دقْن وَلّا شعْر وَلّا الاتْنينْ؟
Would you like to have your hair cut with hair clippers or with scissors and a comb?	*tiɧíbbᵊ tíɧlaʔ bi-mákana wálla maʔáṣṣᵊ wi mišṭ.*	تِحِبّ تِحْلق بمكنة وَلّا مقصّ و مِشْط.
Would you like me to cut it for you on setting 1 or 2?	*tiɧíbb a3míllak 3ála wāɧid aw itnēn?*	تِحِبّ أعْمِلّك على ١ أَوْ ٢؟
Do you want sideburns?	*tiɧíbb a3míllak sawālif?*	تِحِبّ أعْمِلّك سَوالِف؟
How's that?	*ʔē ráʔyak?*	أيْه رأْيَك؟
Would you like me to apply a facial mask?	*tiɧíbbᵊ a3míllak maskᵊ li-lwišš?*	تِحِبّ أعْمِلّك ماسْك لِلوِشّ؟
Do you want a hot towel?	*agíblak fūṭa súxna?*	أجيبْلك فوطة سُخْنة؟

At a Beauty Salon في الكُّوافير

Most hair stylists, whether men or women, are very talkative. They love talking, and it is rare to find one working silently. Your head may be spinning by the end of the session, but of course, this is yet another excellent opportunity to practice your listening skills in Arabic. They may ask you some personal questions, but their intention is just to make friends with you and win you over as a repeat customer.

Beauty salons are typically closed on Mondays in Egypt but open on other days, including the weekend. Some beauty salons are only concerned with شعْر *ša3r* **hair**, وِشّ *wišš* **face**, and ضَوافِر *ḍawāfir* **nails**, while others operate as spas with massage packages, and so on. كُوافير *kuwafīr* a **hairdresser** may be male or female in Egypt, whether the establishment is unisex or caters only to women. Some places even offer a private section for veiled women who prefer to be among other women only. Bring your own equipment for a manicure and pedicure, or buy them there and keep them with you.

GETTING A HAIRCUT

o بُصّي كُنْت عايْزة اقُصّ الأطْراف[1].

◇ مِش حابّة[2] تِعْمِلي قصّة مُعيّنة؟

o لا الأطْراف بسّ و عايْزة اعْمِل قُصّة[3].

◇ حاضِر مِن عينيّا.

o I just wanted to get the tips cut.

◇ You don't want to try a new hair cut?

o No, just the tips, and I want to have bangs.

◇ Certainly! With pleasure!

o *búṣṣi kuntᵊ 3áyza aʔúṣṣ ilʔaṭrāf*[1].

◇ *miš ḫábba*[2] *ti3míli ʔáṣṣa mu3ayyána?*

o *laʔ, ilʔaṭrāf bass. wi 3áyza á3mil ʔúṣṣa*[3].

◇ *ḫāḍir min 3ináyya.*

1 = عايْزاكي تِساويلي الأطْراف *3ayzāki tsawīli -lʔaṭrāf*

2 = عايْزة *3áyza*

3 = عايْزاكي تِقصّيلي قُصّة *3ayzāki tʔuṣṣīli ʔúṣṣa*

2

PAYING

o حِلْو أَوي كِده، تِسْلم إيدِك.
◇ القصّة دي شكْلها يِجنِّن[1] عليْكي.
o طيِّب، إحْنا كِده حِسابْنا كام؟
◇ إحْنا قصّيْنا كاريْة و ظبّطْنا القُصّة. يِبْقى حِسابْنا ٤٠.

o Very nice! Thank you!
◇ This haircut looks incredible on you.
o All right. How much do I owe you then?
◇ We did a bob cut and bangs. That makes it 40 [LE].

o *ḫilw áwi kída, tíslam īdik.*
◇ *ilʔáṣṣa di šakláha ygánnin[1] 3alēki.*
o *ṭáyyib, íḫna kída ḫisábna kām?*
◇ *íḫna ʔaṣṣēna karē wi ẓabbáṭna -lʔúṣṣa. yíbʔa ḫsábna arbi3īn.*

[1] = تُحْفة *túḫfa* = رَوْعة *ráw3a*

3

GETTING A NEW HAIRSTYLE

o بُصّي أنا عايْزة اقصّرْه خالِص[1] و أعْمِل قصّة جِديدة.

◇ أيْه رأْيِك نِعْمِلْه جارْسوْن زيّ الصّورة دي و نِعْمِل هايْلايْت؟

o لا لا مِش لِلدّرجة دي[2] بسّ مُمْكِن القصّة اللي جمْبها.

◇ شكْلها حِلْو فِعْلاً و هتْليق على وِشِّك.

o Well, I want to get it cut really short and have a new hairstyle.

◇ How about we try a pixie cut like the one in this picture and add some highlights?

o No, no, not to that extent, but we can try the picture next to it.

◇ That looks really nice and would suit your face shape.

o *búṣṣi, ána 3áyza aʔaṣṣáru xāliṣ*[1] *w á3mil ʔáṣṣa gdīda.*

◇ *ʔē ráʔyik ni3mílu garsōn zayy iṣṣūra di wi ní3mil haylāyt?*

o *lā lā, miš li-ddaragā-di*[2]*, bass*ᵊ *múmkin ilʔáṣṣa -lli gambáha.*

◇ *šakláha ḫilw*ᵊ *fí3lan wi hatlīʔ 3ála wíššik.*

[1] = عايْزاه قُصيرّ خالِص *3ayzā ʔuṣáyyar xāliṣ*

[2] = مِش أوي كِده *miš áwi kída*

4

Getting a manicure and pedicure

○ ازِّيِّك يا حبيبْتي، عامْلة أيْه؟[1]

◇ الحمْدُ لله يا مدام، تِسْلمي.

○ بُصّي أنا عايْزة اعْمِل مانيكير و بديكير.

◇ تمام مِن عينيّا[2]. ثَواني و هجيب المايّة الدّافْيَة.

○ How are you, dear? How's it going?

◇ I'm fine, ma'am. Thank you.

○ Well, I'd like to get a manicure and a pedicure.

◇ Sure, with pleasure. Just a moment, and I'll bring some warm water.

○ *izzáyyik ya ɦabíbti, 3ámla ʔē?*[1]

◇ *ilɦámdu li-llāh ya madam, tislámi.*

○ *búṣṣi ána 3áyza á3mil manikīr wi badikīr.*

◇ *tamām, min 3ináyya*[2]*. sawāni wi hagīb ilmáyya -ddáfya.*

[1] = أخْبارِك أيْه؟ *axbārik ʔē?*

[2] The response is تِسْلم عينيْكي *tíslam 3inēki.*

5

Getting a perm

o أنا عايْزة أعْمِل السْتايْل ده في شعْري.

◇ أها بسّ ده هيْخلّينا نِسْتخْدِم كِريم فرْد. فيه نوْع مُعيّن بِتْفضّلية؟[1]

o اللي بِتِسْتخْدِمُه كُلّ مرّة تمام، بسّ خلّي بالك[2] عشان فتْلِةْ شعْري مِش قَوية أَوي[3].

◇ لا متِقْلقيش خالِص[4]. إن شاء الله هَيِطْلع[5] زيّ الصّورة و أحْلى.

o I want to get this hairstyle.

◇ Aha... but this will require us to use a perm. Is there a certain type you prefer using?

o The one you use every time, but be careful because my hair thickness is not that strong.

◇ Don't worry... God willing, it will come out just like in the picture, or even better.

o *ána 3áyza á3mil ilistāyl da f šá3ri.*

◇ *ahā, bassᵊ da hixallīna nistáxdim kirīm fard. fī nō3 mu3áyyan bitfaḍḍalī?*[1]

o *ílli bitistaxdímu kullᵊ márra tamām, bassᵊ xálli bālak*[2] *3ašān fátlit šá3ri miš qawíyya áwi*[3].

◇ *lā, ma-tiʔlaʔīš xāliṣ*[4]. *in šāʔ allāh hayíṭla3*[5] *zayy iṣṣūra w áḥla.*

1 تِحِبّي نِسْتخْدِم انْهي نوْع؟ *tiḥíbbi nistáxdim ánhi nō3?* **What type do you want us to use?**

2 = خُد بالك *xud bālak*

3 ضعيفة شُوَيّة *ḍa3īfa šwáyya* **a bit thin**

4 اِتْطمِّني *itṭammíni* **rest assured**

5 = هَيِبْقى *hayíbʔa*

6

GETTING A FACIAL

- ○ عايْزة اعْمِل حمّام بُخار لِوِشّي و تنْضيف.
- ◇ تمام معاكي أدَواتِك[1] وَلّا تِحِبّي أفْتحْلِك جُداد؟
- ○ لا هشْترِي مِن عنْدك و أخلّيهُم[2] معايا.
- ◇ تِحِبّي نِعْمِل ماسْك بعْدها أَوْ نِنضّف بِفتْلة؟
- ○ مُمْكِن ماسْك لطيف[3] كِده.

- ○ I want to have my face steamed and cleansed.
- ◇ Sure, do you have your own tools, or shall I open some new ones for you?
- ○ No, I'll buy some from you and keep them with me.
- ◇ Would you like to make a mask or do some threading?
- ○ We can apply a nice mask.

- ○ *3áyza á3mil ɦammām buxār li-wíšši wi tanḍīf.*
- ◇ *tamām, ma3āki adawātik[1] wálla tiɦíbbi aftáɦlik gudād?*
- ○ *laʔ, haštíri min 3ándak w axallīhum[2] ma3āya.*
- ◇ *tiɦíbbi ní3mil maskᵊ ba3dáha aw nináḍḍaf bi-fátla?*
- ○ *múmkin maskᵊ laṭīf[3] kída.*

[1] = الأدَوات بِتاعْتِك *ilʔadawāt bitá3tik*

[2] = أخُدْهُم *axúdhum*

[3] = حِلْو *ɦilw*

Extended Dialogue

○ أهْلاً وَ سهْلاً. نوّرْتي[1] المكان يا مدام سارة.
◇ بِنورِك يا حبيبْتي، مُتْشكِّرة.
○ النّهارْده مفيش ضغْط شُغْل[2] فا هكون فاضْيالِك و أعْملِّك كُلّ اللي إنْتي عايْزاه.
◇ يا ريْت فِعْلاً. أنا عشان كِده قُلْت أجيلِك النّهارْده بدْري.
○ أؤْمُري.
◇ بُصّي[3] بقى يا سِتّي، أنا عايْزة اعْمِل نْيو لوك و أظبّط كام حاجة كِده.
○ تمام، هنْقُصّ مثلاً؟
◇ لا بُصّي، هنْقُصّ الأطْراف[4] بسّ. لكِن عايْزة اعْمِلُه كيرْلي و هايْلايْت خفيف.
○ طيِّب، الكيرْلي درجات كِتير[5]. فيه حاجة مُعيّنة في دِماغِك[6]؟
◇ آه بُصّي الصّورة دي. شُفْتها و عاجْباني أوَي.
○ تمام هنْحاوِل نوْصل لِأقْرب تعْريجة لِلصّورة. بسّ مِش شرْط تِطْلع بِالظّبْط عشان فتْلِةْ شعْرِك[7] مُخْتلِفة.
◇ طيِّب، خلّينا نِشوف.
○ غيرُهْ[8]؟
◇ و عايْزة أعْمِل حمّام بُخار و تنْضيف لِوِشّي.
○ تِحِبّي ماسْك أَوْ حاجة؟
◇ لا مِش مُشْكِلة[9] بسّ عايْزة أعْمِل كمان مانيكير.
○ تِحِبّي باديكير كمان؟
◇ لا خلّينا نِخلّص دوْل الأوِّل بسّ و بعْد كِده نِشوف.
○ خلاص، مِن عينيّا[10].

(after the hairdresser has finished)

◇ حِلْو جِدّاً! و تِصدّقي الدّرجة اللي قُلْتيلي عليْها في الهايْلايْت طِلْعِت أحْسن فِعْلاً.

o ما أنا قُلْتلِك دي هتْكون ألْيَق[11] على درجِةْ شعْرِك و بشْرِتِك.

◇ تِسْلم إيديْكي[12] حبيبْتي. كِده حِسابْنا كام ؟

o كِده كُلُّه ٢٧٠ جِنيْهْ.

◇ اِتْفضّلي يا حبيبْتي.

o Welcome, Mrs. Sarah.

◇ Thank you, dear.

o Today, we aren't that busy, so I will be all yours to do what you want.

◇ Wonderful! That's why I thought of coming early today.

o I'm at your service.

◇ Look, I'd like to have a new look and get a few things done.

o Okay, are we cutting your hair?

◇ No, we'll just trim the tips, but I want to get a curly perm and apply some highlights

o There are so many levels of curly. Do you have something specific in mind?

◇ Yes, look at this picture. I saw it, and I really like it

o Okay, we will try to get as close to the picture as possible, but it might not come out exactly the same because your hair's thickness is different.

◇ It's okay. Let's see!

o And what else?

◇ I also want to have my face steamed and cleansed.

o Would you like a mask or something?

◇ No thanks, but I also want to get a manicure.

o Would you like a pedicure, too?

◇ No, let's get these done first and then we'll see.

○ With pleasure.

(after the hairdresser has finished)

◇ Very nice! You know what? The shade of highlights that you suggested is really much better.

○ I told you this one would match your hair and skin tones better.

◇ Thanks a lot, dear! How much is the total then?

○ Altogether it's 270 LE.

◇ Here you are, dear.

○ *áhlan wa sáhlan nawwárti*[1] *-lmakān ya madām sāra.*

◇ *bi-nūrik ya ḫabíbti, mutšakkíra.*

○ *innahárda ma-fīš dạxṭᵊ šuɣl*[2]*, fa hakūn faḍyālik w a3míllik kull íll- ínti 3ayzā.*

◇ *ya rēt fí3lan. ána 3ašān kída ʔult agīlik innahárda bádri.*

○ *uʔmúri.*

◇ *búṣṣi*[3] *báʔa ya sítti, ána 3áyza á3mil* [new look] *w aẓábbaṭ kām ḫāga kída.*

○ *tamām, hanʔúṣṣᵊ másalan?*

◇ *laʔ, búṣṣi, hanʔúṣṣ ilʔaṭrāf*[4] *bass. lākin 3áyza a3mílu kírli wi haylāyt xafīf.*

○ *ṭáyyib, ikkírli daragāt kitīr*[5]*. fī ḫāga mu3ayyána fi dmāɣik*[6]*?*

◇ *āh, búṣṣi -ṣṣūra di. šuftáha wi 3agbāni áwi.*

○ *tamām, hanḫāwil níwṣal li-ʔáʔrab ta3rīga li-ṣṣūra. bassᵊ miš šarṭᵊ tíṭla3 bi-ẓẓábṭᵊ 3ašān fátlit šá3rik*[7] *muxtálifa.*

◇ *ṭáyyib, xallīna nšūf.*

○ *ɣēru*[8]*?*

◇ *wi 3áyza á3mil ḫammām buxār wi tanḍīf li-wíšši.*

○ *tiḫíbbi mask aw ḫāga?*

◇ *laʔ, miš muškíla*[9] *bassᵊ 3áyza á3mil kamān manikīr.*

○ *tiḫíbbi badikīr kamān?*

◇ *laʔ, xallīna nxállaṣ dōl ilʔáwwil bassᵊ wi ba3dᵊ kída nšūf.*

○ *xalāṣ, min 3ináyya*[10]*.*

(after the hairdresser has finished)

◇ *ḫilwᵊ gíddan! wi tṣaddáʔi -ddáraga -lli ʔultīli 3alēha fi -lhaylāyt ṭíl3it áḫsan fí3lan.*

○ *m- ána ʔultílik di hatkūn ályaʔ*[11] *3ála dáragit šá3rik wi bašrítik.*

◇ *tíslam idēki*[12] *ḫabíbti. kída ḫisábna kām?*

○ *kída kúllu mitēn wi sab3īn ginēh.*

◇ *itfaḍḍáli ya ɧabíbti.*

1 نوّرْت *nawwárt* (lit. you enlightened) is a formulaic welcome. A common response is بِنورك *bi-nūrak* (lit. with your light). You can also say مِنوّر *mináwwar* and respond مِنوّر بِاصْحابُه *mináwwar bi-ṣɧābu* or مِنوّر بِأهْلُه *mináwwar bi-ʔáhlu.*

2 = الشُّغْل خفيف *iššúɣlᵊ xafīf;* ضغْط شُغْل *ḍaɣṭᵊ šuɣl* (lit. work pressure)

3 = شوفي *šūfi*

4 = الطراطيف *iṭṭaraṭīf*

5 = كذا درجة *káza dáraga*

6 = في بالِك *fi bālik*

7 فتْلِةْ شعْر *fátlit ša3r* = نَوْعية شعْر *naw3īt ša3r* **hair texture, kind of hair**

8 = و أيْه كمان؟ *wi ʔē kamān?* = و أيْه تاني؟ *wi ʔē tāni?*

9 = مِش مُهِمّ *miš muhímm*

10 إنْتي تُؤْمُري *ínti tuʔmúri* = تحْت أمْرِك *taɧtᵊ ámrik* = حاضِر *ɧāḍir*

11 = هتْليق أكْتر *hatlīʔ áktar*

12 تِسْلم إيديْك *tíslam idēk* is the formulaic thank-you to someone who has skillfully done something for you, such as cut your hair or prepare a meal. A common response is الله يِسلّمك *allāh yisallímak.*

Vocabulary

beauty salon; (male) hairdresser	*kuwafīr*	كُوافير
(female) hairdresser	*kuwafīra*	كُوافيرة
to cut	*ʔaṣṣ*	قصّ
haircut	*ʔáṣṣa*	قصّة
bob cut	*karē*	كاريْه
pixie cut	*garsōn*	جارْسوْن
highlights	*haylāyt*	هايْلايْت
hair	*ša3r*	شعْر
type of hair (thickness, etc.)	*fátlit iššá3r*	فتْلِةْ الشّعْر
curly	*kírli*	كيرْلي
perm, straightening	*fard*	فرْد
straightening iron	*bēbi līs*	بيْبي ليس
to dye[1]	*sábaɣ*	صبغ
hair dryer	*sišwār*	سِشْوار
layered	*dēgradē*	ديْجْراديْه
bangs	*ʔúṣṣa*	قُصّة
bun	*káḥka*	كحْكة
ponytail	*dēl ḥuṣān*	ديْل حُصان
part	*farʔ*	فرْق
face	*wišš*	وِشّ

steam facial	*ɧammām buxār*	حمّام بُخار
cleansing	*tanḑīf*	تنْضيف
threading, epilation	*fátla*	فتْلة
eyebrow	*ɧāgib (ɧawāgib)*	حاجِب (حَواجِب)
eyelid	*gifn (gufūn)*	جِفْن (جُفون)
eyelash	*rimš (rumūš)*	رِمْش (رُموش)
pedicure	*badikīr*	باديكير
manicure	*manikīr*	مانيكير
(finger/toe) nail	*ḑufr (ḑawāfir)*	ضُفْر (ضَوافِر)
finger	*şubā3 (şawābi3)*	صُباع (صَوابِع)

[1] Notice that the ص is pronounced *s* (not *ş*) in this word.

Expressions

	○	
I want to have the tips trimmed.	*3áyz- aʔúşş ilʔaţrāf.*	عايْزة أقُصّ الأطْراف.
I want to have bangs.	*kuntᵊ 3áyz- á3mil ʔúşşa.*	كُنْت عايْزة أعْمِل قُصّة.
I want to use the straightening iron.	*3áyz- á3mil šá3ri bēbi līs.*	عايْزة أعْمِل شعْري بيْبي ليس.
(showing a photo) Can you do this haircut?	*ti3ráfi ti3míli -lʔáşşa di?*	تِعْرفي تِعْمِلي القصّة دي؟

I want to apply threading on my face.	*3áyz- á3mil wíšši bi-lfátla.*	عايْزة أعْمِل وِشّي بِالفتْلة.
I want to have my face waxed.	*3áyza á3mil wíšši bi-ššám3.*	عايْزة أعْمِل وِشّي بِالشّمْع.
I'd like my hair washed and blow-dried.	*3áyza áɣsil šá3ri w a3mílu sišwār.*	عايْزة أغْسِل شعْري و أعْمِلُه سِشْوار.
Do you have dye in this color?	*3ándak sábɣit illōn da?*	عنْدك صبْغِةْ اللّوْن ده؟
What colors of highlights do you have?	*ʔē alwān ilhaylāyt ílli 3andúkum?*	أيْه ألْوان الهايْلايْت اللي عنْدُكُم؟

www.ingramcontent.com/pod-product-compliance
Lightning Source LLC
Chambersburg PA
CBHW052054110526
44591CB00013B/2200
* 9 7 8 1 9 4 9 6 5 0 0 4 4 *